A BASIC FRAMEWORK FOR ECONOMICS

RICHARD H. LEFTWICH
Department of Economics
Oklahoma State University

A basic framework
for economics

1980

BUSINESS PUBLICATIONS, INC.
Dallas, Texas   75243
Irwin-Dorsey Limited   Georgetown, Ontario   L7G 4B3

Cover: The photography of H. Armstrong Roberts.

ISBN 0-256-02309-3
Library of Congress Catalog Card No. 79–53969

Printed in the United States of America

1 2 3 4 5 6 7 8 9 0 K 7 6 5 4 3 2 1 0

Preface

In my judgment the principles course should be the most important course in the undergraduate economics curriculum. It is the only formal exposure to economic reasoning that most of its enrollees will encounter. It also is expected to provide the foundation on which upper division courses will build. Through most of my career as a professional economist I have been uneasy, to say the least, with the traditional way that we handle it. Most of our students complete the course knowing very little about everything in the discipline. We simply try to cover too wide a range of topics. And their failure to grasp the embedded fundamental analytical framework of economics makes the course incredibly dull and boring for them.

This book is intended as an alternative to the encyclopedic texts that cover the waterfront. As its name indicates it is an internally consistent core of macroeconomic and microeconomic theory. It is not an easy or a watered-down book, even though it is pitched at a beginning or elementary level. As I have taught the course over the last several years, I have tried to concentrate on those principles that are useful to students—today, tomorrow, and next year—and to pare out those that are not. I have elected to spend more time on basic macro- and micro-economics and less on applied topics like public finance, labor relations, international trade, and the like. I believe that if students understand the principles of scarcity, alternative costs, aggregate demand, aggregate supply, inflation, unemployment, downward sloping product demand curves, upward sloping product supply curves, the effects of price ceilings and price floors, profit maximization under competition and monopoly, resource pricing and allocation, income determination and distribution, and so on, in the principles course, they will have little difficulty with topics treated in upper-division applied courses or theory courses. In addition, I believe that the macro-micro principles covered in this book are essentially those needed by students who take only the principles course, if they are to understand the economic system in which they live and function.

There are a number of ways in which this book can be used. The most obvious use is for a theory-oriented half of a two-semester or two-quarter principles sequence in which the other half is built around current economic issues. Or, supplemented with issues textbooks, this one can provide the theory background or core for an entire two-semester or two-quarter principles sequence. I think it will also be useful for separate one-semester principles courses. It can provide a useful orientation to macro-micro economic principles for MBA students from other disciplines who have had no work in economics, or for those who wish to review their basic economics.

I am grateful to many who have helped me put the text together. The manuscript has been reviewed and many excellent suggestions have been made by Keith C. Brown, Purdue University; Richard Coz, University of Santa Clara; Walter L. Johnson, University of Missouri—Columbia; Allen F. Larsen, St. Cloud State University; James J. McLain, University of New Orleans; William J. Moore, University of Houston; and Donald A. Wells, University of Arizona. Diana Mnich and Nancy Fancy provided excellent secretarial services.

December 1979   ***Richard H. Leftwich***

Contents

of value. Store of value. Money, inflation, and recession: *The equation of exchange. Inflation. Inflation control. Recession. Recession control.*

Government expenditures: *Expenditure trends.* Government
revenues: *Current types of revenues. Trends in revenues. Philosophies of taxation.* Government borrowing and the federal debt:
*The economic effects of borrowing. The economic effects of
the federal debt.*

entry, and exit. Price and nonprice competition. Incentives for and against collusion. Workable competition.

A BASIC FRAMEWORK FOR ECONOMICS

PART ONE

INTRODUCTION: STARTING FROM GROUND ZERO

We start from scratch in Part One. Although some students using this book have been exposed to basic economics before, others have not, and it is desirable that we all have a common foundation on which to build. In the first chapter we review what the discipline of economics is about. In the second chapter we review demand, supply, and price determination fundamentals. With this foundation securely in place we construct the basic framework of economic analysis—macroeconomics—in Part Two and microeconomics in Part Three.

Chapter 1

What is economics about?

The United States economy is in deep trouble. At least so
it would appear to a casual reader of newspapers and
news magazines, or to one who listens to television news casts
and candidates for political office. Inflation is rampant, unemployment is too high, energy is scarce, and too many people
are unable to maintain "decent" standards of living.

What is wrong? What are the forces that cause the problems? Are the problems peculiar to, or a necessary part of,
a capitalistic system? Would they be alleviated if the capitalistic system were supplanted by a socialistic system? Good answers to these questions are not easy to find. A great many
people have answers but they are not always good ones. Consistently good answers can result only from careful study and
examination of the nature of economic activity and the processes through which it is carried on. The pages that follow
are intended to help you consider these in a systematic way.

SCARCITY AND ECONOMIC ACTIVITY

The heart of the economic problem is that most of us want
more goods and services than our incomes will let us have.
Only a few at the very top income levels escape the problem.
It extends beyond individuals; it occurs for any country as a
whole; it exists throughout the entire world. Economic activity
is triggered by unlimited human wants and scarcity of the
means available for satisfying them.

Wants

The sum total of the wants of human beings is insatiable.
Can you or any of your friends purchase enough of different
goods and services to satiate yourselves with all of them simultaneously? Would you like a larger room or house? More or
higher quality furnishings? Additional or more fashionable
clothing? A newer car? Better food? Can you imagine an economy providing all of its inhabitants with such vast quantities
of all goods and services that they could not possibly want
more of anything?

Human wants arise from many sources. First, mere survival
generates minimal demands for food and protection from the
elements. But we human beings want more than mere survival.
We want increasing levels of comfort and security. We want

variety. We want what our neighbors have. We want what our neighbors are likely to want. And the activity we engage in as we attempt to satisfy those wants—for example, fulfilling the want for a university education—generates hosts of new wants. To look at the sources is enough to assure us that the possibility of fully satisfying all human wants is highly remote; unfulfilled wants hang out there in front of us and above us. Wants provide the mainspring of economic activity.

Resources

Limitations on the degree to which an economy can fulfill the wants of its inhabitants are partly determined by the resources available for producing want-satisfying goods and services. *Resources* are the ingredients that go into the production processes that turn out goods and services. For example, sand, gravel, cement, water, a hoe or a concrete mixer, and labor are resource inputs used to produce outputs of concrete. For clarity in thinking we ordinarily classify the resources of an economy into two categories: (1) labor and (2) capital.

Labor resources consist of all efforts of mind and muscle available to be used in production processes. The surgeon who performs an appendectomy provides labor resources in a production process. So does the garbage collector who makes the morning rounds. The labor category includes a great many different occupations and skill levels. Some part of labor power results from the natural or inherited characteristics of human beings while the rest of it is made possible by education and training. The common denominator of the wide variety of labor resources available to an economy is that they are inseparable from the human beings who provide them.

Capital resources are the nonhuman ingredients that enter into production processes. Land areas, minerals, raw materials, wheat crops, semi-finished materials like steel ingots, buildings, machines, tools, energy, and many other items constitute the capital category. Like labor resources capital resources take many different forms.

The quantities of both labor and capital resources available for an economy to use during any given time period—say, one year—are *finite* or *scarce*. The labor force of an economy obviously cannot exceed its total population and will ordinarily amount to less than half of it. The proportion of the population available for work depends on such things as its age distribution, its state of health, and its attitudes toward child labor, female labor, and the labor of the aged. The stock of capital that the economy has available to use during any given year cannot be increased very much during that year, even though it can be added to very substantially over a long period of time. A three to four percent annual increase in an economy's stock of capital is not a bad average over an extended number of years.

Techniques

The remaining limitations on an economy's capacity to produce are the techniques of production available and feasible for it to use. Techniques refer to the means and methods that producers can use in putting resources together to produce goods and services. The development of direct production techniques falls largely in the province of engineering. However, the methods used by a society to organize itself for carrying out consumption, production, and exchange may be referred to as social techniques. Choices among alternative techniques available to be used are economic choices. The level of techniques available to an economy is determined by such things as the inventiveness of the population, its capacity for borrowing and utilizing the techniques of others, the general state of technical knowledge in the economy, and the level of technical education of the population.

Production possibilities

The resources of an economy, together with its techniques, determine its production possibilities, or the many alternative output combinations that it can produce. The resources and techniques of an economy are quite flexible with regard to the different combinations of goods and services they can be used to turn out. They can be shifted from the production of large automobiles to small ones, from other professional services into the production of medical services, and from the production of slide rules into the production of small handheld electronic calculators. They can even be shifted from the production of agricultural products to the production of household appliances. Thus a given complement of resources and a given range of techniques can be used in an economy to provide a large number of alternative combinations of goods and services for its inhabitants.

Consider a very simple economy that produces only two product outputs, food and clothing. Suppose that if all of its resources were used to produce food and if the very best food production techniques were employed the total output of food would be 13,000 bushels. In Figure 1–1, the economy's output would be represented by point A. Alternatively, suppose that if some of the economy's resources are used to produce food while the rest are used to produce clothing, and if the best available techniques are employed in the production of each, the output of the economy is 7,000 bushels of food and 8,000 yards of clothing. The economy's output is shown by point B. Again, suppose that all of the economy's resources are used, along with the best techniques, to produce clothing, and that the output is 11,000 yards. Point D in Figure 1–1 records the result. There are many other possible output combinations,

Figure 1–1
A production possibilities curve

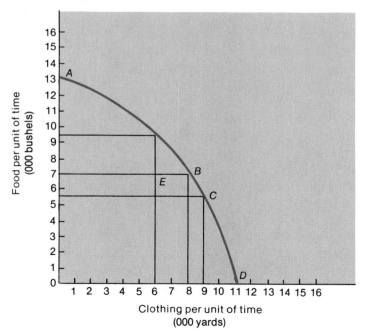

Food per unit of time (000 bushels)

Clothing per unit of time
(000 yards)

all of them together tracing out the curve *AD,* the economy's *production possibilities curve.*

If some of the economy's resources are unemployed and/ or if it does not use the most efficient techniques available it will not be on its production possibilities curve. It will be producing some output combination such as *E.* At combination *E* it is possible to (1) obtain more clothing without giving up any food, (2) obtain more food without giving up any clothing, or (3) obtain more food *and* more clothing. This is the situation that has existed in the United States since 1969 because of the relatively high level of unemployment of both labor and capital. Combinations on the production possibilities curve represent the best the economy can do, given its resources and its techniques. But if combinations such as *E,* lying under the curve, represent all that is produced, the economy's actual output performance is below its potential output performance.

When full employment of resources exists and the economy is using the best available techniques of production, larger quantities of any one item are obtainable only at the expense of smaller quantities of some other item or items. The production possibility curve slopes downward to the right. In Figure 1–1 let the economy initially be at point *B,* producing 7,000 bushels of food and 8,000 yards of clothing. If the society now decides that it wants 9,000 yards of clothing instead of the 8,000 that were being produced, the extra 1,000 yards can be obtained only by giving up 1,500 bushels of food. The decision to produce extra clothing, then, must take into account the sacrifice or the cost of producing it, and this cost is the 1,500 bushels of food that must be forgone. We call such a cost the *alternative cost* of the extra clothing. In general, the alternative cost of a one-unit increase in the output of any one product consists of the value of the product output (other products) that must be forgone in order to produce it. The alternative cost principle is of fundamental importance in economic analysis.

The production possibilities curve in Figure 1–1 is shown bending more sharply downward as the economy moves along it from *A* to *D.* This curvature is correct if, starting from point *A* where no clothing is produced, the alternative costs of clothing rise as the output of clothing is increased and the output of food is decreased. Do rising alternative costs for clothing make sense? Suppose that small quantities of the economy's resources are highly adaptable to food production; small quantities of other resources are highly adaptable to clothing production; and the rest run the gamut of degrees of adaptability to one product or the other.

Starting at point *A* the alternative costs of the first few units of clothing will be relatively small. At *A all* resources of the economy, including those highly adaptable to clothing production, are used to produce food. The production of a unit of clothing requires very little sacrifice of food production because clothing-adaptable resources are pulled out of the production of food and are put to work producing clothing. But as clothing production is increased, resources that are less and less clothing-adaptable and more and more food-adaptable are taken from food production and used for the additional outputs of clothings. This means that more and more food output must be sacrificed for each one-unit increase in clothing output. Presto! Alternative costs of clothing are increasing! And the production possibilities curve is concave to the origin of the diagram.

Frequently, interested groups in a society desire larger outputs of certain goods and services than are being produced. Many believe, for example, that larger quantities of medical services than are being produced would be desirable in the United States. But the alternative costs of such additional medical services tend to be ignored. People assume that the desired expansion of output can be had without decreasing the quantities of other goods and services available. This is so only if there are unemployed resources and inefficient techniques in use that will be tapped to expand the quantities of medical services.

So what is economic activity?

The economic activity that occupies so much of our time consists of using available resources and techniques to satisfy our relatively unlimited wants as fully as possible. But resources available in an economy are scarce and the levels of available techniques have ceilings. These act together to set upper limits on the levels of want fulfillment or the *standards of living* that can actually be reached. In consuming, producing, and exchanging we usually desire that the economy operate in ways that fulfill wants or provide living standards as high as possible. We desire that it provide equity among the persons who live in it. Over time we want to improve and upgrade the productivities of our labor resources; we want to accumulate capital; and we want to improve our techniques of production. Economic activity encompasses all of our attempts to accomplish *efficiency* in production, *economic growth*, and *equity* in the distribution of the economy's output among its population.

ECONOMIC SYSTEMS

The way in which economic activity takes place in any one country is conditioned or shaped by the economic system that it utilizes. The *economic system* used by a country depends on the economic, social, cultural, and political forces at work in the country. Whatever its form—whether it be private enterprise, socialism, or a combination of the two—its purpose is to provide direction and order to economic activity. We shall examine first the functions of an economic system and then consider briefly the alternative systems that exist in the modern world.

The functions of an economic system

Regardless of its form every economic system has certain basic functions to perform. These functions are inherent in the nature of economic activity—they grow out of the scarcity of resources and the level of techniques on the one hand and the unlimited volume of human wants on the other. They cannot be avoided by changing the form of the system.

What to produce.   Every economic system must have some means of determining what its resources and techniques are to be used for. It must be able to evaluate the wants of different individuals and groups and to decide whose wants are relatively most important. It must establish a priority ranking among those wants.

Starting with the current mix of the annual goods and services output of an economy, a number of important questions must be asked—and answered. Would the well-being of the society be increased if more health services were produced? if national defense services were increased? if more food products were produced? if more roads were built? if educational facilities were expanded? The production possibilities curve of the economy informs us that an expansion in any one of these areas usually requires a contraction in others, or has alternative costs in the form of forgone alternative goods and services that would otherwise have been produced. Viewpoints and special interests of individuals and groups differ widely. Some means for effecting compromises and bringing it all together in an orderly system of priorities is essential.

Organization of production. Concurrent with determining what is to be produced, an economic system must organize its production activities. It must have some sort of mechanism for channeling labor and capital resources into their highest priority uses. Consider a country that has been predominantly agricultural and that is now undergoing rapid economic development. As it grows its consumers want more and more industrial products relative to agricultural products. The economic system must have some means of inducing resource owners to transfer the use of some of their resources from the agricultural sector to the industrial sector. In any viable economic system the structure of the want priority ranking will be evolving and changing over time, requiring a constant reallocation of resources away from the production of goods whose priorities are diminishing toward the production of those that are rising on the priority list.

The system should have some means of encouraging production units to use resources efficiently. Resources should be transferred away from the less efficient toward the more efficient production units in a given industry. The system should have some built-in mechanism for inducing producers to use the most efficient combinations of resources available— economizing on those that are becoming increasingly scarce and using relatively larger proportions of those that are becoming more abundant.

Distribution of the product. How is the annual output of an economy to be divided up among the individuals and families that comprise it? What determines who gets the larger shares and who gets the smaller ones? Or does everyone get an equal share? Answers to these questions must be furnished by every economic system along with appropriate means of bringing them about.

The manner in which an economic system performs the distribution function has effects on its efficiency. If the system pays special rewards for superior effort, superior effort is likely to be forthcoming. However, if everyone shares equally regardless of effort, what incentives exist for people to put out superior efforts?

Alternative economic systems

The economic systems of the modern world are a mixture of private enterprise and socialism. There are great variations in the mixture. The systems of Cuba, the Soviet Union, and the Peoples' Republic of China contain large portions of socialism and small portions of private enterprise. In the United States and Canada, the mix is relatively long on private enterprise and relatively short on socialism. But we will understand mixed systems better if we look first at private enterprise and then at socialism in their *pure* or *ideal* form rather than as they actually exist in the real world.

Private enterprise.   A *pure* private enterprise economic system is based on (1) the right of the individual to own property and (2) voluntary exchange. Individuals can own capital resources and/or goods and services. They can also engage in any exchanges that they find mutually beneficial. Production units are put together by and are owned by either individuals or groups of individuals. There are no restrictions on what consumers can consume, what lines of business persons can go into, or where resource owners can place their resources in production. The price system and the profit motive provide the guiding and directing mechanism of the system.

In the determination of what to produce, consumers place values or prices on the existing outputs of goods and services as they spend their incomes. These different prices, relative to the costs of producing the respective goods and services, reflect the relative values of the goods and services and establish the priorities among the many wants of persons as consumers. For example, if over time consumers come to value meat more and vegetables less, they will increase their spending on meat and decrease their spending on vegetables. The price of meat will rise relative to its costs of production while the prices of vegetables will fall relative to their costs of production.

Prices and profits serve to organize production. In the foregoing example meat production becomes more profitable while vegetable production becomes either less profitable or results in losses. Firms in the more profitable lines of endeavor desire to expand and are willing to pay higher prices for resources than those in less profitable or loss-incurring undertakings. Resource owners, desiring to increase their incomes, transfer their resources away from lower-paying uses into higher-paying uses. Thus resources are continually being reallocated from lower- to higher-priority uses. Any given production unit has incentives to operate efficiently because the more efficiently it operates the more profits it will make.

In the distribution of the pure private enterprise economy's output, prices play a key role. Units of labor and units of capital resources tend to be paid according to their respective productivities. Those units contributing more to consumer wants tend to be paid more than those contributing less to consumer wants. So those individuals owning larger quantities of highly productive resources earn higher incomes and can make relatively larger claims on the output of the economy than can those owning smaller quantities of less productive resources. This analysis tells us much about the causes of an unequal distribution of income. An individual at the lower end of the income distribution scale is usually there because he or she owns small quantities of resources that are not very productive. An individual at the upper end of the income distribution scale is usually there because he or she owns large quantities of resources that are highly productive.

Socialism. The basic characteristic of a socialist economic system is that the government owns and/or controls the means of production. It owns the capital of the economy outright. Labor power cannot be separated from the individuals who provide it and is thus not susceptible to government ownership, except under some sort of slave system. It can, however, be controlled by a socialist government. Socialist economic systems usually claim to be more egalitarian in distribution than private enterprise systems. They usually make use of a price system in performing their basic economic functions but they do not give it free rein.

Instead of letting relative product prices show the desired priorities of consumers for different goods and services, the socialist government is likely to control prices. Priorities are likely to be established by government planning agencies. These agencies often establish target outputs for each of the many goods and services that the economy produces. High priorities may be given to such basic products as health care services and housing. Many so-called luxury goods such as private airplanes, fur coats, and palacial mansions may be assigned low priorities. Government agencies, then, play a key role in determining what is to be produced. But if the government is elected democratically, the voices of consumers as voters cannot be totally ignored.

The organization of production in the socialistic economic system is likely to be accomplished largely by government direction with the government manipulating prices to achieve its desired objectives. Since production units are owned by the government, capital resources can be allocated by government planning agencies in accordance with the priorities established for achieving target outputs of final goods and services. Labor allocation may pose a problem since the egalitarian values of a socialistic regime may prevent the use of wage differentials to induce labor to move from one employment area to another. In the absence of wage inducements, it may be necessary for the government to exercise coercion with regard to where and at what labor will work.

Distribution of the economy's output will also be determined largely by the government. Through the control of wage rates and employment possibilities it may partially achieve whatever distribution goals it sets up. In addition, price controls on some products and subsidization of consumption of other products may be used to move toward the desired distribution of output.

Mixed systems.   Most economic systems are neither purely private enterprise nor purely socialistic. The United States leans heavily on private enterprise, but government regulation, control, and ownership of production facilities are widespread. The Soviet Union is predominantly socialistic but it uses the market mechanism rather extensively and even allows a little private enterprise to exist.

In the United States, some 65 to 70 percent of the economy's output is produced by private enterprise, or by the *private sector* of the economy. The output of the private sector includes most of the things that we purchase—automobiles, clothing, food, health care, telephone communications, recreation and entertainment, and the like. Production facilities for these goods and services are privately owned and operated with the price system and the profit motive providing the guiding and directing mechanism.

The other 30 to 35 percent of the output is produced socialistically, or by the *public sector* of the economy. This portion of the output consists to a large extent of services—national defense, police and fire protection, educational services, and regulatory services. In addition, most streets and roads are provided by the government. Most outputs of the public sector are not sold for prices, rather they are said to be provided "free." This is a mistaken idea however. Resources are required to produce them and resources so used are not available to produce private sector goods and services. Thus the costs of public sector services are the values of the resources used to produce them in the best alternative uses of those resources. In some cases, notably in government owned and operated public utilities, the government-produced product is sold to consumers at market prices.

A FRAMEWORK FOR ECONOMIC ANALYSIS

The purpose of this book is to develop a basic framework of principles for the analysis of economic activity. We will be concerned primarily with a mixed economic system, one that is predominantly private enterprise but which has a substantial public sector. The United States economy is, of course, the one that will occupy our attention.

Since the U.S. economy is essentially a market economy we will begin with the basic market tools of analysis or principles. These are the principles governing demand, supply, and price determination for individual goods and services. We will then consider the economy as a whole—the general body of economic principles that is termed *macroeconomics*. The last part of the book consists of the set of principles called *microeconomics* which pertains to individual economic units and their relationships to one another.

Throughout the book we will attempt to establish causal relationships among facts and occurrences. We want to get at what causes what; why the economy behaves as it does; and what, if anything, can be done about it. *Principles* are really statements of causal relationships that appear to hold under most circumstances. Sets of related principles are usually called *theories*. Above all we want our principles and theories to be useful in understanding the world we live in, but this does not mean that they are irrefutable. Hopefully, those we develop will be the best that we can come up with at the present time. But certainly they are susceptible to improvement.

We should distinguish at the outset between *positive* economic analysis and *normative* economic analysis. *Positive economics* is concerned with what *is;* that is, with the causal relations that actually exist, as nearly as we can determine them. *Normative economics* is concerned with what we think *ought to be.* Economic policy making should stem from both positive and normative analysis. We need to determine what is; measure it against what ought to be; and then prescribe policies that will make what is conform to what ought to be. Obviously this is a very tall order!

SUMMARY

In this chapter we sketch out an overview of what economics is about. We consider the nature of economic activity and discuss the general ways in which alternative economic systems carry it out. Finally we consider the general theoretical framework within which economic analysis is conducted.

Economic activity it rooted in the scarcity of the means available for satisfying the unlimited wants of human beings. An economy's scarce supplies of labor and capital, together with its highest attainable levels of technology determine its production possibilities and, consequently, the extent to which it can fulfill human wants. In any economy that is on its production possibilities curve the cost of increasing the production of any one good or service is the value of the goods and services that must be given up to achieve the increase. This alternative cost principle underlies the whole range of consumption, production, and exchange activities.

In the modern world two types of economic systems are used to carry on economic activity. The pure private enterprise system uses markets, prices, and profits to determine what is to be produced, how production is to be organized, and how the economy's output is to be distributed. A pure socialistic system uses central planning to carry out its functions. Most economic systems are mixtures of private enterprise and socialism, although they may lean heavily in either the one direction or the other.

The economic analysis of this book is that of a predominantly private enterprise system. We will be interested in sets of macro- and microeconomic principles. We will also be concerned with both positive and normative economic analysis.

QUESTIONS AND PROBLEMS

1. What are some of the sources of human wants? In what ways do they indicate that the total wants of the persons making up a society are insatiable?

2. Does it seem reasonable to you to expect people to voluntarily restrain their consumption of energy? Food? Housing? Entertainment?

3. For each of the following, determine whether or not it is a capital resource explaining why or why not:
    a. A paper clip used on a term paper.
    b. The bridge on the river Kwai.
    c. A dollar bill.
    d. A corporation stock certificate.

4. In terms of the alternative cost principle what would be the nature of the cost of an increase in health care services in the United States?

5. Discuss the nature of economic activity.

6. What functions must a socialistic economic system perform? How does it perform them?

7. What functions must a private enterprise system perform? How does it perform them?

Chapter 2

The basics—demand, supply, and price determination

CHECKLIST OF ECONOMIC CONCEPTS

Market
Demand
Complementary goods and services
Substitute goods and services
Demand schedule
Demand curve
Change in demand
Supply
Change in supply
Equilibrium price
Equilibrium quantity
Shortage
Surplus
Price ceiling
Price support or price floor
Aggregate demand
Aggregate supply
Full employment output level
Price level
Unemployment

A n economics graduate student stopped at a roadside stand in rural Oklahoma, attracted by a display of beautiful red, vine-ripened tomatoes. The price quoted her by the old farm lady at the stand seemed extraordinarily low as compared with supermarket prices. When asked how she determined the price at which to sell, the old lady replied, "It's all a matter of demand and supply, dearie." As that wise old lady indicated, not much progress can be made in economic analysis without a thorough grounding in the fundamentals of demand, supply, and market price determination.

MARKETS

The *market* for any good or service consists of the area within which its potential buyers and sellers interact with each other and are able to transfer ownership of units of it. Some markets are local in scope. Some are regional. Others are national or international. The scope of a market depends upon the nature of the item being exchanged and on the time horizon we have in mind. The market for haircuts in Billings, Montana, is predominantly local. The market for automobiles is international in scope. Over a short time period—say, six months—we can identify local markets for machinists. Wichita, Kansas, may be one such market. If Boeing and other aircraft manufacturers were to move out unemployment would exist in the market in the short run since machinists and their families may not be willing immediately to consider employment elsewhere. However, over a longer time period—say, two years—the attraction of higher incomes in Denver and Kansas City will surely attract machinists away from lower wage areas where unemployment exists or threatens. The market for the longer period is thus regional in scope.

Selling markets for specific products are classified according to the degree of competition existing among sellers. If there is a large number of sellers of an item—wheat for example— the market for it is said to be *competitive*. If there is a single seller of an item like telephone service, the market is said to be *monopolized*. Where elements of monopoly and elements of competition are mixed, as they are in the production and sale of crude oil, markets are characterized as being *imperfectly competitive*.

DEMAND

Human wants manifest themselves in demands for goods and services. Each good or service produced in an economy can be singled out for an examination of its demand characteristics. Demand for an item obviously refers to the quantities that buyers will purchase; however, the quantities have no meaning unless they are stated in terms of time flows. It makes no sense to say that consumers in a given market for sugar will purchase 10,000 pounds. It does make sense, however, to say that they will purchase 10,000 pounds per month. Quantities demanded must always be stated in terms of rates per unit of time. Convenience and relevance will determine whether the appropriate time unit should be per day, per month, per year, or per some other period. Once the meaning of quantities demanded is understood, we can consider what it is that determines them. Generally speaking, quantities demanded per unit of time are determined by: (1) buyers' psychological tastes and preferences; (2) the number of buyers in the market; (3) the incomes of buyers; (4) the prices of related goods and services; and (5) the item's own price.

Buyers' tastes and preferences, or their psychological attitudes toward particular goods and services, affect the quantities of them that they will buy. An interesting example of the last few years is provided by citizens' band radios. As truckers and automobile drivers became aware of them and came to enjoy their use, the quantities that buyers would purchase increased by leaps and bounds.

The number of buyers in the market for a good affects quantities demanded in a direct and obvious way. Entry of new buyers into the market increases the quantities demanded per unit of time. A baby boom increases quantities demanded of diapers and other essential baby gear. Conversely, when buyers drop out of a market quantities demanded will decrease. What happened to the quantities of engineers demanded when the space program was curtailed in the late 1960s and early 1970s?

Quantities demanded of an item are clearly related to the income or purchasing power of its buyers. They more money buyers have to spend the greater the quantity they will want to buy of most goods and services. When their purchasing power falls, they are inclined to buy less. This phenomenon was amply demonstrated during the economic recession of 1974 and the ensuing economic recovery of 1975 and 1976. Quantities demanded fell during the recession and expanded during the recovery period.

The prices of related goods and services also affect the quantities of any one item that consumers will take. Items may be related in either of two ways. They may be *complementary* which means that they are used together. Bread and butter, tennis rackets and tennis balls, and men's suits and neckties provide examples. Or they may be *substitutes* like beef and pork, nails and glue, and wood and metal. If the price of one of two complementary goods goes up—say the price of men's suits rises—consumers tend to take less of it per unit of time. Thus they will have less desire for—that is, there will be less demand for—neckties. If the price of one of two substitutes rises, the consumers will turn toward and demand more of the substitute for it. An increase in the price of beef would be expected to cause an increase in the quantities demanded of pork because pork has become a relatively better buy for the dollar.

Probably the most important determinant of the amount of a good that consumers will purchase is the price at which it is sold. It should be—but is not—obvious to everyone that buyers will purchase less of a good at higher prices than they will at lower prices. Higher prices of the good induce consumers to turn to relatively lower-priced substitutes. In addition, an increase in the price of a good reduces consumers' purchasing power, causing them to purchase smaller amounts of almost everything, including the one in question. We examine these forces in more detail in Chapter 10.

Definition of demand

The forces that affect the quantities of a good or service that consumers will purchase are summed up in the definition of demand. *Demand for a good means the quantities per unit of time that buyers will take at all possible alternative prices, other things being equal.* Note that the relation between the price of the good and the quantities that buyers will take is the focus of attention. Tastes and preferences, number of buyers in the group, consumers' incomes, and prices of related goods constitute the "other things" that remain equal or constant in defining the demand for the good.

Suppose that an experiment is conducted with a group of consumers to determine their demand for gasoline. The psychological tastes and preferences–the states of mind–of the consumers, together with their number, must be held constant throughout the experiment. So must their incomes and the prices of both substitutes for and complements to gasoline. Let the consumers be confronted with a price level for gasoline that is left in effect long enough to allow their consumption rate to become fully adjusted to it. We record the number of gallons per month they take at that price level. Now let the comsumers be confronted with a different price level and suppose that it, too, is left in effect until a full adjustment to it is made. At the new price level we also record the gallons per month that the consumers take. Still other price levels can be assumed and in each case we observe and record the quantity purchased.

Let columns (1) and (2) of Table 2–1 be the results of the experiment. These two columns are the demand schedule of the group for gasoline—they show the quantities that will be taken per unit of time at alternative price levels, other things being equal. The demand schedule is plotted as *demand curve DD* in Figure 2–1.

It is essential for analytical purposes to distinguish between a movement along a given demand schedule or demand curve and a change in demand. If the demand curve for gasoline is *DD* in Figure 2–1, a change in its price from $0.80 to $0.60

Table 2–1
Demand for gasoline

(1) Price (dollars per gallon)	(2) Quantity (gallons per month)	(3)
$2.00	80,000	85,000
1.80	90,000	97,500
1.60	100,000	110,000
1.40	110,000	122,500
1.20	120,000	135,000
1.10	130,000	147,500
0.80	140,000	160,000
0.60	150,000	172,500
0.40	160,000	185,000
0.20	170,000	197,500

Figure 2–1
Demand for gasoline

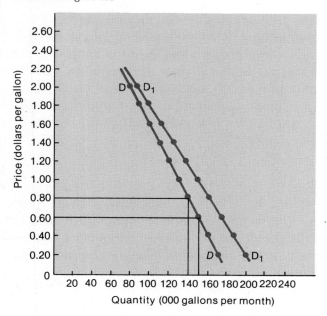

per gallon will increase the *quantity demanded* from 140,000 gallons to 150,000 gallons per month. This increase in quantity is referred to as a *movement along* the demand curve resulting from a change in the price of the product. It is not called a change in demand.

Changes in demand

The term demand is used to refer to an entire curve so a *change in demand* means a shift in the curve, say from *DD* to D_1D_1. A change in demand is caused by a change in one of the "other things" that are held constant in defining a given demand schedule or demand curve. In the gasoline case, suppose that prices are given and at their present level the demand curve is *DD*. Now suppose that consumer incomes rise 10 percent above what they were before and that we conduct a new set of experiments with consumer incomes constant at the higher level. The result will be an increase in the gallons per month consumed at each and every price level. The new demand schedule is represented by columns (1) and (3) of Table 2–1 and is plotted as D_1D_1 in Figure 2–1. A change in consumer tastes and preferences, in the prices of substitutes for gasoline, or in the prices of complements for gasoline will also cause changes in demand for the product, that is, shifts in the entire demand curve.

The slope of a demand curve

The demand curves for most goods and services slope downward to the right. A downward sloping demand curve means simply that consumers will buy more of a good per unit of time at lower prices than they will at higher prices. We call this proposition the *law of demand*. It appears to be perfectly obvious and almost trivial in character. Yet many errors of analysis and policy are made because it is either not known or is ignored by policy makers. For example, what impact would you expect an increase in the federal minimum wage rate to have on the amount of labor that employers will demand?

SUPPLY

Supplies of goods and services are provided by enterprises of many kinds. The supply of any specific good consists of the quantities per unit of time the enterprises that produce and sell it will place on the market. These quantities depend on (1) the price of the item, (2) the prices of resources used to produce them, and (3) the production techniques available to the enterprises that produce and sell them.

Definition of supply

Supply of a good or service is defined as the quantities per unit of time that will be placed on the market at all possible alternative prices, other things being equal. Again the relationship between the price of the good and the quantities of it are singled out for consideration. The prices of resources used to produce the good and the technology available to the producers and sellers comprise the "other things" that are held constant.

To obtain the supply schedule or supply curve for gasoline, suppose we experiment with producers or refiners. Given the prices of resources used—labor, crude oil, refinery costs, and

Table 2–2
Supply of gasoline

(1) Price (dollars per gallon)	(2) Quantity (gallons per month)	(3)
$2.00	185,000	157,500
1.80	180,000	155,000
1.60	175,000	152,500
1.40	170,000	150,000
1.20	165,000	147,500
1.00	160,000	145,000
0.80	155,000	142,500
0.60	150,000	140,000
0.40	145,000	137,500
0.20	140,000	135,000

the like—along with the available refinery technology, they are confronted with alternative gasoline prices. Each price is maintained long enough to allow a full adjustment of supplier to it. Suppose that columns (1) and (2) of Table 2–2 result from the experiment. These columns constitute the *supply schedule* and, plotted in Figure 2–2, they become the *supply curve.*

Figure 2–2
Supply of gasoline

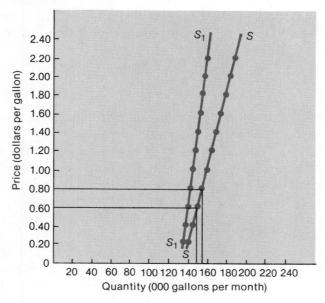

The slope of a supply curve

The supply curves for most goods and services slope upward to the right. The quantity supplied of any one good or service will ordinarily be greater at higher prices than it will be at lower prices. The higher the price offered for a product the more profitable it becomes for producers to make it and place it on the market; consequently, the more strongly inclined they are to do so. The lower the price offered, the less worthwhile production of the item will be and the smaller will be the quantity placed on the market per unit of time.

A change in the price of an item with the "other things" remaining constant generates a *movement along* the supply curve. If the price rises from $0.60 to $0.80 per gallon the resulting change in quantity supplied from 150,000 to 155,000 gallons per month is *not* called change in supply. It must be carefully distinguished from a change in supply.

Changes in supply

A *change in supply* means a shift in the entire supply schedule or supply curve. Such a shift occurs when there is a change in one of the "other things" that we have been holding constant. For example, a rise in the price of crude oil, which is a key resource used in producing gasoline, will reduce the amount of gasoline that will be placed on the market at *all* possible alternative prices of gasoline. Consider the rise in the price of crude oil from approximately $3.50 per barrel to approximately $10.00 per barrel from 1973 to 1974. In Table 2–2 it may change the supply schedule to something like that of columns (1) and (3). In Figure 2–2 the supply curve would shift from SS to S_1S_1.

PRICE DETERMINATION

Prices in competitive markets for goods and services are determined by the interactions of buyers and sellers. They are not set, as many people seem to believe, by the whims of individual sellers or even by sellers seeking to take advantage of the public. First, we will note the equilibrium price and quantity of a product. Second, the repercusions from a lower-than-equilibrium price will be examined. Third, the effects of a price above the equilibrium level will be considered.

Equilibrium price and quantity

The *equilibrium price* of a product is the price at which sellers want to sell the same quantity per unit of time that buyers want to buy. The quantity on which they settle is called the *equilibrium quantity*. If the demand for and the supply of the product are given and are constant over time, its equilibrium price and quantity can be determined. They will not change unless a change occurs in either demand or supply.

Consider the gasoline example. In Table 2–3 columns (1) and (2) comprise the demand schedule and columns (1) and (3) make up the supply schedule. At a price level of $0.60 per gallon, buyers will take 150,000 gallons per month and suppliers will place the same quantity on the market. These are the equilibrium price and quantity, respectively. Figure 2–3 shows the same information in graphic form. At no other price level do the quantity decisions of both buyers and sellers coincide.

A price below equilibrium

If the price of a product is below its equilibrium level a *shortage* of the item will occur. At a price below the equilibrium level, buyers want a quantity greater than the equilibrium quantity while sellers want to place a smaller quantity, only,

Table 2–3
Demand, supply, and equilibrium price for gasoline

(1) Price (dollars per gallon)	(2) Quantity (gallons per month)	(3)
	Demanded	Supplied
$2.00	80,000	185,000
1.80	90,000	180,000
1.60	100,000	175,000
1.40	110,000	170,000
1.20	120,000	165,000
1.00	130,000	160,000
0.80	140,000	155,000
0.60	150,000	150,000
0.40	160,000	145,000
0.20	170,000	140,000

Figure 2–3
Equilibrium price for gasoline

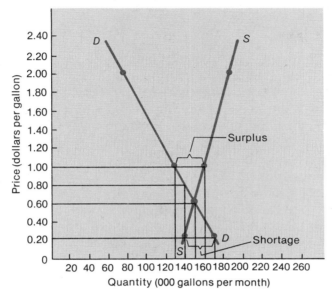

Quantity (000 gallons per month)

on the market. The shortage is equal to the difference between the quantity that buyers want to buy and the quantity that sellers will place on the market.

Referring again to the gasoline case in Table 2–3 and Figure 2–3, suppose that the price is $0.20 per gallon. At that price buyers want 170,000 gallons per month and sellers will place only 140,000 gallons on the market. The shortage amounts to 30,000 gallons per month.

A shortage sets forces in motion that cause the price to rise. At $0.20 per gallon suppliers place only 140,000 gallons per month on the market. What is that quantity worth to buyers? The demand curve provides the answer. For 140,000 gallons per month buyers would be willing to pay as much as $0.80 per gallon. Thus those buyers who are unable to get all they want at $0.20 per gallon are willing to offer more than that price in order to bid gasoline away from other buyers. Bidding by these buyers who are experiencing shortages drives the price up. As the price rises the total quantity desired by all buyers decreases and the total quantity that sellers will place on the market increases. As long as a shortage exists buyers have an incentive to offer higher prices. When the price reaches its equilibrium level the shortage disappears and the rise in price stops.

A price above equilibrium

A product price above the equilibrium level generates a *surplus* of the item. At the higher price buyers will take less than they would take at the equilibrium level, while sellers want to sell more. Thus a surplus equal to the difference between the quantity that sellers want to sell and that which buyers want to buy comes into existence.

Suppose the price of gasoline in Table 2-3 and Figure 2-3 is $1.00 per gallon. Consumers can find uses worth that much or more for only 130,000 gallons. Sellers are induced to place 160,000 gallons on the market at that price. The resulting surplus is 30,000 gallons per month.

A surplus of a product causes its price to move toward the equilibrium level. In the foregoing gasoline market, at $1.00 per gallon some sellers are unable to sell as much as they would like. To get rid of their surpluses they undercut other sellers' prices and the price moves downward. As the price decreases, buyers are willing to increase their purchases and sellers reduce the amounts that they will place on the market. At $0.60 per gallon—the equilibrium price—the surplus no longer exists and the forces that drive the price level downward have disappeared.

EFFECTS OF CHANGES IN DEMAND AND SUPPLY

When demand and supply for a product are constant over time the product price tends to move toward the equilibrium level and stay there. However, demand and supply do not ordinarily remain constant. Changes in either one will cause changes in the equilibrium price and quantity exchanged. In determining the effects of such changes it is convenient first to hold supply constant and change demand; then to hold demand constant and change supply; and finally to consider simultaneous changes in demand and supply. In each case we want to observe the effects on the price and quantity exchanged.

Changes in demand, supply constant

An increase in the demand for a product will cause an increase in its equilibrium price and an increase in the equilibrium quantity exchanged if supply remains constant. In Figure 2–4, let the initial demand curve and supply curve for gasoline be D_1D_1 and S_1S_1, respectively. The equilibrium price is p_1 and the quantity exchanged is g_1. Now suppose that rising consumer incomes and a larger automobile population causes the demand for gasoline to increase to D_2D_2. The old demand curve D_1D_1 is no longer relevant. At price level p_1 a shortage amounting to g_1g_3 occurs. Consumers, bidding against each other for the available supply, drive up the price. As the price rises, sellers place larger quantities on the market and consumers cut back the quantities they want to purchase. When the price reaches p_2 it is in equilibrium. Buyers want quantity g_2 at that price and sellers are willing to place the same quantity on the market.

Suppose, however, that the government imposes a price ceiling on gasoline at level p_1 while the demand for it increases from D_1D_1 to D_2D_2. This is essentially what happened in 1979

Figure 2–4
An increase in the demand for gasoline

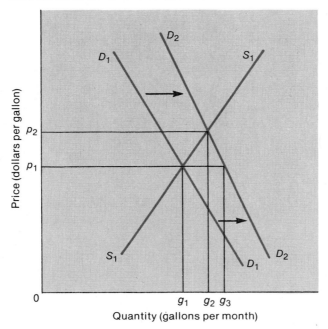

as a set of price ceilings on gasoline became effective. The increase in demand creates a shortage and the price freeze ensures that the shortage will persist over time. The price cannot perform its market function when it is frozen; that is, it cannot rise to (1) stimulate output and (2) to induce consumers to cut back their consumption. An effective price ceiling on a product will *always* cause a shortage of it to come into existence and to persist over time.

A decrease in the demand for a product or service with its supply remaining constant will cause its equilibrium price and quantity exchanged to decrease. Let D_1D_1 and S_1S_1 in Figure 2–5 be the initial demand curve and supply curve for wheat. The equilibrium price is p_1 and the quantity exchanged is w_1. Now suppose that foreigners—say the Russians—decide to drop out of the market. Demand decreases—the initial demand curve D_1D_1 shifts to the left—to D_2D_2. After the decrease in demand, consumers would be willing to purchase only w_3 bushels at price p_1. However, sellers will continue to place w_1 bushels on the market and a surplus of w_3w_1 bushels per year is generated. To get rid of their individual surpluses, sell-

Figure 2–5
A decrease in the demand for wheat

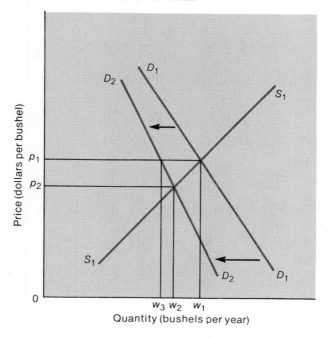

ers undercut each other's prices driving the price level down toward the p_2 level. Buyers increase their purchases above the w_3 bushel level and sellers reduce the amounts they want to sell below the w_1 bushel level. When the price reaches p_2 buyers will want to buy quantity w_2, which is also the quantity that sellers want to sell. The new equilibrium price is p_2.

But what happens if the government supports the price of wheat at the p_1 level after the decrease in demand has occurred? A chronic surplus of w_3w_1 bushels per year exists. Such a price support prevents the price of wheat from carrying out its market function of equating the quantities that sellers want to place on the market with the quantities that buyers want to purchase. If price supports are to be effective they must be above the equilibrium price level of the price-supported product. If they are not, the equilibrium price will prevail in the market. Effective price supports necessarily cause chronic surpluses. Yet, over the long period of time that farm price supports have been used, most people, including farmers, have been perpetually surprised that farm product surpluses were accruing and causing disposal problems. The surpluses have usually been attributed to flaws in the administration and operation of support programs.

Changes in supply, demand constant

An increase in the supply of a good or service with demand remaining constant will cause its equilibrium price to fall and the equilibrium quantity exchanged to rise. Suppose that D_1D_1 and S_1S_1 in Figure 2–6 represent the demand for and supply of hand-held electronic calculators per year. The equilibrium price is p_1 and the quantity per year purchased is e_1. Now suppose that a technological breakthrough in the production of calculators takes place, shifting the supply curve to S_2S_2. If the price remains at p_1 a surplus of e_1e_3 occurs. The surplus induces individual sellers to reduce their prices to sell off their inventories. The lower the price goes the more units purchasers will want and the fewer units producers will place on the market. At price p_2, equilibrium again exists and the quantity exchanged is e_2 units per year. If the price were held at p_1 by legislation or by concerted actions of producers, the surplus would be chronic.

Figure 2–6
An increase in the supply of calculators

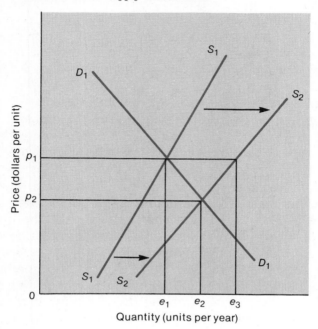

A decrease in the supply of an item will raise its equilibrium price and decrease the equilibrium quantity exchanged. Let the initial demand for and supply of coal be D_1D_1 and S_1S_1 in Figure 2–7. The equilibrium price is p_1 per ton and c_1 tons are exchanged per year. The United Mine Workers' Union now negotiates a substantial increase in coal miners' wage rates and the supply of coal is consequently decreased to S_2S_2 since the cost of producing a ton of coal is now higher than it was before the wage rate increase. At price p_1 there is no change in the amount that purchasers want; however, producers will place only c_3 tons on the market at that price. A shortage of c_3c_1 tons occurs. Individual purchasers, unable to get as much as they desire at p_1, bid for the available supply. As the price rises, producers will place more on the market while buyers are willing to purchase smaller quantities per year. When the price reaches p_2 per ton there will no longer be a shortage. Price p_2 is the equilibrium price and the quantity exchanged will be c_2.

The function of the price in alleviating the shortage would

Figure 2–7
A decrease in the supply of coal

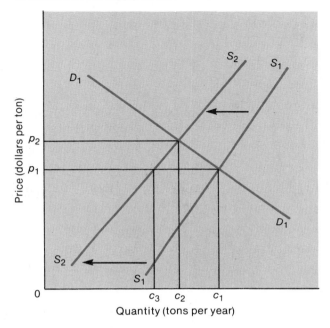

be thwarted if price controls were placed on coal at level p_1. Such a price ceiling would make the shortage chronic. We often witness pressure on governments from large segments of the population calling for price ceilings on products for which prices are rising—crude oil, for example. Whenever this pressure is heeded the result is inevitably a shortage.

Changes in both demand and supply

Simultaneous increases in the demand and the supply for a product will increase the equilibrium quantity exchanged, but the effect on its equilibrium price will depend upon which shows the greater increase. In Figure 2–8 the demand for pencils increases from D_1D_1 to D_2D_2 while the supply of the item increases from S_1S_1 to S_2S_2. The quantity exchanged increases from x_1 to x_2. A decrease in price occurs if the increase in demand is less than the increase in supply in the neighborhood of price level p_1. The determinants of the direction of the price change are most easily seen by asking what would happen to the price if both demand and supply in the neighborhood

Figure 2–8
A simultaneous increase in demand and supply for pencils

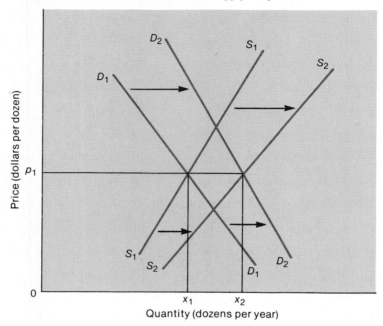

of price p_1 increased by the same amount. Obviously there would be no change in the price. It would remain at p_1 as Figure 2–8 shows. The price will fall if the increase in demand is less than the increase in supply and it will rise if the increase in demand exceeds the increase in supply.

A demand increase accompanied by a decrease in supply will cause the price to rise, but the effect on the quantity exchanged will depend upon which curve shifts upward by the greater amount. The gasoline market during the Arab oil boycott of the winter of 1973–74 provides an excellent illustration of such simultaneous changes in demand and supply. In Figure 2–9 while demand for gasoline was increasing from D_1D_1 to D_2D_2 the boycott was decreasing its supply from S_1S_1 to S_2S_2. The result was an increase in price from p_1 to p_2. The quantity exchanged was reduced from g_1 to g_2 because the upward shift in the supply curve in the neighborhood of quantity g_1 exceeded the upward shift in the demand curve. If the upward shift in the supply curve had been less than that in the demand curve the quantity exchanged would have increased. If the shift had been the same for both curves the quantity exchanged would have remained constant.

Figure 2–9
An increase in demand and a decrease in supply for gasoline

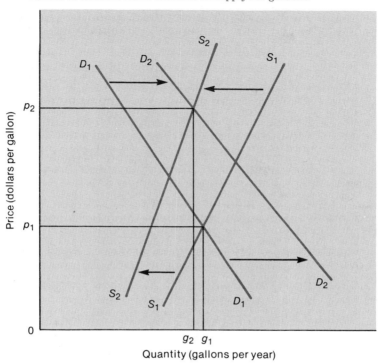

AGGREGATE DEMAND AND AGGREGATE SUPPLY

The concepts of demand and supply can be extended from individual goods and services to the total amount or the aggregate of goods and services that the economy produces. So extended, aggregate demand and aggregate supply concepts will help us understand the causes of such economic illnesses as inflation, recession, and unemployment. Further, they will help us understand what economic medicines may be needed to cure those ills.

Aggregate demand

We noted in Chapter 1 that some of the economy's output is produced by the private sector and the rest is produced by the government or the public sector. Buyers of the economy's output consist of private buyers—households and businesses—and the government. *Aggregate demand* thus refers to the *physical quantities* of the economy's goods and services that will be purchased per year by consumers, businesses, and government units at various alternative price levels, other things being equal. Chief among the "other things" that remain constant in defining any one aggregate demand curve is (1) the level of government spending, (2) the level of government tax collections, and (3) the economy's money supply. The importance of these magnitudes will become evident as we move along in the analysis. If they remain constant or given, it would be expected that the higher the general price level, the lower the total quantities of goods and services purchased, and vice versa. That is, aggregate demand curve for the economy slopes downward to the right.

Aggregate demand is illustrated by the D_1D_1 curve in Figure 2–10. The horizontal axis of the diagram is a composite measure of the goods and services the economy produces. Since pairs of shoes, airplanes, appendectomies, and the like cannot be added together meaningfully, let the output of the economy be divided into "baskets" of goods and services, each basket containing a proportional part of each good and service produced. The price axis is the price per "basket" and thus represents the price level for the composite of all goods and services.

Figure 2–10
Aggregate demand and aggregate supply

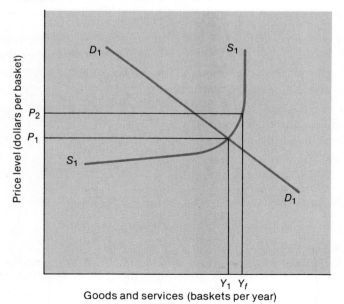

Goods and services (baskets per year)

Aggregate demand curve D_1D_1 shows the quantities (baskets) of goods and services that would be purchased at alternative price levels given (1) the total level of government spending, (2) government tax collections, and (3) the money supply of the economy.

Aggregate supply

The economy's aggregate supply of goods and services is represented by S_1S_1 in Figure 2–10. It shows the quantities of goods and services per year that would be produced at alternative price levels, other things being equal. The major "other things" that must remain constant are (1) resource prices and (2) the state of technology in the economy. At an output level of Y_f, which is generated by a price level of P_2, all of the economy's labor and capital are fully employed. That output level is appropriately called the full-employment level of output and, since larger outputs are impossible to achieve, the supply curve will be vertical at prices higher than P_2. At price levels below P_2, given the prices of labor and capital resources used in production and the state of technology, it is not profitable for producers to use the economy's entire supplies of resources. Unemployment occurs at a price level such as P_1.

Equilibrium price and output levels

The price level of the economy and its output level, also, are determined by aggregate demand and aggregate supply. In Figure 2–10 with aggregate demand curve D_1D_1 and aggregate supply curve S_1S_1 the price level of the economy will be P_1. The output level will be Y_1. Since the output level must be Y_f in order to have full employment of labor and capital, we show unemployment existing at the equilibrium level of output. As we shall see the equilibrium output is not necessarily one at which unemployment occurs—it depends on the position of the aggregate demand curve relative to the aggregate supply curve.

Effects of changes in aggregate demand

An increase in aggregate demand with aggregate supply remaining constant will increase the general price level in

the economy. If aggregate demand and aggregate supply before
the increase are such that unemployment exists, the increase
will also expand the economy's output and decrease the unemployment rate. Suppose in Figure 2–11 that D_1D_1 and S_1S_1
represent the initial state of economic affairs. Now let the
economy's stock of money rise (we will consider the causes
of this in Chapter 5) expanding total spending in the economy.
The aggregate demand curve shifts from D_1D_1 to some position
such as D_2D_2, raising the general price level from P_1 to P_2
and output from Y_1 to Y_f. We show an increase in aggregate
demand sufficient to eliminate unemployment; however it need
not be large enough to do so completely.

   If the initial equilibrium position is one at which output is
at the full employment level, an increase in aggregate demand
will increase the price level but cannot increase the economy's
output. In Figure 2–11 suppose demand and supply are D_2D_2
and S_1S_1 initially. Now let demand increase to D_3D_3. The
price level rises to P_3 but output remains at Y_f.

   A decrease in aggregate demand will decrease the economy's output and the employment level and will tend to de-

Figure 2–11
The effects of changes in aggregate demand

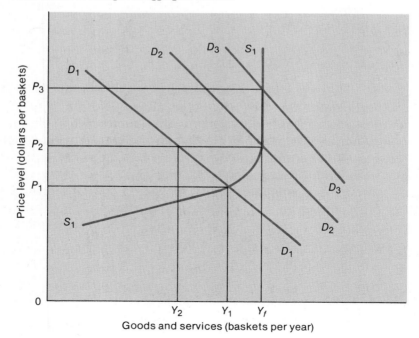

crease the price level. Suppose in Figure 2–11 that the demand is D_2D_2 and supply is S_1S_1. Now let aggregate demand decrease to D_1D_1. If sellers of goods and services refuse to lower their prices buyers will take only Y_2 and output will fall as inventories of goods are built up by sellers. If the surplus goods induce sellers to lower the prices at which they will sell to P_1, output will decrease, but only to the Y_1 level.

Effects of changes in aggregate supply

An increase in aggregate supply with aggregate demand remaining constant will increase the economy's output of goods and services and will tend to decrease the price level. Suppose in Figure 2–12 that D_1D_1 and S_1S_1 are the initial demand and supply curves. Improvements in technology are developed making the economy's labor and capital resources more productive. The full employment level of output for the economy moves from Y_{f1} to Y_{f2} and the aggregate supply curve shifts to the right to S_2S_2. At the original price level P_1 surpluses of goods and services would accumulate and the surpluses would put downward pressure on the price level

Figure 2–12
The effects of an increase in aggregate supply

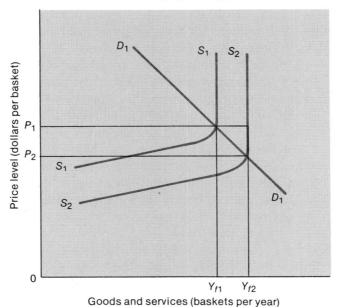

Price level (dollars per basket)

Goods and services (baskets per year)

Figure 2–13
The effects of a decrease in aggregate supply

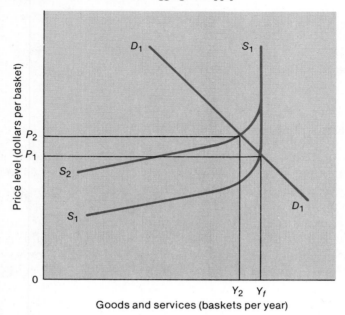

as producers and sellers undercut each others' prices to get rid of their surpluses. At price level P_2 equilibrium would prevail and buyers in the economy would purchase all that is produced. We show both the original equilibrium output and the equilibrium output after the increase in supply at full employment levels. Obviously both could be at less than full employment levels if aggregate demand were less than D_1D_1.

A decrease in aggregate supply with aggregate demand constant will increase the economy's price level. It will also cause an increase in unemployment of resources. In Figure 2–13 the initial aggregate demand and supply curves are D_1D_1 and S_1S_1. Now suppose that economy-wide increases in wage rates take place. The economy's total supplies of labor and capital, together with its level of technology, do not change, so the full employment level of output remains at Y_f. The upward sloping part of the aggregate supply curve is shifted upward (to the left) by the higher wage rates and becomes S_2S_1. Shortages at the initial equilibrium price level P_1 cause the price level to rise to P_2. The new equilibrium output will be Y_2 and, since it is smaller than Y_f, unemployment is generated.

SUMMARY

Demand, supply and price determination are basic concepts in economic analysis. They can be applied to the markets for individual goods and services. They are also useful for economy-wide types of problems.

Demand for a product summarizes what the buyers of it are willing to do. The demand schedule and demand curve for the product show the quantities per unit of time that buyers will take at alternative prices, other things being equal. Changes in the "other things" will shift the demand curve. Changes in demand must be kept separate from movements along a given demand curve.

Supply of a product summarizes what producers and sellers of the good are willing to do. The supply schedule and supply curve show the quantities that will be placed on the market at alternative price levels, other things being equal. Changes in supply—shifts in the supply curve—result from changes in one or more of the "other things."

Buyers and sellers of a product interacting in the market for it determine its equilibrium price and quantity. A price below the equilibrium level creates shortages and upward pressure on the price. A price above the equilibrium level generates surpluses and downward pressure on prices. Changes in demand, supply, or both cause changes in equilibrium prices and outputs.

For the economy as a whole, aggregate demand and aggregate supply curves of representative "baskets" of goods provide important tools of analysis. They help us get at the causes of changes in the general price level. They also help us understand how the economy's output and employment levels are determined.

QUESTIONS AND PROBLEMS

1. Show with a diagram and explain the difference between a change in demand and a movement along a demand curve.

2. Show with a diagram and explain the difference between a change in supply and a movement along a supply curve.

3. In a free market (no collusion among buyers and sellers and no governmental intervention) for crude oil would you expect

price to be above, below, or at an equilibrium level? Explain what happens in each case.

4. Explain for each of the following events whether gasoline demand, supply, or both is affected and what the impact will be on the price and quantity exchanged if free markets exist within the United States:

   a. An increase in consumer incomes.
   b. A decrease in the importation of foreign crude oil.
   c. Both a and b combined.
   d. An improvement in domestic crude oil recovery techniques.
   e. Deterioration of the nations refining capacity.

5. Draw an aggregate supply curve and explain its shape.

6. If resource costs rise what happens to the aggregate supply curve? Explain and illustrate.

PART TWO

MACROECONOMICS: THE WHOLE BALL OF WAX

The macroeconomic part of the analytical framework of economics enables us to think logically and consistently about the economy as a whole. Macroeconomic analysis has at least two major closely related objectives. The first is to provide a means of measuring the overall performance of the economy. The second is to examine the nature, causes, and control of economic fluctuations. Both of these objectives are pursued in Part Two. In more advanced treatises a third objective, the analysis of economic growth, must be included. But we will have our hands full with the first two.

Chapter 3

How well does the economy perform over time?

CHECKLIST OF ECONOMIC CONCEPTS

Gross national product (current dollars)
Consumer goods and services
Gross investment goods
Government goods and services
Net national product (current dollars)
Capital consumption
Net investment goods
Price index numbers
Implicit price deflator
Real *GNP*
Real *NNP*
Per capita real *GNP*
Per capita real *NNP*
Inflation
Consumer price index
Wholesale price index
Demand-pull inflation
Cost-push inflation
Full employment
Unemployment
Recession
Depression

The progression of economic events in the United States since the last half of the 1960s has not been very satisfactory, to say the least. The economy has been plagued with inflation and with recession. It has encountered unemployment problems and energy problems. It has undergone a meat crisis. From time to time labor problems have emerged. The effects of production and consumption on the environment have caused concern. But how can we measure and evaluate the economy's performance over time? What are the most important forces affecting its performance? These are the questions that we attempt to answer in this chapter.

MEASURES OF PERFORMANCE

The most important aspect of an economy's performance is the level of want satisfaction or the standard of living that it can provide. The resources and the technology available to the economy are the ultimate determinants of its living standards. Economic problems and crises are significant in that they affect the uses of the economy's resources and technology and, consequently, the standard of living that it can provide. The level of want satisfaction that an economy actually provides is measured in terms of its gross national product and its net national product. These concepts and refinements of them will be considered in turn.

Gross national product

The value of goods and services per year produced in final form in an economy is called its *gross national product* or *GNP*. Gross national product includes the annual outputs of both the private sector of the economy and the public sector. In the private sector most of the output will be *consumer goods and services,* or *C.* Some of it will be *capital goods*—buildings, machinery, tools, and the like. These are often called *gross investment goods* or *GI.* The public sector's contributions to *GNP,* called *government goods and services,* or *G,* include national defense services, police and fire protection, roads, public education services, and a variety of other items—whatever it is that governmental units produce. Thus in any given year

$$GNP = C + GI + G.$$

Some indication of how well an economy performs over time can be obtained by observing the course of its *GNP* over time. Table 3–1, plotted in Figure 3–1, shows that U.S. *GNP* in *current dollars*—that is, 1960 *GNP* valued in 1960 dollars, 1970 *GNP* valued in 1970 dollars, etc.—has increased continuously since 1950. The increase for the 28-year period was a little over fivefold; the economy's output appears to have experienced very substantial growth.

Net national product

Not all of *GNP* represents net output for a year. In producing *GNP*, there is wear and tear on the economy's plant and equipment. Some of it becomes obsolete. Inventories of raw and semifinished materials may be drawn down. The dollar value of these occurrences is referred to as *capital consumption*.

Net national product or *NNP* is what is left of *GNP* after the value of capital consumption has been deducted from it. As we noted above, some of *GNP* consists of *GI*, or total capital goods produced during the year. We call this *GNP* component *GI* because it is the total or *gross* output of capital or investment goods. Suppose we want the economy's stock of capital at the end of the year to be exactly what it was when the

Table 3–1
GNP, NNP, and implicit price deflators, 1950–1978

	GNP			NNP		
Year	Current dollars	Implicit price deflator	1972 dollars	Current dollars	Implicit price deflator	1972 dollars
1950	286.2	53.64	533.5	262.3	53.5	489.9
1955	399.3	60.98	654.8	364.0	60.7	599.8
1960	506.0	68.67	736.8	458.3	68.1	672.5
1965	688.1	74.32	925.9	630.6	74.2	850.0
1970	982.4	91.36	1,075.3	891.1	91.2	977.8
1971	1,063.4	96.02	1,107.5	964.7	95.9	1,005.9
1972	1,171.1	100.00	1,171.1	1,065.7	100.0	1,065.7
1973	1,306.3	105.92	1,233.4	1,189.3	106.3	1,122.5
1974	1,406.9	116.20	1,210.7	1,272.9	116.3	1,094.0
1975	1,528.8	127.15	1,202.3	1,366.3	126.5	1,079.7
1976	1,700.1	133.76	1,271.0	1,522.3	132.9	1,145.1
1977	1,887.2	141.61	1,332.7	1,692.0	140.6	1,203.8
1978	2,087.5*	150.98	1,382.6*	1,874.2*	149.8	1,251.1*

* Second quarter annualized rate.

Source: U.S. Department of Commerce *Survey of Current Business*, vol. 56, no. 1, Part I, pp. 39–40, Part II, pp. 8–13, 94; vol. 57, no. 11 (November 1977), pp. 4–5; vol. 58, no. 11 (November 1978), pp. 4–5, 11.

Figure 3–1
GNP and *NNP*, 1950–1978

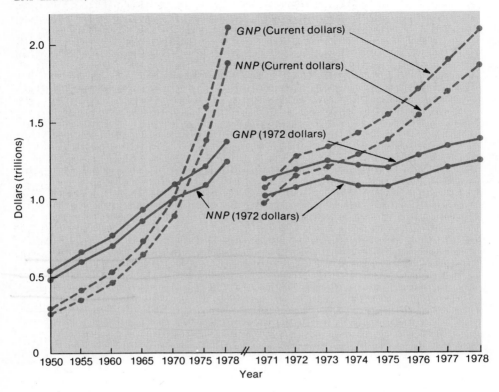

year began. Some of the *GI* component of *GNP* must be used
to replace the capital used up or what we have called capital
consumption. Plant and equipment would be repaired or replaced. Inventories would be brought up to their beginning-
of-the-year levels. The remainder of *GI*, after capital consumption has been met from it, is called *net investment* goods, or
simply *I* as distinguished from *GI*. Thus *NNP* is the *net amount*
of annual output produced and available for the economy to
use if it keeps its productive capacity exactly intact over time.
To repeat:

$$GNP = C + GI + G$$

and

$$NNP = C + I + G.$$

NNP data may provide a somewhat more accurate measure of an economy's performance over time than *GNP*. In Table 3–1 and in Figure 3–1, we note a continuous increase in U.S. current dollar *NNP* that is similar to the increase in *GNP*. It also shows slightly more than a fivefold increase from 1950 to 1978. As Figure 3–1 shows, the pattern of the increase in *NNP* is almost identical to that of *GNP*. The superiority of *NNP* data as a measure of economic performance does not lie in what it tells us about trends. Instead, if it has any superiority, it rests on the fact that *NNP* gives us more accurate information on how much is available for us to use annually than does *GNP*.

Price level changes

The more than fivefold increases in *GNP* and *NNP* overstate the increases in output that actually occurred from 1950 to 1975. All of us are painfully aware of the price level increases that have occurred, especially those since 1968. For any given year, *GNP* or *NNP* is obtained by multiplying physical outputs of goods and services by their respective prices. Over time *both* outputs *and* prices have increased; thus, some part of the increases in *GNP* and *NNP* are attributable to price level increases.

Since all prices do not increase at the same rate, *price index numbers* are constructed to measure the average annual increase in the price level. For example, to obtain a set of price index numbers, or what is called the *implicit price deflator* for *NNP*, consider first the year 1972 in Table 3–1. That year was selected by national income statisticians as the *base year* or the reference year against which the price levels of other recent years would be compared. The first step in the computation of the *NNP* implicit price deflator was the selection of a sample of goods and services representative of the entire *NNP*, with each item of the sample weighted according to its relative importance in NNP. The sample was valued in 1972 prices and, since its value in 1972 prices is 100 percent of its value in 1972 prices, the price index number for 1972 was determined as 100.0. The same sample of goods and services was then valued in 1973 prices and its total value in that year was 106.3 percent of its total value in 1972. The price index number for 1973 is thus 106.3. The other numbers in the *implicit price deflator* column for *NNP* were computed in a similar way.

The sample was valued in each of the various years in the respective prices of those years. Each year's value of the sample was divided by the base year value to obtain the percentage figures that are listed as the price index numbers. The price level of 1950 was 53.5 percent of the price level of 1972. The price level of 1975 was 126.5 percent of the price level of 1972.

The implicit price deflators for NNP form an important set of numbers. They can be used to adjust a series of current dollar NNP figures to eliminate the effects of price level changes. The adjusted series then provides us with comparative NNPs in terms of actual outputs of goods and services. The fact that the price level of 1975 was 126.5 percent of the 1972 base year price level means that the current dollar NNP in 1975 was 126.5 percent of what it would have been if it were valued in 1972 prices. Dividing the 1975 NNP current dollar figure of $1,366.3 billion by 126.5 percent, or 1.265, yields a result of $1,079.7 billion, which is 1975 NNP valued in 1972 dollars. For each of the listed years the current dollar NNP is divided by the implicit price deflator for the same year to obtain NNP for that year in 1972 dollars. The NNP (1972 dollars) column thus represents real output differences for the series of years. The effects of rising prices over the years on NNP has been eliminated

The adjustment of the current dollars NNP series to eliminate the effects of price level changes throws a whole new perspective on the performance of the economy from 1950 to 1978. Looking at the NNP (1972 dollars) column, NNP in 1978 was $1,251.1 billion. In 1950, it was $489.9 billion. The actual or real net output of the economy in 1978 was only about 2.5 times the 1950 real net output. Further, in 1974, the real NNP was less than it was in 1973, and in 1975, it was still smaller. Over the years from 1950, real NNP increased through 1973; declined slightly in 1974 and 1975; and resumed its upward trend in 1976 and the following years. The NNP solid lines in Figure 3–1 show these trends graphically.

The GNP (current dollars) column of Table 3–1 can be converted into GNP (1972 dollars) with a procedure like that used on the NNP series. Note that there is a slight difference between the set of GNP implicit price deflators and that of NNP. The difference occurs because the GNP sample of goods and services is slightly different from the NNP sample. Like the

NNP (1972 dollars) series, the *GNP* (1972 dollars) series peaked in 1973 and declined slightly in 1974 and 1975. This, too, is illustrated in Figure 3–1 by the *GNP* solid lines.

Per capita *GNP* and *NNP*

Although real *GNP* and *NNP* data provide information on what happens to an economy's real output of goods and services over time, they may mislead us with regard to the living standards that are possible and how these change over time. The population and population changes of the economy from year to year have been left out of account.

Both *GNP* and *NNP* are converted to a *per capita* basis in Table 3–2 and Figure 3–2. The real *GNP* and real *NNP* data for each year are divided by the population for that year, and we obtain both series in per capita terms. The per capita columns of Table 3–2, plotted in Figure 3–2, show that both per capita *GNP* and *NNP* rose steadily until 1973, peaked in that year and declined in 1974 and 1975. By 1976 they were both at approximately their 1973 levels, and in 1977 and 1978 they continued to move upward. Again, per capita *NNP* provides more accurate information about the living standards

Table 3–2
Real per capita *GNP* and *NNP*, 1950–1978

				Per Capita	
Year	GNP (billions of 1972 dollars)	NNP (billions of 1972 dollars)	Population (millions)	GNP (1972 dollars)	NNP (1972 dollars)
1950	533.5	489.9	152.3	3,503.0	3,216.7
1955	654.8	599.8	165.1	3,966.1	3,132.9
1960	736.8	672.5	180.7	4,077.5	3,721.6
1965	925.9	850.0	193.5	4,785.0	4,392.8
1970	1,075.3	977.8	204.9	5,247.9	4,772.1
1971	1,107.5	1,005.9	207.0	5,350.2	4,859.4
1972	1,171.1	1,065.7	208.8	5,608.7	5,103.9
1973	1,233.4	1,122.5	210.4	5,862.2	5,335.1
1974	1,210.7	1,094.0	211.9	5,713.5	5,162.8
1975	1,202.3	1,079.7	213.5	5,556.9	4,984.5
1976	1,271.0	1,145.1	215.1	5,908.8	5,323.6
1977	1,332.7	1,203.8	216.8	6,147.1	5,552.6
1978	1,382.6*	1,251.1*	218.4	6,330.6	5,728.5

* Second quarter annualized rate.

Sources: U.S. Department of Commerce *Survey of Current Business*, vol. 56, no. 1 (January 1976), Part I, pp. 39–40, Part II, pp. 8–13, 94; vol. 57, no. 11 (November 1977), pp. 4–5; vol. 58, no. 11 (November 1978), pp. 4–5. *Statistical Abstract of the United States*, (1972), p. 10.

Figure 3–2
Per capita *GNP* and *NNP*

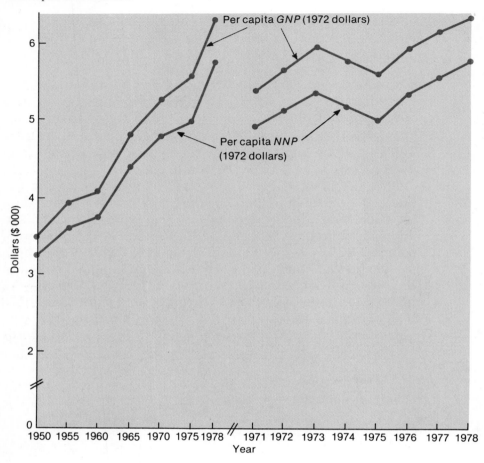

that the economy provided. Both series reflect the changes
that occurred over time.

INFLATION

Since the last half of the 1960s there has been great concern
in the United States about inflation. This concern was evi-
denced in much public discussion and by news media coverage
in the last two years of the Johnson administration—1967 and
1968—and throughout the Nixon, Ford, and Carter administra-
tions. The Johnson administration and Congress vacillated

over an increase in the personal income tax to fight inflation from 1966 to 1968, finally passing a measure calling for a small increase. The first Nixon administration came to office pledged to stop inflation. The issue has continued to occupy the national spotlight since that time.

Why all this concern about inflation? Why does inflation generate fear and distress? We must first of all define the term precisely. Then we can consider its causes and its consequences.

A period of *inflation can be defined very simply as a period of rising prices*. To put the concept in proper perspective, consider a hypothetical situation in which there is a two-year period with a constant price level, followed by a two-year period with a rising price level, followed by another two-year period with a constant price level. There is no inflation during either the first or the third two-year periods. Inflation occurs only during the second two-year period.

The use of price index numbers in measuring inflation is illustrated in Table 3–3. We show three different series of price index numbers: (1) the *GNP* implicit price deflator, (2) the consumer price index, and (3) the wholesale price index. The first is constructed by the U.S. Department of Commerce and is the broadest possible measure of price level changes over time. The latter two are computed by the U.S. Department of Labor and each includes a much smaller range of goods

Table 3–3
Price index numbers and the rate of inflation

Year	GNP *price level**		Consumer *price level*		Wholesale *price level*	
	Implicit price deflator	*Inflation rate (percent)*	*Price index†*	*Inflation rate‡*	*Price index†*	*Inflation rate‡*
1970	91.36	—	118.1	5.8	111.0	3.3
1971	96.02	5.1	122.4	3.6	114.4	3.1
1972	100.00	4.1	126.6	3.4	120.0	4.9
1973	105.92	5.9	136.6	7.9	139.5	16.2
1974	116.20	9.7	153.0	12.0	170.2	22.0
1975	127.15	9.4	164.6	7.6	178.9	5.1
1976	133.76	5.2	173.3	5.3	185.2	3.5
1977	141.61	5.9	184.5	6.5	196.3	6.0
1978	150.98	6.6	200.9	8.9	213.2	8.6

* Yearly averages.
† October for each year. Not seasonally adjusted for 1977 and 1978.
‡ October to October.
Source: *Federal Reserve Bulletins.*

than the *GNP* implicit price deflator. All three series show constantly increasing price levels since 1970.

Inflation is frequently referred to in terms of annual percentage changes in the price level. The annual inflation rate for each of the three price index series is shown in Table 3–3. Inflation rates are also reported on a monthly basis by the government and these monthly rates are annualized for purposes of comparison. For example, suppose the rate of increase in the consumer price index for the month of April is 0.6 percent. To put the increase on an annual basis we simply multiply 0.6 percent by 12 obtaining 7.2 percent. The 7.2 percent rate means that if inflation were to continue for a full year at the April rate the price level would rise by 7.2 percent from the first day of the April just passed to next April the first.

Note that the three price indexes show different inflation rates during any given year. These differences point up the fact that the prices of different groups goods and services usually do not change at the same rate. Most of us as consumers are interested in what happens to consumer prices rather than what happens to wholesale prices. However, the wholesale price index reflects price changes in goods one step prior to final sales in the production and sales chain. As such it is used frequently to predict what is likely to happen to consumer prices since wholesale prices tend to lead the retail prices that consumers pay by a few months.

THE CAUSES OF INFLATION

Many different events and/or groups of persons receive the "blame" for inflation. The oil embargo by the Arabs and a worldwide decrease in food production in 1973–74 received much blame for causing the inflation of the seventies although inflation was already in existence and was a matter of extreme national concern *before* the Arab boycott and the alleged reductions in world food production occurred. Labor unions often get blamed and so do "monopolistic" businesses. Farmers are often blamed and in self-defense they try to shift the blame to that perennial inflation scapegoat, the "middleman."

In any sort of ultimate economic sense, the cause of inflation is a rate of increase in aggregate purchasing power in the economy that exceeds the rate of increase in the physical volume of goods and services available to be purchased. This basic underlying cause still leaves substantial room for events and persons to receive blame. If an Arab boycott and crop failures throughout the world keep supplies of goods and services from increasing as fast as purchasing power increases, the result is inflation. The same sort of reasoning may be applied to various other specific objects of blame.

In an economic analysis of the causes of inflation, the concepts of aggregate demand and aggregate supply developed in the last chapter are very useful. These concepts help us to distinguish between the causes and consequences of *demand-pull inflation and cost-push inflation.*

Demand-pull inflation

Almost every period of inflation begins as demand-pull inflation; that is, the initiating force is an increasing level of aggregate demand for goods and services over time to which aggregate supply cannot or does not respond with equal speed. The increasing level of demand is usually the combined result of (1) increases in government expenditures that are not matched by increases in tax collections and (2) increases in the stock or supply of money in the economic system. Both of these will be examined in detail in subsequent chapters.

Suppose that aggregate demand and aggregate supply in the economy are initially D_1D_1 and S_1S_1 in Figure 3–3. The actual level of NNP is Y_1 and is below the full employment level; that is, some unemployment of labor and capital exists. Now suppose that aggregate demand increases to D_2D_2. The price level rises from P_1 to P_2. Businesses become more profitable, expand outputs, and real NNP increases to Y_2. A further increase in aggregate demand to D_3D_3 causes the price level to rise to P_3 and real NNP to increase to the full employment level Y_f. If aggregate demand now increases to D_4D_4, the price level goes up to P_4. However, there can be no further increase in real NNP beyond Y_f since at that output level *all* resources are fully employed. The impact of the increase in aggregate demand from D_3D_3 to D_4D_4 is concentrated entirely on the price level. The effects of increases in aggregate demand can be very different depending on the level of the economy's operation when they occur.

The inflation of the 1960s was a classic case of demand-pull inflation. When President Kennedy took office in 1961

Figure 3–3
Demand-pull inflation

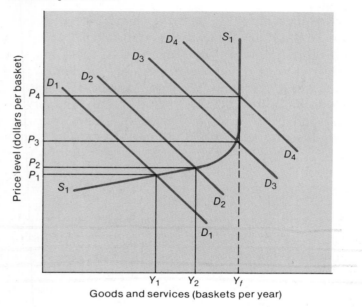

Goods and services (baskets per year)

about 6 percent of the labor force was unemployed—a rather high rate of unemployment by historic standards. There was no inflation. The Kennedy administration and the Johnson administration took deliberate steps to reduce taxes a little, increase government expenditures to some extent, and to generate somewhat more rapid increases in the money supply than had been occurring. The resulting increase in aggregate demand yielded a little inflation, sizable increases in *NNP*, and lower rates of unemployment. By 1966 the economy was near or at a full employment level of *NNP*. However, during the second Johnson administration things got a little out of hand. Escalation of the Vietnam War brought in increased government spending and even more rapid money supply increases. In 1967 and 1968 we found ourselves in a full employment, pure-inflation situation like that depicted in Figure 3–3 for the increase in demand from D_3D_3 to D_4D_4.

Cost-push inflation

While demand-pull inflation theory provides much information on what was happening in the 1960s as the U.S. economy

moved from a serious unemployment level of output to a full
employment level of output, it cannot explain adequately what
happened in the 1970s. In the 1970s cost-push aspects of inflation came to the fore generating a very different set of economic problems. Cost-push inflation is unlikely to occur by
itself. Ordinarily it is superimposed on demand-pull inflation.
But it can be understood better if it is considered first in isola-
tion.

Suppose that initially the economy's aggregate demand and
aggregate supply curves are D_1D_1 and S_1S_1, respectively, in
Figure 3-4. It is producing the full employment output level
Y_f and the price index stands at P_1. If for some reason—say,
an increase in petroleum prices—costs of production rise, the
aggregate supply curve shifts upward to positions like S_2S_1
and S_3S_1. These shifts, with aggregate demand remaining at
D_1D_1, cause the price level to rise to P_2 and P_3. Thus, increases
in costs are the forces that in turn cause the inflation.

Cost-push inflation, as Figure 3-4 shows, generates unemployment. Employers will purchase smaller quantities of resources at higher resource prices than they will at lower resource prices. They will produce smaller quantities of goods
and services when costs are higher than they will when costs

Figure 3-4
Cost-push inflation

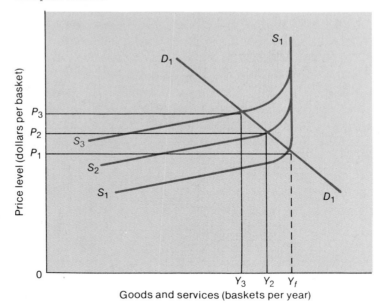

Goods and services (baskets per year)

e lower. Consequently, increases in resource prices, other ings being equal, result in smaller outputs like Y_2 and Y_3 or the economy and lower levels of resource employment.

Dei... pull and cost-push combined

The inflation-unemployment problem of the 1970s has been represented by many as a new phenomenon that defies analysis with conventional economic tools. But this is not so. It is readily explainable in terms of combinations of demand-pull and cost-push forces.

In the inflationary process, changes in aggregate demand *lead* changes in aggregate supply in point of time in both upward directions and downward directions. The meaning and the importance of this statement are illustrated in Figure 3–5. Suppose that $D_1 D_1$ and $S_1 S$ were representative of the U.S. economy in 1960. Aggregate demand then increased to $D_2 D_2$. Resource prices did not increase immediately so the aggregate supply curve remained at $S_1 S$. The price level rose from P_1 to P_2 because of demand-pull forces and output rose from Y_1 to the full employment level Y_f. From 1966 to 1969

Figure 3–5
Demand-pull combined with cost-push inflation

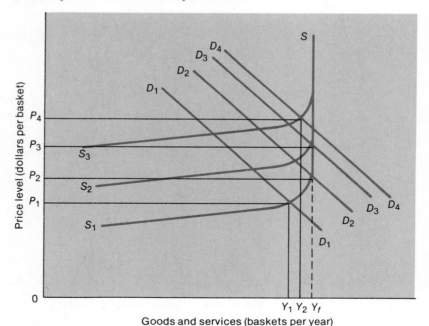

Goods and services (baskets per year)

aggregate demand continued to increase to a level represented by D_3D_3. Resource prices began to increase also and the aggregate supply curve shifted upward to S_2S. Pure inflation was occurring—after the initial time lag, resource prices were rising at approximately the same rate as the general price level—but the economy continued to operate at a full employment level of output. Suppose now that the rate of increase in aggregate demand slacks off—as it did in 1969 and 1970—and it increases from D_3D_3 to D_4D_4 only. Resource suppliers, still thinking and acting in terms of the former higher rates of increase in aggregate demand, continue to increase resource prices at that former higher rate. Consequently, the aggregate supply shifts upward to S_3S—by more than the upward movement in aggregate demand. The price level rises to P_4, propelled by both demand-pull and cost-push forces. In this latter case the cost-push aspects of inflation predominate over its demand-pull aspects, causing the economy's output to fall and unemployment to occur.

Events of the 1970s make sense when viewed in this framework. Unemployment increased in 1970 and 1971 when cost-push forces were stronger than demand-pull forces. In 1972 and 1973, unemployment receded as demand-pull forces outstripped cost-push forces. In 1974, the shoe was back on the cost-push foot. From March of 1975 until the end of 1978 demand-pull was the stronger force and unemployment was reduced somewhat. The effects of the 1979 Carter administration's anti-inflation program remain to be seen.

THE CONSEQUENCES OF INFLATION

What is wrong or right about inflation? Why has it caused so much consternation? Actually, inflation does not always lower the economic welfare of the country. In order to determine the circumstances under which it has adverse influences and those under which it has positive influences on economic welfare, we can classify its effects into two categories: (1) those affecting income distribution and (2) those affecting the economy's output.

Distributional effects

When inflation is occurring, some redistribution of income among households occurs. If inflation were to cause all household incomes to increase at the same rate as the general price level, the distributional effects would be negligible. However, it usually causes the incomes of some households to rise faster than the price level and such households gain. The incomes of other households lag behind the inflation rate and they tend to lose because of inflation. It is easier to identify those groups in the economy that are likely to lose than those that are likely to gain.

So-called fixed income households lose because of inflation. Those who live on such income sources as pensions, interest from bonds, and annuities fall in this category. Frequently, these are composed of older persons. Salaried persons, too, often find that their salaries do not rise as rapidly as the price level does. Thus, the purchasing power of their incomes dwindles with inflation.

Creditors, or those to whom money is owed, tend to lose because of inflation. Suppose, for example, that a creditor loans $100 at the beginning of the year to be repaid at the end of the year. During the year the price level rises by 5 percent so that at the end of the year it takes $105 to buy what $100 would have purchased at the beginning of the year. But the creditor receives only $100 in repayment—which will now purchase less than it would at the time the loan was made. The creditor's loss is, of course, the debtor's gain.

Not much can be said about the impact of inflation on working people in general. Some gain and some lose. Those fortunate enough to be employed in making products for which demand increases relatively the most will gain. By the same token, those whose labor makes products for which demand expands relatively the least will lose.

The redistribution of income or purchasing power is capricious or arbitrary. Inflation does not reward those who "deserve" to be rewarded or punish those who do not. It rewards those who happen to furnish resources to industries highly responsive to inflation and punishes those who do not.

Output effects

Under some circumstances inflation causes changes in the levels of *GNP* and *NNP*, and under other circumstances it may have no appreciable effects on them. The critical determinants of the output effects of inflation are (1) the state of the economy when the inflation begins and (2) whether the inflationary pressure is generated by demand-pull or cost-push forces.

Suppose, as we did in the discussion of demand-pull inflation, that the economy is initially at a less than full employment level of output and that there is virtually no inflation occurring. As Figure 3–3 shows, an increase in aggregate demand from D_1D_1 to D_2D_2 with aggregate supply fixed at S_1S_1 will generate relatively small increases in the price level and relatively large increases in output. The price level rises from P_1 to a level such as P_2. Production activity becomes more profitable; resource units that were unemployed are drawn into use; and output expands from Y_1 to Y_2. Thus the output effects of demand-pull inflation under these circumstances are positive.

As the economy approaches a full employment level of output the effects of increases in aggregate demand are relatively larger and larger increases in the price level, accompanied by relatively smaller and smaller increases in output. In Figure 3–3, suppose aggregate demand rises from D_2D_2 toward D_3D_3. Again profits rise in production activities and producers seek to expand their outputs. The best, or the most productive, units of different kinds of resources are already employed so in order to expand output employers put inferior resource units that were previously unemployed to work. Production bottlenecks arise as some kinds of resources become fully employed before full employment levels are reached for other kinds. Thus the output effects of demand-pull inflation become smaller and smaller as a full employment level of output is approached.

When an economy is producing a full employment level of output, increases in aggregate demand succeed only in increasing the price level. Output cannot increase. Thus, in Figure 3–3, an increase in aggregate demand from D_3D_3 to D_4D_4, has no positive output effects. This situation is sometimes referred to as *pure inflation.*

An economy that has experienced a high rate of inflation, say over 5 percent per year for a number of years, is peculiarly susceptible to adverse output effects from cost-push inflation. The U.S. economy of the 1970s has been in this situation. If the time lag between increases in aggregate demand and increases in costs of production has ceased to exist, and if costs are rising as rapidly as the prices of final goods, the economy is extremely vulnerable. Suppose that aggregate demand now begins to increase less rapidly while the rate of increase in costs of production continues at its former rate. This classic cost-push situation not only feeds the inflation, but it also reduces the economy's output and resource employment levels. The recession of 1974 provides an excellent, but tragic, illustration.

RECESSION

In 1974, there was general agreement that an economic recession was in progress. It was not the only recession ever witnessed in the United States; however, it is a recent clear-cut example. In this section, the first order of business is to define the term. Then we shall examine its causes and its consequences.

Definition

When the term "recession" is used by the news media, by politicians, and by the general public, the meaning is not really clear. In Washington, D.C., the political party of the president of the United States is usually reluctant to admit the existence of a recession, but the opposition party is overeager to hang the weight of recession around the administration's neck. Consequently, the administration's party spokesmen may insist that no recession exists while at the same time those of the other party declare that a recession is in progress. Squabbling of this nature is understandable and is of no great consequence.

Economists define recession as a period in which economic activity declines, but there is not unanimity on what constitutes such a decline. Is it a decline in real *GNP*? Or real *NNP*? Or per capita *GNP*? Or per capita *NNP*? A situation is possible in which *none* of these are declining yet the performance of the economy is progressively becoming more unsatisfactory. Consider Figure 3–6, for example. Line *AF* shows the course of the economy's potential *GNP* over a four year period. Potential *GNP* is the maximum *GNP* that the economy's available resources and techniques of production will allow. It would be expected to rise over time as the economy accumulates additional capital resources, improves its labor resources, and

Figure 3–6
Recession and recovery

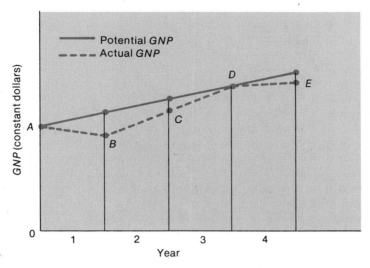

undergoes technological advancement. All *GNP* values are assumed to be in constant dollars to remove the distorting effects of price level changes. During Year 1, the actual course of *GNP*, reflected by line *AB*, is downward. Year 1 is clearly a period of recession by anyone's definition. Year 2 and Year 3 show actual *GNP* rising relative to potential *GNP*. These years constitute a period of *recovery*. In Year 4 actual *GNP*, though rising in absolute terms, is falling relative to potential *GNP*. Should such a period be called one of recession? We think so and will include it in our discussion.

Causes

Recession may stem from either or both of two basic causes. First, it may result from decreases in aggregate demand in the economy. Second, it may come about because of upward shifts in the aggregate supply curve. Third, both of these forces may be at work simultaneously.

The effects of a decrease in aggregate demand are illustrated in Figure 3–7. Let D_1D_1 and S_1S be the initial aggregate demand and supply curves with the output of the economy at the full employment level Y_f. Now suppose that the money supply of the economy is decreased, shifting the aggregate demand

Figure 3–7
The causes of recession

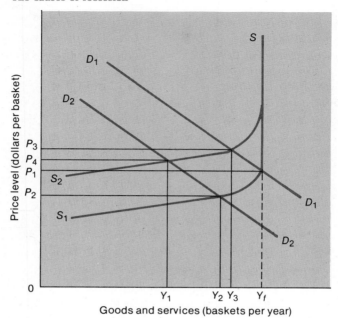

curve to the left toward D_2D_2. If aggregate supply stays at S_1S, the economy's output falls toward Y_2 which is less than the full employment output level Y_f. The period during which output is declining is one of recession.

Suppose that instead of a decrease in aggregate demand there is an upward shift in aggregate supply from S_1S toward S_2S because of such forces as rising wage rates and higher raw materials prices. Let the aggregate demand curve remain at D_1D_1. The economy's output of goods and services declines toward Y_3—below the full employment potential output level of Y_f. Thus recession—the period during which actual output is declining—is caused by cost-push type forces.

To illustrate the simultaneous effects of decreasing aggregate demand and upward shifting aggregate supply, suppose that while the aggregate supply curve is shifting upward from S_1S to S_2S the aggregate demand curve is shifting to the left from D_1D_1 to D_2D_2. Output will decline from Y_f to Y_1 and the period of decline can be identified as recession.

It should be clear on the basis of the foregoing cases that aggregate demand need not decrease in order for recession to occur. As a matter of fact, aggregate demand could be increasing, as it was throughout the 1970s, and recession could still happen, as it did in 1974. If the aggregate supply curve shifts upward more rapidly than does the aggregate demand curve these results will occur. Whenever cost-push forces exceed demand-pull forces, output will fall and prices will rise; that is, we will have a combination of recession and inflation.

Consequences

The consequences of recession consist primarily of output effects. However, some distributional effects occur at the same time.

The output effects are obvious from the definition of recession. The actual output level falls below the potential output level and the population of the economy as a whole experiences a level of economic well being or welfare below that which the economy is capable of providing.

From the distributional point of view few, if any, households stand to gain from recession; however, some may lose relatively more than others. Particularly hard hit are those who lose their jobs as output declines. During recession, demands for some products fall more rapidly than demands for others. For example, demands for consumer durable goods—houses, automobiles, and large appliances—fall relatively more than demands for staple food products like bread and potatoes. Demands by industry for capital goods like buildings and machinery fall relatively more than demands for most consumer goods. Consequently, those who have been furnishing resources—labor and capital—to the consumer durable and capital goods industries are most likely to lose jobs and experience the greatest decrease in incomes.

DEPRESSION

Not much needs to be said about depression. Most of the discussion of recession is, on a magnified scale, applicable to depression. The dividing line between recession and depression is fuzzy and is usually drawn on the basis of how far actual *GNP* falls below potential *GNP*. However, the precise level at which it is drawn is arbitrary.

The U.S. economy experienced its last depression in the

1930s. It was a disastrous decade. Unemployment had increased to about 25 percent of the labor force by 1933. Between
1929 and 1933 the economy's real output fell precipitously to
about 70 percent of its 1929 level. The major causal factor
appears to have been a series of large decreases in aggregate
demand. Not until World War II did the economy recover
fully from the huge decline that occurred from 1929 to 1932.

SUMMARY

There are several measures of how well an economy performs over time. Gross national product measures its total
output in dollar terms. Subtracting out annual capital consumption we arrive at net national product information. Both can
be adjusted for price level changes leaving us with real *GNP*
and real *NNP* for a series of years. If we divide real *GNP*
and *NNP* by population we obtain real per capita *GNP* and
NNP. These data provide the best information we have on
living standards over time.

Inflation refers to price level increases over time. It is measured by implicit price deflators for *GNP* and *NNP*, the consumer price index, and the wholesale price index. The appropriate index to use depends upon the group of goods and services that are being considered. Inflation results whenever
the economy's purchasing power increases at a faster rate
than its physical output of goods and services. We usually
distinguish between demand-pull and cost-push inflation.
Whenever demand-pull forces exceed cost-push forces unemployment will decrease. If cost-push forces exceed demand-
pull forces unemployment will rise. Inflation generates effects
on (1) income distribution in the economy and (2) the output
of the economy.

Recession and depression refer to serious slowing of economic activity. Recession brings about income distribution effects and output effects also. Depression is essentially a
deeper, more prolonged economic event than a recession.

QUESTIONS AND PROBLEMS

1. Explain each of the following:
    a. Gross national product and its component parts.

      b. Captial consumption

      c. Net national product and its component parts.

2. What would it mean if we were told that the consumer price index in 1980 is 187?

3. Compute real *GNP* in terms of the base year for the following:

Year	GNP (billions of current $)	Implicit price deflator	GNP (real)
1975	100	95	___
1977	110	100	___
1978	115	110	___
1979	130	117	___
1980	150	130	___

4. Illustrate with a diagram and explain the impact on price and output of demand-pull forces when

      a. Recession exists but there is no inflation.

      b. Full employment exists.

5. How would you explain a situation in which there is both unemployment and inflation?

6. Illustrate and explain the effects of cost-push inflation on net national product and the employment level.

7. What is "bad" about inflation?

8. How can you determine whether or not the performance of the economy is improving or deteriorating over time?

Chapter 4

Money and how it affects the economy's performance

CHECKLIST OF ECONOMIC CONCEPTS

Money
Currency
Demand deposits
Barter
Liquidity
Value of money
Income velocity of money
Inflation
Recession
Equation of exchange
Deflation

The causes of economic fluctuations and the appropriate means of controlling them are not well understood. The continuing debate in U.S. government circles and throughout the country on the appropriate policies needed to reduce the rate of inflation and to avoid recession is a reflection of how difficult it is to understand and to control the underlying forces that cause them. We will construct a basic analytical framework within which a relatively simple and self-contained analysis of economic fluctuations can be developed but which will also accommodate and assimilate successively more complex and sophisticated analytical material. Thus at whatever level we care to push our analysis we will have a reasonably well-integrated model. The broad outlines of the analytical framework—the aggregate demand and aggregate supply apparatus—have already been constructed. In this chapter, we incorporate a basic monetary model into it. First we look at the nature of money. Second, the functions of money are examined. Third, the pieces of the monetary model are put together and used to examine the problems of inflation, recession, and unemployment.

WHAT IS MONEY?

At first glance, it seems rather silly to ask the question, "What is money?" Surely everyone knows the answer. But for purposes of economic analysis the answer is not quite as simple as one might imagine. The Federal Reserve System, which exercises control over the nation's money supply, has five definitions of it. So, we must first settle on the definition that we will use. Then, we will look briefly at both the historical and the modern components of the money supply.

Definition of money

We will define *money* as anything used as a medium of exchange that is generally accepted as such by the general public. Note that the definition contains two elements. First, the items that constitute money must be something in terms of which goods and services are exchanged. Instead of exchanging goods for goods, goods are exchanged for the money items which are then exchanged for other goods. It facilitates exchange. Second, most people must be willing to accept the

money items in exchange for goods. Without general accept-
ability, it cannot serve its purpose of being a medium of exchange.

Historical money

Historically, many items have been used as money. Among
these are seashells, cloth, tobacco, and beads. Some money
items have been living creatures—cows, camels, and even
women in male-oriented societies fell in this category. As civi-
lizations advanced, societies used bronze, silver, and gold as
money items. In prisoner-of-war camps during World War II,
cigarettes were a common money item for exchanges among
prisoners. All of these have two things in common: (1) they
were used as media of exchange and (2) they were generally
acceptable as such.

Modern money

Present day economies have come to rely more and more
on pieces of paper and less and less on items with intrinsic
value to serve as money. The money supply of most countries
can be classified into two components: (1) currency and (2)
demand deposits or checking accounts.

It is not at all difficult for most of us to conceive of currency
as money. The *currency* supply in the United States is made
up of paper bills and coins of various denominations. The
one-dollar, two-dollar, five-dollar and other bills are Federal
Reserve Notes issued by the Federal Reserve System.[1] They
are completely acceptable to sellers and we use them extensively in making on-the-spot payments for goods and services
of all kinds. In addition, the United States Treasury mints
and issues such coins as pennies, nickels, dimes, quarters,
half dollars, and dollars. These are for our convenience in
making change and for use in myriad kinds of coin-operated
machines.

The other component, the major component, of the money
supply consists of the *demand deposits* or checking accounts
that we have in banks. It is not quite clear to many people

---

1. The Federal Reserve System, as a quasi-independent agency of the federal
government, will be considered in detail in the next chapter.

Table 4–1
Components of the money supply *(M₁)*,
August 1979 ($ billions)

Currency.....................	103.6
Demand Deposits	270.7
Total	374.3

Source: *Federal Reserve Statistical Release,* H.6
(508), (September 20, 1979).

that these are really money, but logical thought will establish
that they are. Suppose that I buy an automobile from you
for $2,000. I write a check to you, decreasing my demand depos-
its in Stillwater National Bank by $2,000, and you deposit the
check in your bank, increasing your deposits in your bank
by $2,000.[2] Demand deposits are transferred from person to
person in payment for goods and services and they are generally acceptable to the public as such.

Table 4–1 lists the money supply components as they were
in late 1978.[3] The demand deposit component is considerably
larger than the currency component. That the public prefers
most of its money in the form of demand deposits is clearly
indicated. All large payments as well as a great many medium-
size and small ones are made by means of checks, which
are the instruments for transferring demand deposits from one
person to another.

THE FUNCTIONS OF MONEY

Modern economies are often referred to as *money*
economies, implying that economies may have existed that
functioned without the explicit use of money. This was indeed
the case in some primitive societies in which each household
was largely self-sufficient. But when economies developed to
the point at which a considerable amount of exchange was
carried on among households, money systems evolved with
money performing three closely related functions: (1) it serves
as a medium of exchange; (2) it provides a measuring stick
for values; and (3) it is used as a store of value.

---

2. A full explanation of the process is contained in the next chapter. At this
point, we need only to highlight what almost everyone already knows about such
a transaction.

3. The money supply definition that we use is that which the Federal Reserve
calls M_1.

Medium of exchange

In moneyless transactions, the exchange of goods, services, and resources among economic units is carried on through *barter*. One kid trades a sack of marbles to another for a pocketknife. Someone works eight hours for a farmer in exchange for ten bushels of wheat. A family trades an automobile for a year's rental of a house. Many such trades occur—even in modern economies.

Although the first trading relationships in human societies were carried on by barter, as trade developed money evolved. The reasons for its evolution are not hard to understand. In the first place, it is often difficult for one trading party to find a second party who has what the first one wants and who wants what the first one desires to exchange. Money helps solve this problem. The goods of the first party can be sold for money to whomever will buy it. The money can then be used to buy whatever it is the first party wants. Matching pairs of persons are not necessary for the consummation of an exchange. In the second place, it is not often that one party's valuation of the goods or services it offers just matches the second party's valuation of what it desires to exchange. The first party may want to exchange a dugout canoe for a whole set of fishing gear but the second party may have only one fishing spear to give up. Under barter arrangements the trade may not be consummated; however, in a money economy, the canoe is sold for money; whatever is needed of the money to buy the spear is so used; and the remainder of the money can be used to buy other items of fishing gear from whomever may have it to sell.

Money as a medium of exchange is really a *technology* of exchange. It facilitates trade. It makes exchanges possible that would not take place without it. Thus, the efficiency with which trade is accomplished is higher in a money economy than it is in a barter economy.

Measure of value

Monetary units such as dollars and cents enable us to measure and compare the values that society as a whole places on thousands of kinds of goods and services. The price of any item reflects the value that the society places on it. In our roles as consumers, the comparative prices of different kinds of goods help us determine the ways in which we will spend our incomes. In our roles as resource owners, prices offered for our resources in different uses reflect the values of our resources in those different uses and help us decide where we will put them to work. Businesses use the selling prices of goods on the one hand and the buying prices of resources on the other to determine whether or not they can make profits. Without a price system in which prices measure values, economic activity would be much less effcient than it is.

Although money serves as a measuring stick of value, it falls short of perfection in performing this function. The problem is that the value of the monetary unit itself changes over time because of inflation. If the economy is experiencing an inflation rate of 5 percent per year, an item that carries a price tag of $105 would have carried a price tag of only $100 a year ago, if its value relative to other goods and services has not changed over the year. So, when inflation (or deflation) is occurring, we find that we are using an elastic ruler to measure values.

It has been commonly believed that the value of money depends upon the intrinsic value of the material from which the money is made. For example, until very recently, most people in the United States believed that gold and silver "backing" of the money supply determined its value. Actually, in any meaningful sense of the term, the value of a dollar refers to what it will buy in goods and services, not to what you can get for it in gold or silver if you turn the dollar over to the government. During inflation, as prices rise the value or purchasing power of the dollar declines. This would be the case regardless of whether money has gold or silver "backing."

Store of value

Persons who save a part of their incomes and accumulate assets find various ways of storing the purchasing power of their accumulated assets. The most common way of storing purchasing power is to invest in capital resources of one kind or another—land, buildings, corporate ownership, and the like. But investments carry risks. There is a danger that the value of the investment will decline. Consequently, some people like to keep some part of their assets in the form of money, assuming that a dollar is a dollar is a dollar.

Most people keep some part of their assets in the form of money for *liquidity* purposes. Money is immediately spendable for whatever its holder desires to spend it for and is therefore a perfectly liquid asset. Assets held in the form of land, stocks, bonds, buildings, and equipment are not. So, to be in a position to take advantage of bargains, or to meet unforeseen contingencies, the public desires to hold a part of its assets in liquid form; that is, in money.

During inflation, those who store their assets in the form of money will certainly lose because of the declining purchasing power of the dollar. During a period of stable prices, assets stored in money form will hold their value; however, they will earn no income for their holders.

MONEY, INFLATION, AND RECESSION

We return now to the role of money in the performance of the economy over time. What are the relationships of the money supply to aggregate demand and aggregate supply? Do these relationships affect economic fluctuations? Do they provide any clues as to how inflation and recession may be controlled? To answer these questions, we establish first a monetary model—the equation of exchange. Then we use it to analyze the causes of and possible means of controlling inflation and recession.

The equation of exchange

The total dollar amount of spending per year by buyers of goods and services is necessarily equal to the total dollars received by the sellers of those goods and services. This truism is the basis of the equation of exchange. The equation itself relates the components of total spending to the components of total receipts.

On the total spending side, let M represent the average *supply of money* available per year to spend—the average amount of currency in existence plus the average dollar volume of demand deposits outstanding. Let V be the number of times per year the average dollar is spent on *NNP* items. We call

V the *income velocity of money.* Total spending per year on *NNP* is by definition:

$$M \times V.$$

On the receipts side of the picture, we designate *NNP* in real or physical terms as T, or the total *volume of trade* of *NNP* items. It will be helpful to think of T as so many identical baskets of goods and services, as we did in the discussion of aggregate demand and aggregate supply. The *price level* or the price per basket of goods sold is labelled P. The value of goods sold per year is thus:

$$P \times T.$$

Since the total amount of money spent per year by buyers must be equal to the total amount of money received by seller, then:

$$M \times V = P \times T.$$

This is the famous (or in some circles infamous) *equation of exchange.* It brings together in the simplest possible form the determinants of the price level and the level of output in the economy. By itself, it furnishes no information about the direction or the order of causal relationships.

Inflation

The equation of exchange provides a basis for deepening our understanding of the causes of inflation. Suppose that M increases while V and T remain constant. The result can only be an increase in P; that is, inflation. Or suppose that households decide to hold their dollars for shorter periods of time—they increase their rate of spending. Velocity and total spending increase and, again, if T remains constant P must rise. On the other hand if MV or total spending remains constant and T declines, then P must increase. Inflation occurs whenever MV is rising relative to T, or whenever T is falling relative to MV.

Increases in the money supply are the usual triggering mechanism for the demand-pull inflation that we discussed in the preceding chapter. Money supply increases shift the aggregate demand curve to the right, pulling up the price level. The rising price level makes the sale of goods more profitable, so to increase their profits sellers place larger quantities of products on the markets. They deplete their inventories and to build them up again they increase their orders from producers. Producers try to increase their outputs in order to increase their profits. If there are unemployed resource units available in the economy, producers tend to draw them into production, increasing T which dampens down the amounts by which P must increase in order for the total value of goods sold to absorb the increase in total spending. If there are no unemployed resources in the economy, individual producers, as they try to attract additional quantities of resources into their individual production activities, succeed only in bidding up the prices of resources. The volume of trade cannot expand except as the accumulation of capital resources, improvements in the quality of labor resources, and improvements in technology take place over time. The burden of responding to an increasing $M \times V$ must be born in this case by the rising price level; that is:

$$\overbrace{M \times V}^{\uparrow} = \overset{\uparrow}{P} \times T.$$

Inflation control

If inflation is generated by a rate of increase in $M \times V$ that exceeds the rate of increase in T, it would seem reasonable to expect that inflation could be controlled by reducing the rate of increase in M. This medicine will work but it will cause an increase in unemployment in the economy while it is doing its job. The money supply in the United States is under the control of the Federal Reserve Board of Governors and the techniques of control will be detailed in the next two chapters.

Suppose for present purposes that $M \times V$ is increasing and that T is not. The price level P is increasing at the same rate as $M \times V$. If the rate of increase in $M \times V$ is reduced through tighter control of M, P will continue to increase for a time at more or less its former rate because of inflationary expectations and because of the lagged response of resource prices to changes in aggregate demand that we discussed in the last chapter. Cost-push forces will exceed demand-pull forces for a time. With the reduction of the rate of increase of $M \times V$ below that of P, T must decline. As T declines unemployment rises.

Rising unemployment resulting from reductions in the rate of increase of M is the penalty that must be paid by an economic system for permitting inflation to occur in the first place. Up to this point in time, at least, no country has been able to bring a prolonged inflation under control without an increase in unemployment. Once inflation has been reduced to a tolerable rate, prices and costs should adjust over time to levels that would permit reasonably full employment of resources. The unemployment caused by inflation control through reduction in the rate of increase in the money supply will be minimized if the reduction is effected little by little over a substantial period of time.

Recession

The equation of exchange is also a useful aid to understanding the causes of and the control of recession. Suppose that initially the economy is at a full employment level of output and that there is no inflation. Now suppose that a decrease occurs in M or V or in both; that is, total spending decreases. If the price level does not decrease fewer goods and services will be purchased. Inventories will accumulate and orders to producers will be reduced. Thus T will decline and unemployment will rise. A recession will be in progress.

The surpluses of goods and services and the unemployed resources exert downward pressure on the price level. If the downward pressure can be realized—that is, if prices can indeed go down—the resulting *deflation* may keep the recession from being as serious as it would otherwise be. The decline in T that results from the decline in total spending will be less if P as well as T declines on the right hand side of the equation of exchange.

As we have noted previously recession may also occur together with inflation. This will be the case when cost-push forces exceed demand-pull forces for an extended time period. When inflationary expectations of economic units and the lag of cost responses behind changes in total spending cause P to rise at a greater rate than does total purchasing power, T will decline. Unemployment rises and recession is in progress.

Recession control

A recession that occurs when there is no inflation is much easier to control than one that is accompanied by inflation. In the former case increases in M by the government's monetary authorities may be sufficient to pull the economy out of recession. They will cause increases in total spending, generating some increases in P. Business becomes more profitable; T expands; and unemployment falls as unemployed resources are put to work.

A recession combined with inflation is much more difficult for the monetary authorities of the government to handle. Suppose the price level is increasing at a high rate—say 8 to 9 percent per year; $M \times V$ is increasing at the same rate and T is below the full-employment level. In order to increase T the rate of increase in M must be accelerated even further so that $M \times V$ is rising faster than P. This result may be very difficult to achieve. Inflationary expectations may cause the rate of increase in P to rise as fast as that of $M \times V$ making it impossible for T to expand. But even if T does expand, an increase in the rate of inflation will most certainly be unpopular in an economy already plagued by a high inflation rate. There are no easy, painless means of controlling recession and inflation simultaneously.

SUMMARY

Changes in an economy's money supply over time play a key role in the causes of and the control of inflation and recession. They operate directly on aggregate demand for the goods and services that constitute NNP. An economy's money supply consists of currency and demand deposits with demand deposits as its most important component part. Control over the money supply is exercised by the national government. Money performs three important functions in an economic system. It serves as a (1) medium of exchange, (2) measure of value, and (3) store of value.

The equation of exchange brings together the elements of total spending and total value of goods sold per year. From it we obtain an overview of the impact of money supply changes in causing and/or controlling economic fluctuations. Increases in the money supply that cause total spending to increase faster than the volume of trade will cause inflation. Whenever the price level increases relative to total spending, the volume of trade will fall causing unemployment to rise. Inflation control by monetary authorities through slowing the rate of increase in the money supply will generate temporary increases in unemployment because changes in cost-push forces tend to lay behind changes in demand-pull forces. Expansion of the money supply can be used successfully to control recession if the economy is initially in a noninflationary situation. However when recession occurs together with inflation, increases in the money supply are a much less certain means of bringing it under control.

QUESTIONS AND PROBLEMS

1. What is money?

2. What is the composition of the money supply in the United States? Is your bank account a part of the U.S. money supply? Explain.

3. Compare and contrast exchange by means of barter with exchange by means of money.

4. Has money functioned well as a store of value over the last 15 years? Explain.

5. State the equation of exchange and explain each part of it.

6. Using the equation of exchange as a tool of analysis, explain the effects of increases in the money supply on economic activity.

7. Suppose that inflation has been occurring and that increases in the money supply are now significantly decreased or stopped. Using the equation of exchange as a tool of analysis, explain what happens in the economy.

Chapter 5

The banking system and the money supply

It is apparent that the money supply is a key element both in causing and controlling inflation and recession. Why does the money supply get out of hand? Who is responsible for keeping it under control? In the United States, management of the money supply is a unique responsibility of a partially independent government agency, the Federal Reserve Board of Governors. It encounters tremendous problems, partly of a technical nature and partly because of political pressures from the Congress and the administrative branch of the federal government, in exercising it. To comprehend these problems it is necessary that we understand the structure of our banking system and how it works. Then we can examine its role in determining the money supply.

STRUCTURE OF THE BANKING SYSTEM

The banking system in the United States consists of two levels of banks. Commercial banks make up the lower level and Federal Reserve banks form the upper level. The Federal Reserve Board of Governors exercises policy control over Federal Reserve banks and those commercial banks that are members of the Federal Reserve System. Many commercial banks operate outside of and largely independent of the Federal Reserve System.

Commercial banks

The public does its banking business with commercial banks. It makes deposits with them and from time to time it borrows from them. It writes checks on the deposit accounts that are held for it by commercial banks.

Altogether there were 14,698 commercial banks in the United States as of June 30, 1978. Of these 4,616 were national banks, chartered by the federal government under the National Bank Act of 1863. The remainder were state banks, established through charters from the individual states in which they were incorporated.[1] National banks are required by law to be members of the Federal Reserve System. State banks are free to choose whether or not they will be members of the system.

---

1. Federal Reserve Bulletin, Number 12, Volume 64 (December 1978) A14-A15.

Federal Reserve banks

The Federal Reserve Act of 1913 divided the United States into 12 geographic areas called Federal Reserve Districts and established a Federal Reserve bank in each one. The purposes of the Federal Reserve System as stated in the Federal Reserve Act are: (1) to provide an elastic currency for the country; that is, to make sure that sufficient currency exists to meet the needs of the public; (2) to provide facilities for discounting commercial paper; that is, to make loans to commercial banks letting those commercial banks use certain of their notes receivable or promissory notes receivable as guarantees of repayment; and (3) to improve the supervision of banking. Essentially the 12 Federal Reserve banks together operate as the central bank of the United States.

Each Federal Reserve bank is a privately incorporated institution with its own president and its own board of directors. But each is operated so as to put into effect the policy decisions of the Federal Reserve Board of Governors. In each Federal Reserve district the stock of the Federal Reserve bank is owned by the member banks of the system in that district. Each member bank is *required* to buy stock in the district Federal Reserve bank. Federal Reserve banks are not operated for purposes of making profit and any net earnings that exceed the sum of expenses, dividends of 6 percent to stockholders, and certain additions to surplus, go to the United States Treasury. Any losses that occur are covered by the United States Treasury.

The Board of Governors

General supervision over the activities of the Federal Reserve banks and of commercial bank members of the system is exercised by the Federal Reserve Board of Governors. Each member of the seven-member Board is appointed by the President of the United States and must be confirmed by the United States Senate. Appointments are for 14-year terms staggered so that one term expires every two years. The President designates one of the members as Chairman to serve as such for four years, but with the possibility of being redesignated chairman throughout the member's service on the Board.

The Federal Reserve System

The Board of Governors, the Federal Reserve banks, and a large number of commercial banks combine to form the Federal Reserve System. Policy decisions for, supervision of, and regulation of the system emanate from the Board of Governors. Federal Reserve activities that carry out Board of Governors' decisions are largely effected through the 12 Federal Reserve banks. Decisions of the Board of Governors and the operations of the Federal Reserve banks affect directly what commercial banks are able to do.

As we indicated above not all commercial banks are members of the Federal Reserve System. All national banks are required to be members, but state banks are free to choose for themselves whether or not the benefits of membership are worth the costs. Of the approximately 10,000 state banks in existence, only about 1,000 have elected to join.

Until the Federal Reserve Act of 1913 was passed the United States was almost unique among the advanced countries of the world in that it had no central bank. In fact, the framers of the Federal Reserve Act did not really intend to establish a central bank. Instead they set up the 12 Federal Reserve districts with the 12 regional Federal Reserve banks, each intended to perform certain central bank functions for the banks of its district. Over time the activities of the 12 Federal Reserve banks have come to be coordinated and controlled by the Board of Governors in such a way that, as arms of the Board, they act essentially as one central bank. The nature of these activities will be discussed in detail in the next chapter.

COMMERCIAL BANK OPERATIONS

The demand deposit component of the money supply, amounting to almost 75 percent of the total, is provided by commercial banks. It has been *created* by them and they are able to increase or to decrease it. In this section we shall see how banks perform this important act and shall look at the limits to the money creation that they can accomplish.

The bank as a business concern

A bank is a business concern operated for the purpose of providing a return to those who own its capital resources. It is no different in this respect from other business establishments. It sells services for which the general public is willing to pay and it uses resources, both capital and labor, that are costly to it in the production and sale of those services.

The money-creating items of banks can be brought into focus with a "T-account" technique. A T-account will be used to record a bank's assets, liabilities, and net worth. The *assets* of a bank (or any other economic entity) consist of what it owns—its buildings and equipment, its cash on hand, the promissory notes owed it by borrowers, the bonds or stocks that it owns, and the like. Its *liabilities* are made up of what it owes. A very large part of a bank's liabilities are the demand deposit accounts that it owes its depositors. The *net worth* of any business is the difference between its assets and its liabilities. The T-account form for a hypothetical bank is shown in Figure 5–1.

Figure 5–1
The T-account for a bank

State Bank of Glencoe

Assets		Liabilities	
Buildings	$200,000	Demand deposits	$300,000
Cash	100,000	*Net worth*	
Notes receivable	100,000	Common stock	150,000
Government bonds	100,000	Accumulated surplus	50,000
Total Assets:	$500,000	Total Liabilities and Net Worth	$500,000

The totals of the two T-account columns must be equal since net worth is defined as the difference between assets and liabilities. If the bank's assets exceed the total of its liabilities and the book value of its common stock the excess is reflected by its accumulated surplus. If its assets are less than the sum of its liabilities and the book value of its common stock, the deficiency is shown by an accumulated loss in lieu of the accumulated surplus.

We will be concerned primarily with *changes* in the banks assets and liabilities. Its net worth accounts will be treated as though they were constant over time. Thus *changes* in asset totals will be matched by equal *changes* in liability total and vice versa.

A monopoly bank and money creation

Consider an economy in which there are no banks initially. Let the money supply be $100,000 consisting entirely of currency. All payments are made in currency. Now suppose that a bank is established and that it is the only bank in existence. This monopoly bank must be used by anyone desiring to make use of a bank.

Primary deposits. Smith and Jones make deposits in the monopoly bank. Smith's deposit amounts to $1,000 in currency. Actually the currency is given to the bank in exchange for a deposit. The currency becomes the property of the bank to do with as it sees fit and is thus a bank asset. The deposit account of Smith at the bank records a bank liability owed to Smith. Smith can claim the entire amount or any part of the bank debt to her at any time she so desires. She can also have the bank pay the total amount or any part of it to any third party that she designates. In Figure 5–2 the items marked (1) come into existence. When Jones deposits $1,000 in currency in the bank the transactions marked (2) in Figure 5–2 are generated.

The deposits of Smith and Jones are money in every sense of the term. They can be used as a means of exchange and will be accepted by the public as such—if the public accepts and has confidence in the bank. Let Smith make a purchase from Jones amounting to $500. Smith writes a check to Jones for that amount and Jones deposits the check in the bank. The bank increases Jones' deposit by $500 and reduces Smith's deposit by the same amount, as transaction (3) in Figure 5–2 indicates. The bank has simply transferred—as Smith's check requests—$500 of the debt it owes Smith to the amount it owes Jones.

Deposits made in cash or currency cause no net change

Figure 5–2
Primary deposits and the effects of transfers

Monopoly Bank

Assets		Liabilities	
		Deposits:	
Cash	$1,000 (1)	Smith	$1,000 (1)
	1,000 (2)		− 500 (3)
		Jones	1,000 (2)
			+ 500 (3)

in the money supply of the economy as long as the cash is simply held by the bank as an asset. In the example of Figure 5–2, currency amounting to $2,000 was taken out of circulation and demand deposits of $2,000 were substituted for it. Both before and after the deposits were established the money supply is $100,000. Deposits of this kind are called *primary deposits*.

Loans and secondary deposits. It is often thought that the cash deposited at a bank must be kept on hand to meet the demands for cash withdrawals from those deposits that depositors may make. Although those who make deposits may ask whenever they wish that all or a part of those deposits be redeemed in cash, the bank soon finds that the entire amount of cash deposited is not needed to take care of cash withdrawals. Smith may write a check to "Cash" for $500 and present it at the bank. In this case the bank gives her $500 of its cash and reduces her deposit by the same amount. This is shown by transaction (1) in Figure 5–3. If Smith now makes a $500 payment to Jones in cash, Jones will in all probability deposit the cash in the bank, increasing the bank's cash account and Jones' deposit account by $500 each as we show in transaction (2). A bank typically finds that the cash withdrawals by some of its depositors tend to be offset by the cash deposits of others. When those who withdraw cash spend it, those who receive the cash payments usually deposit it in their own accounts at the bank. Usually withdrawals and deposits in cash are occurring simultaneously.

Since all of the banks depositors are unlikely to request that all of their deposits be paid to them in cash at the same time, the bank does not really need to have cash on hand equal to 100 percent of its total deposit liabilities. Therefore the bank can engage in lending activities. Suppose that Ms.

Figure 5–3
The effects of cash withdrawals

Monopoly Bank

Assets		Liabilities	
		Deposits:	
Cash	$2,000	Smith	$1,000
	− 500 (1)		− 500 (1)
	+ 500 (2)		
		Jones	1,000
			+ 500 (2)

King asks to borrow $1,000 to help pay for a new automobile. The bank checks out her financial condition and, finding her to be a good credit risk, makes the loan. If the loan were made in cash the bank's cash would be reduced by $1,000. Ms. King would sign a *promissory note* promising to repay the $1,000 loan by a stated date along with interest on the loan. The note is a bank asset and would be carried on the bank's books as a part of its Loans account.

The usual method of bank lending is illustrated in Figure 5–4. The bank loans Ms. King $1,000 and obtains a promissory note from her for that amount. Instead of making the loan in cash it simply increases her checking account or her demand deposit by $1,000. In effect the bank has exchanged IOUs with Ms. King and the IOU that it provides her is a deposit that can be spent. Transaction (1) shows the effects of the loan

Figure 5–4
Secondary deposits and lending activities

Monopoly Bank

Assets		Liabilities	
		Deposits:	
Cash	$2,000	Smith	$1,000
Loans	+ 1,000 (1)	Jones	1,000
		King	+ 1,000 (1)

and the establishment of the corresponding deposit. Deposits of this nature, arising from lending activities of a bank, are called *secondary deposits*.

Note that the loan to Ms. King *increases* the economy's money supply. Prior to the establishment of the bank the money supply was $100,000. When the bank was established and $2,000 in primary deposits were made, the bank withdrew $2,000 in currency from circulation replacing it with $2,000 in deposit liabilities. At this point no change has occurred in the money supply. But consider now the secondary deposit established by the loan to Ms. King. It *increases* the deposit component of the money supply by $1,000 *without a corresponding decrease* in the currency component. Secondary deposits generated by bank loans represent *net additions* to the money supply; or, in other words, they represent *money creation* by the bank.

Bank reserves. Are there limits to how much money our monopoly bank can create? There are indeed and the limit is determined by two things: (1) the bank's reserves and (2) its reserve ratio. A bank's reserves are what a bank has available to pay those depositors who want their deposits paid to them. Our monopoly bank's *reserves* are its cash assets. The ratio of a bank's reserves to its deposits is called its *reserve ratio.* In Figure 5–5 the entries indicate that primary deposits of $10,000 have been made and that secondary deposits of $40,000 have been generated by lending activities of the bank. Reserves are $10,000. Total deposits are $50,000. The reserve ratio is $10,000/$50,000 = $\frac{1}{5}$ = 20 percent.

The managers of a bank must strike a balance between operations that are prudent or safe and operations that earn it the greatest possible income. Most of a bank's income is

Figure 5–5
Reserves and the reserve ratio

	Monopoly Bank		(R.R. = 20%)
Assets		*Liabilities*	
Cash	$10,000	Deposits	$50,000
Loans	40,000		

earned from the interest it receives on the loans that it has made. The larger the amount of its loans (and the larger the amount of its secondary deposits) the more income it earns. But the bank must also be prepared to meet the demands that depositors will make on it for cash. The larger the total amount of its deposits the greater the demands for cash will be. The bank must make sure that its reserves are adequate to meet those demands; that is, it must not let its reserve ratio drop below what it considers to be a safe level.

What is a safe reserve ratio? It will vary depending upon the community in which the bank is located and upon the customers that it serves. Reserve ratios as low as 5 percent may be sufficient where the bank's total volume of deposits is quite stable. Where the volume of deposits is volatile it may be desirable to keep the reserve ratio as high as 25 percent.

How do the monopoly bank's reserves and its desired reserve ratio determine the amount of money that it can create?

Figure 5–6
Limits to money creation

	Monopoly Bank	(R.R. = 20%)

Assets		*Liabilities*	
Cash:	$10,000 (1)	Deposits	$10,000 (1)
	(R = 2,000)		+ 40,000 (2)
	(X = 8,000)		
Loans:	+ 40,000 (2)		

R.R. = desired reserve ratio.
R = reserves required to maintain R.R.
X = excess reserves.

Suppose that the monopoly bank wants to maintain a reserve ratio of at least 20 percent. In Figure 5–6, entry (1) shows primary deposits of $10,000. The $10,000 of cash reserves of the bank can be separated into two parts: (1) required reserves R and (2) excess reserves X. Required reserves are the minimum reserves necessary to maintain the desired reserve ratio. With total deposits of $10,000 and a desired reserve ratio of 20 percent they amount to $2,000. *Excess reserves* are the reserves over and above the required reserves. They amount to $8,000 in the example.

The bank can make loans and create secondary deposits, but for every dollar of secondary deposits that it creates, 20 cents of the excess reserves must be shifted into the required reserves category. Suppose the bank makes loans and creates $40,000 in secondary deposits, as entry (2) indicates. All of the $8,000 that were excess reserves become required reserves. The bank now has total deposits of $50,000, reserves of $10,000, and a reserve ratio of 20 percent. Since its desired reserve ratio is also 20 percent it has reached the limit of its money-creating capabilities.

For a monopoly bank which is the only bank of the economy, the deposit-creating possibilities can be easily determined by using the formula:

$$\Delta D = X \cdot \frac{1}{R.R.}$$

in which

X = excess reserves,
$R.R.$ = desired reserve ratio,
ΔD = potential deposit creation.

Suppose, for example, that a monopoly bank has $7,000 in excess reserves and a desired reserve ratio of 10 percent. Then:

$$\Delta D = \$7,000 \cdot \frac{1}{1/10}$$
$$= \$7,000 \cdot 10$$
$$= \$70,000;$$

that is, on the basis of the $7,000 in excess reserves and the 10 percent reserve ratio, the bank could make new loans, generating new secondary deposits, in the amount of $70,000.

A multiple-bank system and money creation

Most present day economies have a multiple-bank system rather than a monopoly bank. The basic mechanics of the system as a whole are the same as those for the monopoly bank; however, any one individual bank is more limited in its money-creating powers than is the system as a whole. The reason for this is that any one bank of a multiple-bank system may experience adverse clearing balances. We shall consider first the nature of clearing operations. Next we shall look at the deposit-expansion limits of a single bank of the system. Finally, the limits of deposit expansion for the system as a whole will be established.

Clearing operations. In a multiple-bank system, checks written on one bank are often deposited in another. This situation does not arise in the monopoly-bank system since everyone uses the same bank. But in the multiple-bank system, a mechanism for handling such interbank transactions is necessary. This mechanism is referred to as *clearing operations.*

Clearing operations are illustrated in Figure 5–7. Suppose Jones, who has a deposit in Bank A, writes a $1,000 check to Smith, who has a deposit in Bank B. As the entries marked (1) indicate, Smith deposits the $1,000 to his account in Bank B. Bank B sends the check to Bank A, on which it was written, for collection. Bank A reduces Jones account by $1,000 and sends $1,000 of its reserves to Bank B. Consequently, Bank A's reserves are decreased by $1,000 while Bank B's reserves are increased by $1,000.

Suppose that while the foregoing transactions are taking place Stevens, who has a deposit at Bank B, writes a check for $500 to Garfinkel, who has a deposit in Bank A. Garfinkel

Figure 5–7
Clearing operations

Bank A

Assets			*Liabilities*		
Reserves	$10,000		Deposits	$40,000	
	− 1,000	(1)		− 1,000	(1)
	+ 500	(2)		+ 500	(2)
Loans	30,000				

Bank B

Assets			*Liabilities*		
Reserves	$20,000		Deposits	$60,000	
	+ 1,000	(1)		+ 1,000	(1)
	− 500	(2)		− 500	(2)
Loans	40,000				

deposits the check at Bank A increasing her account by $500. Bank A sends the check to Bank B for collection. Bank B reduces Stevens' account by $500 and sends $500 on reserves to Bank A. Thus, Bank A's reserves are increased by $500 and Bank B's reserves are reduced by $500. The entries market (2) show the complete set of transactions.

Obviously it is unnecessary for one bank to send reserves to another every time a check drawn on it is deposited in another bank. At the same time that checks drawn on Bank A are being deposited in Bank B, checks drawn on Bank B are being deposited in Bank A. All that is really necessary is that the banks settle with each other periodically for the net amount that one may owe the other. If daily settlements are made and if the only transactions are those shown by entries (1) and (2) in Figure 5–7, at the end of the day a single transfer of $500 in reserves from Bank A to Bank B would take care of the obligations of both banks. Bank A is said to have an *adverse clearing balance* in this case since its reserves have been reduced by $500. By the same token Bank B has a *favorable clearing balance.*

Limits to deposit expansion: single bank. In a multiple-bank system, the possible occurrence of adverse clearing balances severely limits the deposit expansion that a single bank can generate when it has excess reserves. In Figure 5–8, entry (1) records a primary deposit of $10,000 at Bank A. Suppose

Figure 5–8
Effects of adverse clearing balances on deposit creation

	Bank A		(*R.R.* $= 20\%$)
Assets		*Liabilities*	
Reserves	$10,000 (1) − 10,000 (3)	Deposits	$10,000 (1) + 40,000 (2) − 10,000 (3)
Loans	+ 40,000 (2)		

	Bank B		
Assets		*Liabilities*	
Reserves	+$10,000 (3)	Deposits	+$10,000 (3)

that Bank A's desired reserve ratio is 20 percent. Its required reserves for the $10,000 deposit would be $2,000 and it would have excess reserves of $8,000. If the bank expands loans and deposits by $40,000 as entry (2) indicates its reserve ratio will be at the 20 percent lower limit, but no problem appears to exist. But some of those persons who borrowed from Bank A will make payments to persons who do their banking at other banks. Suppose that the transactions marked (3) take place. Payments of $10,000 are made by Bank A depositors to persons who bank with Bank B. An adverse clearing balance of $10,000 arises for Bank A completely wiping out the reserves that Bank A would have for the remaining $30,000 of deposits. Clearly Bank A cannot make the $40,000 in loans shown by entry (2).

By how much can a single bank of a multiple-bank system safely increase its loans when it has excess reserves? The correct answer is *by an amount equal to the excess reserves.* Consider Figure 5–9. Entry (1) shows a $10,000 primary deposit in Bank A that gives rise to $8,000 in excess reserves for the bank. Bank A can safely make loans of $8,000 as shown by the (2) entries. Now if the borrowers of the $8,000 from Bank A make payments by check to persons who keep their accounts at Bank B, Bank B's deposits increase by $8,000. It sends the checks through to Bank A for collection. Bank A sends reserves of $8,000 to Bank B while at the same time reducing the deposits of those who wrote the checks by a total of $8,000. Bank B's reserves are increased by $8,000. The four entries marked (3)

Figure 5–9
Deposit creation in a multiple-bank system

		Bank A			(R.R. = 20%)
	Assets			*Liabilities*	
Reserves		$10,000 (1)	Deposits		$10,000 (1)
		− 8,000 (3)			+ 8,000 (2)
Loans		+ 8,000 (2)			− 8,000 (3)

		Bank B			(R.R. = 20%)
	Assets			*Liabilities*	
Reserves		+$ 8,000 (3)	Deposits		+$ 8,000 (3)
		− 6,400 (5)			+ 6,400 (4)
Loans		+ 6,400 (4)			− 6,400 (5)

		Bank C			(R.R. = 20%)
	Assets			*Liabilities*	
Reserves		+$ 6,400 (5)	Deposits		+$ 6,400 (5)

in Figure 5–9 record these changes. Study them until you understand them completely. Bank A still has reserves of $2,000 to support the remaining $10,000 in deposits.

Limits to deposit expansion: The banking system. The banking system as a whole *is able to do* what a single bank of the system *cannot do*. When excess reserves exist the system as a whole can expand loans and deposits by an amount equal to the excess reserves multiplied by the reciprocal of the reserve ratio. The system as a whole can accomplish the same results as those accomplished by the monopoly bank.

Returning to Figure 5–9 we look again at Bank A. Currency amounting to $10,000 was deposited in the bank establishing $10,000 in reserves and $10,000 in deposits. As we indicated above, Bank A loaned an amount equal to its excess reserves or $8,000. The loan created new money amounting to $8,000. When the borrowers of the $8,000 made payments to persons who keep their deposits in Bank B, Bank B's deposits and reserves were each increased by $8,000. With a desired reserve ratio of 20 percent only $1,600 of the $8,000 in reserves are required reserves; the other $6,400 constitute excess reserves. Thus Bank B can expand its loans and its deposits by $6,400— the amount of the excess reserves. These expansions are designated by the (4) entries.

The borrowers from Bank B are now assumed to make payments of the entire $6,400 that they borrow to persons who keep their accounts in Bank C. As indicated by the entries marked (5), Bank C's deposits increase by $6,400; the checks are sent to Bank B for collection; Bank B's deposits are reduced by $6,400; Bank B sends $6,400 of its reserves to Bank C; and Bank C's reserves increase by that amount.

The process continues. Bank C has excess reserves of $5,120 and can expand loans and deposits by that amount. The next bank in the chain can expand loans and deposits by $4,096; the next by $3,276.80; the next by $2,261.44; and so on. Eventually, the expansion that a single bank can make approaches zero.

The total of all the expansions of loans and deposits that can be generated by the initial $8,000 in excess reserves of Bank A will be $40,000. The total is obtained as follows:

$$\$8,000 + \$8,000 \cdot 4/5 + \$8,000 \cdot (4/5)^2 + \$8,000 \cdot (4/5)^3 + \cdots +$$
$$\$8,000 \cdot (4/5)^n = \$8,000 \cdot \frac{1}{1 - 4/5} = \$8,000 \cdot 5 = \$40,000.$$

The total of the expansions generated by the individual banks is the sum of a convergent geometric series and approaches $40,000 as the increase which any single bank can generate approaches zero. Thus, when excess reserves appear in a multiple bank system: (1) any one bank can expand loans and deposits by an amount equal to the excess reserves; however, (2) the banking system as a whole can expand loans and deposits by an amount equal to the excess reserves times the reciprocal of the reserve ratio. The banking system as a whole can create exactly the same amount of money as could the monopoly bank that we discussed earlier since there are no adverse clearing balances for the system as a whole. Each individual bank is limited, because of the possibility of adverse clearing balances, to the amount of its excess reserves in its contributions to the total expansion.

How banks destroy money

The process of money destruction is precisely the opposite of money creation. When a bank customer repays what has previously been borrowed from the bank the customer's deposit account is used to make the payment. Thus, both deposits and loans of the bank are reduced by the amounts that are repaid.

Figure 5–10 shows a hypothetical combined T-account for all commercial banks of the banking system. Given a desired reserve ratio of 20 percent for all banks, the initial unnumbered entries inform us that the system has created as much as it can—an amount of money equal to $400,000. Suppose that $10,000 of the loans it has made become due. Anticipating that their loans must be repaid, borrowers will have built up their checking accounts sufficiently to make the payments. Those whose loans fall due write checks for $10,000 to the banks from which they have borrowed. As the entries marked (1) indicate both deposits and loans are reduced by $10,000. The economy's money supply is reduced by that amount.

The withdrawal of reserves from banks will also cause banks to destroy money if the withdrawal results in a reserve deficiency. In Figure 5–10 banks have total deposits of $490,000 left after the loans of $10,000 are repaid. Required reserves are $98,000 and actual reserves are $100,000 so banks have $2,000 in excess reserves. Suppose now that a customer comes in and writes a check to cash for $10,000. As the entries designated (2) show, deposits and reserves are both reduced by $10,000. Total deposits are now $480,000 and required reserves become $96,000. But the banks have total reserves of only $90,000 so a reserve deficiency of $6,000 exists.

The reserve deficiency forces banks to reduce further the amounts of their deposits. The reduction can be accomplished by the process of banks letting loans be paid off as they fall due without making new loans in their stead. The entries marked (3) show that $30,000 in old loans are repaid reducing deposits by the same amount. Total deposits are now $450,000;

Figure 5–10
How money is destroyed

All Commercial Banks			($R.R. = 20\%$)
Assets		**Liabilities**	
Reserves	$100,000 − 10,000 (2)	Deposits	$500,000 − 10,000 (1) − 10,000 (2) − 30,000 (3)
Loans	400,000 − 10,000 (1) − 30,000 (3)		

reserves are $90,000; and the actual reserve ratio is equal to the desired reserve ratio of 20 percent. Note that the *deposit contraction* forced on banks by the reserve deficiency *is equal to the reserve deficiency multipled by the reciprocal of the reserve ratio.*

Runs on banks

Since the commercial banks of a banking system create deposits that are several times greater in amount than their reserves, they would not be able to meet the demands of depositors if a large number of their depositors ask that their deposits be paid to them in cash—immediately. A situation in which such demands are made is termed a *run on banks.* It arises when bank depositors lose their confidence in banks' abilities to pay them cash for their deposits. The last major run on banks occurred during the Great Depression of the 1930s.

Figure 5–11 illustrates the nature of a run on banks. Suppose that banks initially have reserves of $100,000, deposits of $500,000 and a desired reserve ratio of 20 percent. Now some of the banks' customers lose confidence in the abilities of banks to meet their deposit liabilities and withdraw $100,000 of their deposits in cash. As the entries marked (1) show, banks lose $100,000 in deposits and $100,000 in reserves. In fact, the withdrawal leaves banks with no reserves whatsoever. They cannot meet the demands of depositors to whom the other $400,000 is owed without outside help.

Runs on banks have been eliminated by a very simple device—insurance covering the deposits that people maintain in banks. The Federal Deposit Insurance Corporation was established in 1934 following the disastrous runs on banks between 1929 and 1934. A bank which uses its services pays deposit insurance premiums to the FDIC. In return the FDIC insures the deposits of the bank's individual depositors—up

Figure 5–11
A run on banks

All Commercial Banks				(R.R. = 20%)
Assets			*Liabilities*	
Reserves	$100,000	Deposits		$400,000
	− 100,000 (1)			− 100,000 (1)
Loans	400,000			

to $40,000 per depositor at the present time. Fear of bank failure, the cause of runs on banks, no longer exists. The depositor is guaranteed recovery of his deposit no matter what happens to the bank. Most banks now insure their deposits with the FDIC.

Destabilizing effects of commercial bank activities

An uncontrolled system of commercial banks leads to instability in an economy's money supply and its level of economic activity. Commercial banks create and destroy money. Unfortunately, they tend to create money at precisely those times when, in the interests of economic stability, money ought not to be created. They tend to destroy money at precisely those times when, in the interests of economic stability, money ought not to be destroyed.

During periods of economic expansion and inflation banks create money rapidly, increasing aggregate demand and adding fuel to inflationary fires. There are two primary reasons for this. First, most bank lending and the consequent deposit expansion is in response to business demands. During an economic expansion, when business is booming, businesses want to borrow to finance inventories and to meet other needs for money associated with their increasing volumes of business. Second, banks want to expand their lending. During periods of economic expansion the likelihood of borrowers defaulting when their loans fall due is relatively small. Banks earn their incomes from their loans and other investments and the larger these are the more income they can earn. The favorable climate of an economic expansion enables them to expand loans and deposits with relatively more safety than at other times.

During periods of recession banks slow the rate of increase and may actually reduce the money supply. As economic activity slows during recession there is less business demand for loans. Banks become more reluctant to make loans because the risks of nonpayment are higher. The resulting restraints on the money supply have adverse effects on aggregate demand and make a recession worse than it would be if they were not operating.

The destabilizing effects of an uncontrolled, unregulated commercial banking system arise from the nature of the banking business itself and not from any malevolent desires on the part of the banking community. Banks, like other businesses, exist to earn income for their owners. Like other businesses they tend to expand when business is booming and contract when the economic outlook is bleak. Unfortunately in doing so they create and destroy money thus adding to other destabilizing undercurrents that are operating in the economy.

SUMMARY

Since demand deposits make up a large part of the money supply it is important that we understand the banking system and the role that it plays in bringing about changes in the money supply. The U.S. banking system has a number of commercial banks with which the general public carries out its banking business. It also has 12 Federal Reserve banks which operate as a central bank. All national banks and those state banks that so desire are members of the Federal Reserve system. The Federal Reserve Board of Governors is the policy making unit of the Federal Reserve System.

Commercial banks create new money through their lending activities. Their capacity to create money is limited by the amounts of reserves that they have and by the minimum reserve ratio that they want to maintain. Money is destroyed as loans are repaid or as the public withdraws reserves from their banks.

Commercial banks left uncontrolled or unregulated have destabilizing effects on the economy. An economic expansion encourages net increases in lending activity, and the consequent creation of new money augments an already increasing aggregate demand. A recession causes banks to retrench, letting old loans be paid off without making new loans in their place. The money supply is reduced, reducing aggregate demand and augmenting the recession.

QUESTIONS AND PROBLEMS

1. Make a chart showing the structure of the U.S. banking system. Include in the chart:
   a. The Federal Reserve Board of Governors.
   b. Federal Reserve banks (show at least two).

    c. National banks.

    d. State banks (show both member and non-member banks).

2. The country of Utopia initially uses currency, only, as money and the currency unit is the dracula. One million draculas are in circulation. A monopoly bank is now established.

    a. Ms. Poe and Mr. Frank decide to use the bank and each makes a primary deposit of 10,000 draculas. Show and explain the appropriate changes in the monopoly bank T-account. What has happened to the total money supply?

    b. Mr. Frank now buys a piano from Ms. Poe paying for it with a 1,000 dracula check which Ms. Poe deposits in her account. Show and explain the appropriate T-account changes. What has happened to the total money supply?

    c. The bank now makes a loan of 5,000 draculas to Ms. Fisk. Show and explain the appropriate T-account changes. What is the bank's actual reserve ratio? What has happened to the total money supply?

    d. Suppose the bank's required reserve ratio is 50%. Given the deposits of Ms. Poe and Mr. Frank, along with the loan to Ms. Fisk, how much more can the bank lend? Show appropriate T-account entries for the additional lending, setting up the new deposits that are created under the heading "other deposits."

3. In a multiple-bank system the State Bank of Ripley has excess reserves of $10,000. No other bank in the system has excess reserves. All banks have a required reserve ratio of 25 percent.

    a. By how much can the State Bank of Ripley increase its loans and its demand deposits? Explain.

    b. By how much can the banking system as a whole increase its loans and its demand deposits? Explain.

Chapter 6

The Federal Reserve System and monetary policy

CHECKLIST OF ECONOMIC CONCEPTS

Bankers' bank
Government's bank
Member bank reserves
Clearing operations
Government securities, negotiable and nonnegotiable
Open market sales
Open market purchases
Current interest rate or yield
Discount rate
Borrowed reserves
Monetary policy
Easy money policies
Tight money policies

As the central bank of the United States the Federal Reserve Board of Governors and the Federal Reserve banks (acting as a unit) are in a unique position to counteract the destabilizing effects of unregulated commercial bank activities. To facilitate understanding of how this is done we divide Federal Reserve functions into two categories. The first category consists of banking functions. The second is that of controlling the money supply. We shall look at each of these in turn and shall then consider the general nature of Federal Reserve monetary policies.

FEDERAL RESERVE BANKING FUNCTIONS

The Federal Reserve banks (hereinafter called the FRB) perform two important banking functions. One of these is to serve as a bankers' bank for commercial banks that are members of the Federal Reserve System. The other is to act as the government's bank. Both of these functions facilitate control of the money supply by the Federal Reserve authorities.

Bankers' bank

Member banks of the Federal Reserve System use the FRB in much the same way as private parties use commercial banks. Member banks maintain deposits with the FRB. They also borrow from the FRB from time to time.

Deposits. The Federal Reserve Act requires that member banks deposit the bulk of their reserves with the FRB. The exception is the small amount of currency that member banks keep on hand to accommodate customers who want cash. Banks use their FRB deposits to make payments to each other, or to draw on when they need to replenish their currency supplies to meet customer needs.

The establishment of member bank deposits at the FRB are illustrated in Figure 6–1. The National Bank of Torrance and the National Bank of Whitehall initially have currency reserves of $100,000 and $50,000 respectively, as the unnumbered entries show. Their initial loans and their deposits are also unnumbered. Both banks now deposit their currency reserves at the FRB. The FRB T-account thus shows deposits of $100,000 and $50,000 respectively, for the two banks; that is, the FRB owes

Figure 6–1
Clearinghouse operations of the FRB

	National Bank of Torrance		$(R.R. = 20\%)$
Reserves	$100,000	Deposits	$400,000
	− 1,000 (1)		− 1,000 (1)
Loans	300,000		

	National Bank of Whitehall		$(R.R. = 20\%)$
Reserves	$ 50,000	Deposits	$200,000
	+ 1,000 (1)		+ 1,000 (1)
Loans	150,000		

	Federal Reserve Bank		
Cash	$150,000	Deposits:	
		N.B. of Torrance	$100,000
			− 1,000 (1)
		N.B. of Whitehall	50,000
			+ 1,000 (1)

the banks these amounts. Member bank deposits with the
FRB—what it owes them—are counted as reserves of the
member banks in the same way that their currency has been
counted in our analysis up to this point. So the act of member
banks depositing currency with the FRB causes no change
in what we show as member bank reserves in the member
bank T-accounts.

Since both banks maintain deposits with the FRB, that institution can assist them with their *clearing operations.* Suppose
that a customer of the Torrance bank writes a check for $1,000
to a customer of the Whitehall bank. The latter deposits the
check in the Whitehall bank. As shown by the transactions
marked (1), Whitehall deposits are increased by $1,000. White-
hall now sends the check to the FRB. The FRB increases Whitehall's deposit by $1,000 which also increases Whitehall's re-
serves by that amount. The FRB reduces Torrance's deposit
by $1,000 which has the effect of reducing its reserves by the
same amount. The check is sent by the FRB to Torrance which
reduces the account of its check-writing customer by $1,000.
Thus the clearing balance of $1,000 from Torrance to Whitehall
is paid through a bookkeeping transaction at the FRB. No currency needs to be sent from one bank to the other.

Loans.   The other important aspect of FRB operations as

Figure 6–2
Commercial bank borrowing from the FRB

National Bank of Torrance

Reserves	$100,000	Deposits	$500,000
	+ 10,000 (1)		
Loans	400,000	Borrowings	
		from FRB	+ 10,000 (1)

Federal Reserve Banks

Cash	$100,000	Deposits:	
		N.B. of Torrance	$100,000
			+ 10,000 (1)
Loans to			
M.B.s	10,000 (1)		

a bankers' bank consists of loans made to member banks. The unnumbered entries in Figure 6–2 show the initial position of the Torrance bank and the corresponding FRB accounts relating to the Torrance bank. If the Torrance bank now borrows $10,000 from the FRB, a liability account, which we shall call "Borrowings from the FRB" comes into being for it. The Torrance bank accepts the loan in the form of an increase in its deposit at the FRB and this, in turn, increases the reserves of the Torrance bank by $10,000. Since the $10,000 loan is owed the FRB, it is an FRB asset which we set up as the "Loans to Member Banks" account. The transactions marked (1) show the complete set of changes. The interest rate that the FRB charges member banks when they borrow from it has come to be called the *discount rate*.

Government's bank

As the government's bank, the FRB performs services similar to those that any bank performs for its customers. The government maintains deposits at the FRB and writes checks on them. It also borrows from the FRB on occasion.

The establishment of government deposits at the FRB is illustrated in Figure 6–3. The unnumbered entries show the initial positions of the Torrance bank and the FRB. Suppose that a customer of the Torrance bank writes a $10,000 check to the government in payment of personal income taxes. The

Figure 6–3
Government deposits at the FRB

Federal Reserve Banks

Cash	$100,000	Deposits:	
		N.B. of Torrance	$100,000
			− 10,000 (1)
		Government	+ 10,000 (1)

National Bank of Torrance

Reserves	$100,000	Deposits	$400,000
	− 10,000 (1)		− 10,000 (1)
Loans	300,000		

government deposits the check at the FRB thus establishing
a deposit account of $10,000. The FRB, noting that the deposited
check was written on the Torrance bank, reduces the Torrance
bank deposit by $10,000 and sends the check to the Torrance
bank. The Torrance bank, in turn, reduces the deposits of the
customer who wrote the check, and also its own reserves,
by $10,000.

Governments usually borrow money by selling Treasury
bills and bonds to individuals, businesses, and other organiza-
tions. The FRB is among the purchasers of such government
securities, although it is not a major purchaser, and is thus
a lender of funds to the government. In Figure 6–4, the initial
position of the FRB consists of the unnumbered entries. If the
FRB now purchases $100,000 worth of government securities
from the Treasury, they become a "Government Securities"
asset account. Payment is made to the government by increasing its deposit account by $100,000. These changes are indi-
cated by the entries marked (1).

Figure 6–4
Government borrowing from the FRB

Federal Reserve Banks

Cash	$200,000	Deposits:	
		Member banks	$100,000
Government securities	+ 100,000 (1)	Government	100,000
			+ 100,000 (1)

CONTROL OF THE MONEY SUPPLY

The functions of the FRB as a bankers' bank and as the government's bank facilitate control of the money supply by the FRB. Three major tools of control are available. These are: (1) open-market operations, (2) variation of the discount rate, and (3) variation of the required reserve ratio. The first two enable the Federal Reserve to control the volume of total deposits by controlling the total reserves of member banks given the required reserve ratios of those banks. The third allows it to control the volume of deposits that can be created by member banks given the amount of reserves that they have available.

Open-market operations

The FRB, like any other organization or person, can buy or sell existing government securities. But such buying and selling on the part of the FRB, termed *open-market operations,* has important effects on the money supply of the economy. The sale of some of the government securities that the FRB owns tends to contract the money supply. Purchases of government securities by the FRB tends to increase the money supply.

An understanding of the use of open-market operations requires some knowledge of the market for government securities. The government borrows money by selling Treasury bills and government bonds. Most of these are *negotiable;* that is, they are not issued in the names of specific buyers and once they are issued, they can be bought and sold by anyone at whatever price buyers and sellers can agree on. Some government bonds such as savings bonds are issued to specific buyers and are therefore *nonnegotiable.* But these are a small part of the total government securities outstanding and are not involved in open-market operations.

Government securities are issued to pay fixed amounts of interest based on the face values of the securities. For example, if the government issues a series of bonds at an interest rate of 8 percent, a $1,000 face value bond of the series pays $80 per year in interest to its holder until the bond becomes due and is redeemed by the Treasury. The bond, however, need not be bought and sold for $1,000. It may bring a higher price or it may bring a lower price, depending on the supply of and demand for government bonds.

If a person buys such a bond for a price below its face value, say for $800, the interest rate earned by the buyer is greater than the interest rate specified in the bond. The interest income on the bond is $80 per year, providing a current yield of 10 percent to the person who purchases it for $800. Thus whenever government securities sell below their face values the current interest rate to purchasers is above the fixed rate indicated on the securities. The lower the market price of securities are relative to their face values, the higher the current interest rate will be and the more attractive the securities are to potential buyers.

The buyer who pays more than the face value for such a government security receives a current interest yield that is below the interest rate specified for the security. Suppose the buyer of the $1,000 bond with a specified interest rate of 8 percent pays $1,200 for the bond. The interest income of $80 per year provides a current yield of only 6⅔ percent on the buyer's investment. The higher the market price of the security is relative to its face value, the lower the current interest yield will be and less attractive the security becomes to potential buyers.

The unnumbered entries in Figure 6–5 provide a starting

Figure 6–5
Open-market sales

Federal Reserve Banks

Cash	$100,000	Deposits:	
		Member Banks	$100,000
			− 10,000 (1)
Government			
securities	100,000	Government	100,000
	− 10,000 (1)		

Member Banks			(R.R. = 20%)
Reserves	$100,000	Deposits	$500,000
	− 10,000 (1)		− 50,000 (2)
Loans	200,000		
	− 50,000 (2)		
Government			
securities	200,000		
	+ 10,000 (1)		

point to illustrate how open-market operations work. Both member banks and the FRB are assumed to hold substantial quantities of government securities among their assets. The acquisition of government securities by member banks from other private parties generates new secondary deposits for those banks in much the same manner as does the making of new loans. When banks buy already existing government securities they pay the sellers by creating new deposits for them. Thus, in Figure 6–5, the member bank deposits of $500,000 can be thought of as coming from primary deposits of $100,000, from secondary deposits generated by lending activities in the amount of $200,000, and from secondary deposits generated by the purchase of government securities from other private parties in the amount of $200,000. It is important to keep in mind that open-market operations are transactions involving already existing government securities—securities that were issued by the Treasury at some time in the past. They do not refer to the sale of new securities by the government.

How do open-market sales of government securities by the FRB bring about reductions in the country's money supply? In Figure 6–5, suppose that $10,000 in government securities are sold to member banks by the FRB. Member banks pay for the securities with a part of their deposits at the FRB. Consequently, the member bank deposits and government securities are each reduced by $10,000 in the FRB T-account. In the T-account of member banks, government securities are increased by $10,000 and, since member bank deposits at the FRB are also member bank reserves, member bank reserves are decreased by a like amount. These changes are indicated by the transactions marked (1).

Assuming that the required reserve ratio of member banks is 20 percent, the $10,000 reduction in reserves that member banks used to pay for the government securities leaves them with a reserve deficiency. In order to bring the reserve ratio back to the 20 percent level member banks, with reserves of only $90,000, must let some of their old loans be repaid before they make new ones. The $90,000 of reserves will support only $450,000 in total deposits so the banks must let $50,000 in old loans be repaid, reducing both their loans and their deposits by that amount. The entries marked (2) show the reductions. The $10,000 open-market sale by the FRB to member banks has thus forced a $50,000 reduction in the money supply.

Open-market purchases of government securities from member banks by the FRB tend to have the opposite impact on the money supply. In Figure 6–6, the unnumbered entries represent the initial position of the FRB and member banks. Now let the FRB purchase $10,000 in government securities from member banks. The FRB pays for the securities by increasing member bank deposits at the FRB by $10,000. As the entries marked (1) indicate, both government securities and member bank deposits in the FRB T-account are increased by $10,000. The increase in member bank deposits at the FRB represents an increase in member bank reserves. At the same time member banks' holding of government securities are reduced by $10,000. These changes in the member banks' T-account are also marked (1). Member banks now have excess reserves of $10,000 which can be used as a base for generating additional deposits. In fact, with this amount of excess reserves, member banks can make additional loans of $50,000, creating $50,000 in new deposits as the entries marked (2) illustrate.

Although the FRB can always engineer a contraction, prevent an expansion, or put an upper limit on the rate of expansion of member bank demand deposits, it cannot force an expansion of deposits to occur. When the FRB puts excess reserves in the hands of member banks, it is possible for them

Figure 6–6
Open-market purchases

Federal Reserve Banks

Cash:	$100,000	Deposits:	
		Member Banks	$100,000
			+ 10,000 (1)
Government		Government	100,000
securities	100,000		
	+ 10,000 (1)		

Member Banks   (R.R. = 20%)

Reserves	$100,000	Deposits	$500,000
	+ 10,000 (1)		+ 50,000 (2)
Loans:	200,000		
	+ 50,000 (2)		
Government			
securities:	200,000		
	− 10,000 (1)		

simply to hold the excess reserves without expanding loans and deposits. But if the FRB induces reserve deficiencies for member banks, they must contract their loans and deposits in order to get their reserve ratios back to the required minimum level.

Open-market operations provide FRB officials with a powerful tool for controlling the money supply of the economy. The sale of government securities to member banks always reduces member bank reserves and, to the extent that reserve deficiencies are brought about, forces them to contract their loans and their deposits by a multiple of the reserve deficiencies. Open-market purchases from member banks always increase member bank reserves, making it possible for member banks to expand their loans and their customers' deposits by a multiple of their excess reserves.

Discount rate variation

The Federal Reserve authorities are authorized by the Federal Reserve Act to control discount rates—the rates of interest charged by the FRB when it makes loans to member banks. As we noted earlier, when member banks borrow from the FRB the amounts they borrow become member bank reserves.[1] Some borrowing is always occurring so some part of member bank reserves always consists of borrowed reserves.

Changes in the discount rate change the cost to member banks of borrowing from the FRB. One would expect an increase in the discount rate to discourage borrowing, thus bringing about a decrease in member bank reserves. A decrease in the discount rate would be expected to encourage borrowing which would in turn increase member bank reserves. Decreases in reserves can force member banks to contract their total loans and the deposits of the public. Increases in their reserves make possible the expansion of loans and deposits.

In using discount rate variation as a means of controlling the money supply, Federal Reserve authorities should increase it to restrain money supply growth or to bring about actual reductions in the money supply. It should lower the discount rate to encourage expansion of the money supply. In practice discount rate variation is much less effective as a tool of con-

---

1. See Figure 6–2.

trol than are open-market operations. Member bank borrowing, and consequently the volume of member bank reserves, is not very sensitive to discount rate changes. Discount rate changes are, however, generally interpreted by banks and by the financial community as signals of what Federal Reserve authorities intend to do. Increases signal that the FRB intends to hold member bank reserves and the money supply in check. Decreases signal the encouragement of expansion.

Required reserve ratio variation

The Federal Reserve Board of Governors sets the minimum reserve ratios that member banks must maintain. Member banks are separated into two classes: (1) reserve city banks and (2) other banks. Reserve city banks are those with net deposits of over $400 million while others are those with deposits of $400 million or less. Under the provisions of the Federal Reserve Act the Federal Reserve Board of Governors can require a minimum reserve ratio of any magnitude from 10 to 22 percent for reserve city banks and from 7 to 14 percent for other banks.

Given the total amount of member bank reserves, changes by the FRB in the required reserve ratio affect the total volume of demand deposits that member banks have outstanding. In Figure 6–7, let the reserves of member banks be $100,000. Suppose that the minimum required reserve ratio is 12 percent. Loans of $733,333.33 with total deposits of $833,333.33 are possible as the entries marked (1) show. If the FRB raises the minimum required reserve ratio to 14 percent, member banks must reduce their loans to $614,285.71 and the volume of their deposits to $714,285.71 as the entries marked (2) illustrate.

Figure 6–7

Member Banks

Reserves	$100,000	Deposits:	$ 833,333.33 (1)
			714,285.71 (2)
			1,000,000.00 (3)
Loans and	733,333.33 (1)		
investments:	614,285.71 (2)		
	900,000.00 (3)		

(1) R.R. = 12%
(2) R.R. = 14%
(3) R.R. = 10%

However, if the required reserve ratio were reduced to 10 percent, loans could be expanded to $900,000 and total deposits could be increased to $1,000,000 as the entries marked (3) indicate. Like open-market operations and discount rate variation, when increases in the required reserve ratio bring about member bank reserve deficiencies, member banks are forced to contract their loans and their deposits. However, a decrease in the required reserve ratio can only shift some of member bank reserves into the excess reserve category. While excess reserves may encourage member banks to expand their loans and their deposits, they are not required to do so.

MONETARY POLICY[2]

The control that Federal Reserve authorities exercise through open-market operations, discount rate variation, and reserve ratio variation is known as *monetary policy*. The monetary policies they pursue are of tremendous importance in the nation's economic health over time. They can help to combat recession. They can generate inflation. And, as we have been witnessing for the last 10 to 15 years, they can be a major factor in causing unemployment when they are used to control inflation.

Combatting recession, no inflation

Easy money policies by the FRB are in order when the economy is showing signs of recession but is not experiencing inflation. The main indicator of such a recession will be an unemployment rate that is climbing above acceptable levels. The years in the late 1950s and early 1960s provide an example—we were in a prolonged recession uncomplicated by inflation.

Easy money policies are those leading to a relatively more rapid expansion of the money supply. Their judicious use when there is recession with no inflation makes much sense. The Federal Reserve can (1) engage in open-market purchases of government securities, (2) lower the discount rate, and (3) lower required reserve ratios. All of these actions will increase the excess reserves of the banking system and encourage banks to make new loans which would generate additional

2. Before beginning this section of the chapter it will be useful to review the section of Chapter 4 entitled "Money, Inflation, and Recession."

demand deposits.[3] An increasing money supply increases aggregate demand, causing the prices of final goods and services to rise. The increasing profitability of business activity, virtually assured because cost increases will lag behind the rising prices of final goods and services, stimulates expansion in the level of production and reductions in the level of unemployment. As unemployment approaches an acceptable level, monetary policy should become progressively less expansionary.

Generating inflation

If the FRB pursues easy money policies when full employment exists inflation will result, as the years in last half of the 1960s will illustrate. In 1966, the U.S. economy enjoyed virtually full employment. The escalation of the Vietnam War in that and succeeding years was costly, however, and in 1967 and 1968 the government under the Johnson administration borrowed large amounts of money to meet those costs; that is, the government sold large amounts of new government securities to the general public. The increased supplies of government securities placed on the market forced the security prices down, causing current interest rates on them to rise. In an attempt to provide some support of government security prices and to hold interest rates in check the FRB was induced to engage in substantial amounts of open-market purchases. These purchases served to increase commercial bank reserves setting the stage for relatively large increases in the money supply.

The banking system did in fact respond to the larger reserves available to it. Whereas the money supply had been increasing at an annual rate between 1.7 and 4.7 percent from 1960 through 1966, it increased at an annual rate of over 7 percent per year in 1967 and in 1968. The accelerated increases in the money supply generated additional increases in aggregate demand in the economy, but since resources were fully employed the demand increases could not be matched by increases in aggregate supply. In terms of monetary theory, increases in $M \times V$, without corresponding increases in T could

---

3. But note again that an increase in demand deposits cannot be *forced* on the banking system. Banks can, if they so desire, simply sit on the excess reserves that they accrue. However, it seems clear that in most circumstances the larger the amounts of excess reserves available to banks, the greater their volume of demand deposits will be.

only serve to increase P. By the end of 1968 the inflation rate, which stemmed largely from the easy money policies of 1967 and 1968, reached a level of 4 to 5 percent per year.

Controlling inflation and generating unemployment

When inflation is occurring—that is, when $M \times V$ is increasing at a faster rate than T—tight monetary policies are thought by many economist to be the appropriate medicine to stop it. *Tight monetary policies* are those intended to slow substantially or stop the growth in the money supply that invariably accompanies inflation. Tight monetary policies are put into effect by means of (1) open-market sales of government securities by the FRB, (2) increases in the discount rate, and (3) increases in the required reserve ratios of member banks of the Federal Reserve System.

A substantial tightening of monetary policies during a period of inflation will tend to result in unemployment. This effect was demonstrated in 1969 and 1970. The first Nixon administration came to office in 1969 determined to stop the inflation generated during the Johnson administration in 1967 and 1968. Tight monetary policies by the FRB in 1969 and 1970 reduced the growth rate of the money supply substantially below that of 1967 and 1968 thus reducing the rate of growth of $M \times V$ and the rate of increase in aggregate demand. Although the rise in aggregate demand was checked, costs of production were not immediately affected, since changes in costs of production follow changes in aggregate demand only after a time lag. Businesses at all levels of production and sales either found their profits squeezed or replaced by losses. Economic activity was reduced and workers were laid off. So, the tighter money policies of 1969 and 1970 served to increase unemployment with little immediate abatement in the rate of inflation.

The tight money policies of the first two years of the Nixon administration were abandoned in 1971, even though there is considerable evidence that by mid-1971 they were beginning to bring down the rate of inflation. The problem leading to the abandonment of tight money was a level of unemployment that was unacceptably high for the upcoming election year of 1972. Easy money policies were in effect during 1971, 1972, and 1973. Price controls from August of 1971, to April of 1973, held the general price level somewhat in check, but the pressures of rising $M \times V$ and aggregate demand were overwhelming. By late 1973 and early 1974 inflation rates jumped above 10 percent per year.

Tight money policies were again followed in the last half of 1974, and unemployment rose to over 9 percent of the labor force, its highest rate since the Great Depression of the 1930s. From 1975 to 1979 monetary policies were erratic but might be characterized on balance as being more or less neutral. Slow recovery from the severe 1974 recession has been underway since about March of 1975.

Some lessons from experience

The U.S. economy's experience with monetary policies over the last two decades points toward several conclusions. First, the most efficient tool in the Federal Reserve monetary policy kit appears to be open-market operations. Second, monetary policies can have undesirable as well as desirable impacts on economic activity. Third, when used to control inflation, the sooner monetary policies are put into effect the less their undesirable effects will be.

Open-market operations are undoubtedly the most efficient means available to the Federal Reserve authorities for controlling the money supply. Discount rate variations and required reserve ratio variations serve essentially as secondary or back-up means of control. Open-market sales or purchases can be implemented quickly in whatever quantities the Federal Reserve authorities desire and, since member banks respond voluntarily to the incentives provided by the FRB to buy or sell, they lead to minimal disruptions in the business planning of member banks. The effectiveness of discount rate variation tends to be restricted by the fact that member bank borrowing from the FRB is not very responsive to discount rate changes. Reserve ratio changes, if used regularly, would soon lose their effectiveness because member banks, in order to be certain of meeting reserve requirements, would find it necessary to keep sufficient reserves available to meet the highest anticipated required reserve ratio.

Monetary policies can generate undesirable effects on the economy. As the experience of 1967 and 1968 illustrates, easy money policies can be a fundamental cause of inflation. On the other hand, tight money policies can play a major role in causing recession and rising unemployment when they are applied vigorously in a full-employment high-inflation situation.

Ideally, monetary policies can be used to prevent both inflation and recession. But ideal solutions to these problems are seldom achieved. To prevent recession, easing of monetary policies must be started before the recession has much of a chance to get underway. To stop inflation, tightening of monetary policies must be effected before the inflation becomes serious. But the signs that indicate the onset of recession or the beginning of inflation are often not clear, and even in cases where they are clear, the appropriate monetary policies for economic stability may not be suitable for attaining the ends desired by politicians seeking to win the next election.

SUMMARY

The 12 Federal Reserve banks, acting together under the policies prescribed by the Federal Reserve Board of Governors, from the central bank of the United States. As such they function as a bankers' bank, as the government's banker, and as a quasi-independent agency of the government that controls the nation's money supply.

Federal Reserve authorities have three primary means of controlling the money supply. These are: (1) open-market operations, (2) variation of the discount rate, and (3) variation of the required reserve ratio of member banks of the system. Open-market operations are the most effective and consistently used of the three. The other two provide support to whatever open-market policies the Federal Reserve authorities elect to pursue.

The policies followed by Federal Reserve authorities in controlling the money supply are called monetary policies. Easy money policies encourage expansion of the money supply. Tight money policies are those designed to restrict or prohibit money supply growth over time. Easy money policies are appropriate when the economy is experiencing recession with no inflation. With full employment, however, easy money policies will generate inflation. Tight money policies will inhibit or restrict inflation. But in doing so they will generate unemployment.

QUESTIONS AND PROBLEMS

1. In what sense are Federal Reserve banks bankers' banks? the federal government's bank?

2. Explain the relationship between open market purchases and sales by the FRB and
   a. the interest rate.
   b. member bank reserves.
   c. the total volume of demand deposits in the economy.

3. How does an increase in the discount rate affect
   a. member bank reserves?
   b. the total volume of demand deposits in the economy?

4. Suppose that the banking system has reserves of $60 billion, no excess reserves, and a required reserve ratio for all banks of 25 percent. With the aid of T-accounts, explain the potential effect on the money supply of
   a. open market sales of $5 billion worth of government securities by the FRB to member banks.
   b. a decrease in the required reserve ratio to 20 percent.

5. Can the FRB force increases in the demand deposit component of the money supply? Can it force decreases? Explain why or why not in each case.

6. If the Federal Reserve Board of Governors were to seek out your advice on the policies they should follow at the present time, what would be your recommendations?

Chapter 7

How the level of national income is determined

Monetary forces alone are insufficient to provide a complete explanation of the performance of the economy over time—the level of economic activity, economic instability, and the control of instability. The framework of national income analysis not only enables us to develop greater insight into how monetary forces work, but it permits us to incorporate additional causal forces into the collection of those that influence the course of the economy's performance. In this chapter we develop a model for a more detailed analysis of national income problems. First we consider national income from the point of view of value of products produced. Next, we look at it from the point of view of income earned. Then, we turn to how the level of national income is determined.

THE VALUE OF PRODUCTS VIEWPOINT

The concepts of gross national product and net national product were introduced in Chapter 3. We defined *GNP* as the value of all goods and services produced and sold in final form during a year's time. Then we defined *NNP* as that which remains of *GNP* after depreciation of the economy's plant and equipment has been subtracted from it. The components of *GNP* and of *NNP* were identified as follows:

$$GNP = C + GI + G$$
$$NNP = C + I + G$$

We shall consider each component in turn.

Consumer goods and services

The largest part of the economy's annual output consists of the goods and services that we buy as consumers. We refer to the total dollar value of these as personal consumption expenditures, or *C*. About three fourths of *C* are *nondurable* items like clothes, food, and medical care. The other one fourth is made up of *durable* goods like washing machines, refrigerators, and housing. The *C* component of *GNP* and *NNP* for any given year contains only those consumer goods and services produced and sold during that year. It specifically does not include the values of goods produced and sold in prior years but which are resold during the given year.

Investment goods

The total value of capital goods produced and/or discovered during any given year is called *gross investment,* or *GI.* As such it is a component part of *GNP.* But, as we noted in Chapter 3, in producing *GNP* a part of the economy's stock of capital is used up, depreciated, or rendered obsolete. All of this is referred to as capital consumption or *depreciation.*

Net investment, or *I,* is equal to *GI* minus depreciation. It is the net dollar value addition or flow into the economy's stock of capital. The new capital goods include the net amounts of new machinery and tools produced, new buildings built, new land discovered, new developments on old land, additions to inventories of all kinds and other items of a similar nature. They are called investment goods because the purchase of them is really investment in them by the purchasers.

Government goods and services

The third component part of the economy's annual output is the value of goods and services produced in a given year by governmental units. All levels of government—local, state, and national—are in the business of producing goods and services that we use. Municipal and county governments provide fire and police protection. They build and maintain roads, streets, and bridges. Sometimes they sell water and electricity. State governments in conjunction with local governments produce and distribute primary, secondary, and even post-secondary education. They also build roads and perform a wide range of additional services. At the national level, government produces national defense, highways, law enforcement services, regulatory services, and a host of other items. The total annual value of government goods produced is referred to as *G.* Since many of the items produced by government for its citizens are not sold in market places for prices, we simply value them at what it costs to produce them.

Double-counting problems

As we consider *GNP* and *NNP* from the value of products point of view we must be careful not to double count items produced during the year. For example, the value of bread

Table 7–1
The value-added concept

	Product value	Value added
Wheat	$ 5.00	$ 5.00
Flour	10.00	5.00
Bread	15.00	5.00
Total	$30.00	$15.00

sold to consumers *contains* in its price the value of flour sold to the baker. The value of flour sold to the baker in turn contains the value of wheat that the miller has used in producing it. If all of these were added together, *GNP* and *NNP* would be greatly overstated; many items would have been double counted. To avoid double counting we must consider the values of goods and services in their final forms, only. Or, alternatively, we can total the *values added* at each stage of the production process for each item that requires a multi-stage production process.

The numbers involved in double-counting problems are illustrated in Table 7–1. On the one hand we can consider as a part of *GNP* and *NNP* the $15 value of bread in the Product Value column. If we count the value of wheat and the value of flour also we get a $30 total value. But the $30 total has double counted the value of flour and has triple counted the value of wheat. It is incorrect. On the other hand we can put together the values added at each stage of the production process. The farmer generates a $5 value of wheat; the miller adds $5 in value to it by turning it into flour; and the baker adds another $5 value to it by making it into bread. The total of the values added is $15—the same as the final product value.

THE INCOME EARNED VIEWPOINT

Every sale of an item to its ultimate user during any given year generates an amount of income equal to its selling price. This amounts to saying that what buyers pay, sellers receive. But who are these sellers that earn the income? In reality they are the resource owners who furnished the resources to produce the item. Consider the sale of a new automobile for $7,000. The $7,000 received by the auto dealer covers payments already made to many resource owners—those who furnished labor, steel, rubber, glass, copper, and all of the other ingredients going into the production of the car. The dealer's "profit" is really a payment to the dealer for furnishing the resources that get the automobile off the factory truck and into the hands of the ultimate buyer. Thus the entire $7,000 value of product item has generated income amounting to $7,000 for the resource owners who produced it. We can identify income earned equivalents of *GNP* and *NNP*.

Gross national income

The production and sale of *GNP* in any given year generates an equal amount of income that we can call *gross national income* or *GNI*. Each item comprising *GNP* generates its income counterpart. Just as we total the values of all items produced and sold in final form to determine *GNP*, so can we total the corresponding incomes generated to determine *GNI*. In Figure 7–1 we represent the equivalence of the two concepts by rectangles of equal size.

Figure 7–1
Value of product equals income earned

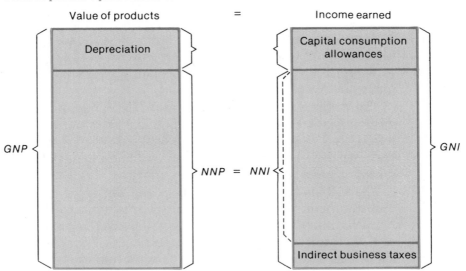

Net national income

The entire amount of gross national income generated is not available to be spent by those who earned it if the economy's stock of capital is to remain intact over time. The owners of the economy's stock of capital must purchase enough of the capital goods produced during the year to take care of depreciation if the stock of capital is to be maintained. We refer to this amount of spending out of gross national income as *capital consumption allowances.* Thus in computing the *net* income generated that income receivers have available to spend each year we must reduce *GNI* by the amount of capital consumption allowances, leaving us with *net national income,* or *NNI,* as shown by the solid bracket on the left side of the Income Earned rectangle of Figure 7–1.

Actually income earners have less income per year to spend than *NNI* data as shown by the solid bracket would lead us to believe. Many goods and services are subjected to excess taxes or sales taxes by all levels of government. As consumers or buyers we view the tax on an item as a part of its selling price, and in the computation of *GNP* and *NNP* the price or value of an item includes the excise or sales tax placed on it. Obviously the tax part of the price of an item never gets into the hands of a resource as income earned. Instead, it goes directly to the government. Taxes of these kinds, on "things" rather than on persons, are called *indirect business taxes.* To arrive at net income earned during a year that consumers have available to spend, indirect business taxes must be subtracted from *NNP* or *NNI* as shown by the solid bracket in Figure 7–1. Thus the dotted bracket in Figure 7–1 correctly identifies *NNI.*

The difference between *NNP* and *NNI* when indirect business taxes are taken into account is not important for our purposes. We will assume that *NNP* and *NNI* are equal. Further, we will assume that the entire amount of *NNI* earned during a year is available for spending.

The full set of relationships between the value of products and the income earned viewpoints are summarized in Figure 7–1. We think first in terms of *GNI* generating an equal amount of *GNI.* Subtracting depreciation and capital consumption allowances, respectively, from each side leaves us with *NNP* equal to *NNI,* ignoring the effects of indirect business taxes.

Transfer payments

As we total up *GNI* or *NNI* there are certain *transfer pay-ments* that do not constitute income earned by their recipients and which must not be included as a part of these two con-cepts. Transfer payments occur in both the private sector and the public sector of the economy.

Two types of private transfer payments can be identified. First, gifts from one person to another reduce the purchasing power of the giving party and increase that of the recipient. No new purchasing power is generated and what the receiver of the gift receives should not be counted as a part of income earned for the year. Second, property produced in previous years may be transferred from one private party to another. Suppose, for example, that during this year one student sells a 1976 model automobile to another. Nothing has been added to *GNP* for this year. A 1976 *GNP* item has simply changed hands and an amount of purchasing power equal to its value has been transferred from the buyer to the seller.

Government transfer payments are payments made by the government to private parties for which the recipients make no current contributions to the economy's output. Basically a government transfer payment can be thought of as a transfer of purchasing power from taxpayers to subsidy receivers. Con-sider for example that social security payments made in any given year are financed by social security tax collections. The recipient's purchasing power increases, although the recipient performs no current services. The taxpayer's purchasing power is reduced. The payment of interest on the federal government debt is also a transfer payment. Purchasing power is trans-ferred from taxpayers to government bondholders who receive the interest. Like private transfer payments, government trans-fer payments should not be counted as a part of income earned during the year.

THE LEVEL OF NATIONAL INCOME

The level of *NNP* and *NNI* is determined by the relationships between what the society earns and what the society wants to spend. We will let the symbol *Y* represent the dollar amount of this level. When the society wants to spend exactly what it is earning, *Y* will be in equilibrium. It will fall if people

want to spend less than they are earning and it will rise if
people desire to spend more than they are earning. We shall
develop an analytical framework for each of these three possibilities. Initially we shall assume that there is no public sector
of the economy; the government will be left out of consideration. Later the public sector will be incorporated into the
analytical model that we construct.

Determinants of consumption spending and saving

What determines the economy's annual level of spending
on consumption goods and services? The level of C depends
upon two very general variables. The first is Y, or the level
of income being earned by the population of the economy.
The second is the population's inclination to consume or its
propensity to consume.

The relationship between the level of C and the level of
Y is called the *consumption function* of the society, using the
term *function* in a mathematical sense to indicate the dependence of C on Y. The first two columns of Table 7–2 illustrate
the nature of the relationship. At relatively low levels of Y
for a country—for example in a depression—the population
may consume more than its income. At relatively high levels
of Y its consumption will be less than its income.

How can the inhabitants of an economy consume more than
they earn? They can do so by failing to produce enough capital

Table 7–2
Hypothetical consumption and savings functions ($ billions)

(1) Level of Y	(2) Level of C	(3) MPC	(4) Level of S	(5) MPS
100	120	—	−20	—
200	200	.8	0	.2
300	280	.8	20	.2
400	360	.8	40	.2
500	440	.8	60	.2
600	520	.8	80	.2
700	600	.8	100	.2
800	680	.8	120	.2
900	760	.8	140	.2
1,000	840	.8	160	.2
1,100	920	.8	180	.2
1,200	1,000	.8	200	.2
1,300	1,080	.8	220	.2
1,400	1,160	.8	240	.2

goods to take care of depreciation over time. If the *GNP* of the country does not include enough capital goods to take care of depreciation, then the consumption goods and services component of *GNP* exceeds the total *NNP*. In effect, by failing to take care of depreciation, the economy is "eating up" some of its capital. It converts some of its capital into consumption goods and services in addition to consuming all of its *NNP*. This phenomenon actually occurred in the United States in the 1930's.

Economists have observed that when the level of *Y* of an economy changes, consumption changes by less than the change in *Y*. The amount of the change in *C* induced by a change in *Y* depends on the public's *marginal propensity to consume,* or *MPC*, defined as the change in *C* per one-unit change in *Y;* that is:

$$MPC = \frac{\Delta C}{\Delta Y}$$

for any change in *Y*. In Table 7–2 the *MPC* is assumed to be 0.8 or ⅘, meaning that a one-dollar change in *Y* changes *C* by 0.80. Note that an increase in *Y* from \$700 to \$800 increases consumption from \$600 to \$680.

The consumption function of Table 7–2 is plotted in Figure 7–2 as line *CC*. National income is measured along the horizontal axis and consumption is measured along the vertical axis. The *slope* of the consumption function measures the marginal propensity to consume. For example, if *Y* increases from 700 to 800, consumption increases from 600 to 680. Thus, at point A, a movement of 100 in the horizontal direction causes a movement of 80 in the vertical direction. So the slope of the *AB* section of the consumption function of $\frac{\Delta C}{\Delta Y}$ is 0.8, or ⅘, which is, of course, the *MPC*.

Saving is defined as that part of a society's income not spent on consumption. However, there is more than this to be said about savings. Savings decisions of households and of the society as a whole are made at the same time as and along with consumption decisions. Several forces make people want to save. One of these is the desire to be able to meet unforeseen contingencies such as illness or unemployment. Another is to provide old age security. Still another is the desire to build an additional source of income by saving and

Figure 7–2
The consumption function

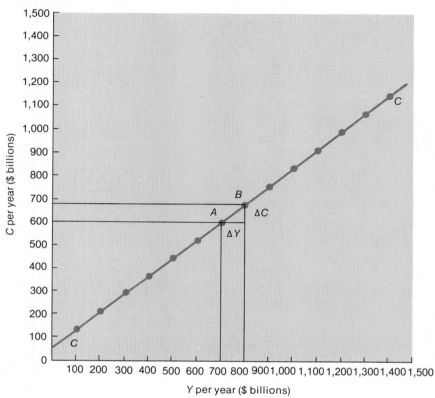

investing the savings in income-yielding assets. To the extent
that these forces induce people to save they also induce people
not to consume.

In Table 7–2, savings, or *S*, at various levels of *Y* are listed
in column (4). At each level of income *S* is simply the difference
between *Y* and *C*. Note that at relatively low income levels
where *C* exceeds *Y*, *S* is negative. Where *C* is less than *Y*, *S*
is positive.

For a change in *Y* the *marginal propensity to save*, or *MPS*,
for the society is defined as the change in savings per unit
change in income, or:

$$MPS = \frac{\Delta S}{\Delta Y} \cdot$$

In Table 7–2 the *MPS* is 0.2 or ⅕. If *Y* increases from $700 to

Figure 7–3
Consumption and savings functions

A.

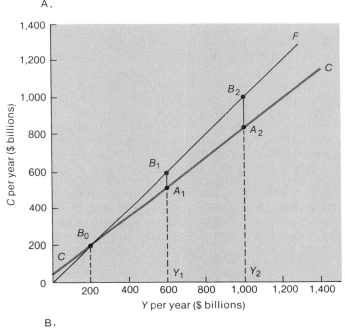

B.

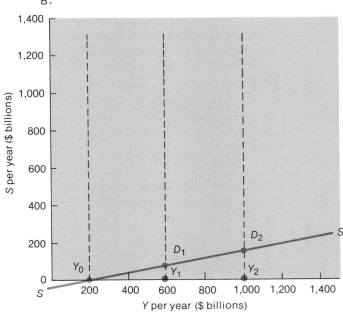

$800, S increases from $100 to $120. The MPS plus the MPC must always be equal to one. We can easily determine that this is the case by considering a one-unit increase in income. The MPC tells us what part of it will be spent on C and the MPS tells us what part of it will be saved. Thus, the definitions of the two terms require that

$$MPS + MPC = 1.$$

From Table 7–2 we plot the society's savings curve SS in Figure 7–3(B) along with a repetition of the consumption curve CC in Figure 7–3(A). The SS curve of Figure 7–3(B) is derived from the CC curve of Figure 7–3(A). In Figure 7–3(A) draw a 45 degree straight line OF. Thus at any given level of Y such as Y_2, the distance Y_2B_2 represents the same number of dollars as does the distance OY_2. Thus we can think of vertical distances such as Y_0B_0, Y_1B_1, and Y_2B_2 as measures of Y equivalent of Y_0, OY_1, and OY_2, respectively. Determination of savings at each possible level of Y now becomes a simple task. At income level Y_2 savings are measured by the vertical distance A_2B_2, which is the difference between that income as measured by Y_2B_2 and consumption level Y_2A_2. Savings at income level Y_2 are $160 billion. Similarly, at income level Y_1, savings are A_1B_1, or $80 billion. At income level Y_0, savings are zero. At smaller income levels, savings are negative. Once we have determined the magnitude of savings at each income level in Figure 7–3(A) we can plot the numbers in Figure 7–3(B) at each income level, obtaining the savings curve SS. The SS curve can be thought of as the vertical subtraction of CC from the OF curve.

Determinants of investment

Decisions to invest in new plant and equipment or in additional inventories of goods are made for the most part by business firms—including family businesses such as the corner grocery store and the family farm. Investment means the purchase of the net annual output of capital resources produced, or an increase in the economy's capital resources. New buildings are built or old ones are improved; land is improved; new machinery is produced and put in place; new tools are acquired; inventories are expanded. All of these serve to increase the economy's productive capacity.

Decisions to invest are heavily influenced by: (1) business expectations and (2) the prevailing rate of interest at which businesses can obtain funds for investing. Expectations of favorable business conditions have a positive effect on investment. If the economy is expanding; the business climate is good; and the future of the economy looks healthy, more will be invested per year than would be the case if the outlook were gloomy. The interest rate—the rate of return that businesses must pay on money that they use to invest—is also important. Higher interest rates mean higher costs to businesses of obtaining funds to invest and thus tend to inhibit investment. Conversely, lower interest rates tend to lower the costs to businesses of obtaining funds for investment and thus encourage investment. The amount of investment per year that takes place will depend upon the combined effects of these two forces.

Income determination—the private sector only

The pieces that go into determination of the level of national income for a private sector, only, economy are now available. We can begin to assemble them into a model. We shall show first the determination of an equilibrium level of Y. Then, we shall look at the consequences of income levels below and those above the equilibrium level.

Equilibrium Y. In Table 7–3 we use a period analysis to show how an equilibrium level of Y is determined. In period analysis, the level of Y in any given period is determined by the level of spending on C and on I in that period; that is, in Period II

$$Y_{II} = C_{II} + I_{II}.$$

Then we assume that income earned in any given period is

Table 7–3
Period analysis—*NNP* constant ($ billions)

	Period				
	I	*II*	*III*	*IV*	—
Y	1,000	1,000	1,000	1,000	—
C	—	800	800	800	—
S	—	200	200	200	—
I	—	200	200	200	—

available for spending in the next period; that is, Y_{II} is available for spending in Period III. The purpose of period analysis is to separate earning and spending conceptually.

Suppose now that $1,000 billion was earned in Period I. Assume that of this amount the public decides in Period II to spend $800 billion on consumption goods and services. The remainder of the $1,000 billion, or $200 billion, is saved. Now suppose that investors decide in Period II to invest in $200 billion worth of new capital goods. All of Period II savings can be thought of as having outlets into or as being channeled into the purchase of the new capital goods. All of the Period I income available for spending in Period II is spent—$800 billion on consumption goods and services and $200 billion on new capital goods. The income earned by the resource-owning public in Period II is also $1,000 billion. The $800 billion spent on C generates $800 billion in income for those who provide the resources to produce C. The $200 billion spent on I yields $200 billion in income to those who furnished the resources to produce I. Thus total income earned in Period II is $800 billion plus $200 billion or $1,000 billion; that is,

$$Y_{II} = C_{II} + I_{II}.$$

The channels through which savings go into the purchase of I may be direct or they may be rather roundabout. Savers may use their savings directly to purchase new farm machinery or additions to the family business. Or they may purchase newly issued corporation stocks and bonds, the proceeds of which are used by corporations to expand their plant, equipment, and inventories. Or savers may deposit their savings in savings accounts at banks or at savings and loan associations. These financial institutions may then use the savings to invest in an expansion of the economy's stock of capital. Many possibilities such as these exist.

The income earned in Period II is available to be spent in Period III. Suppose, again, that $800 billion is spent on C leaving $200 billion saved. Let I continue to be $200 billion per period. The value of goods produced and sold and the income generated in Period III is again $1,000 billion. The income earned in Period III is available to be spent in Period IV. As long as the amount that is earned in one period is just spent in the following period, Y will remain constant over time or is said to be in *equilibrium*. Note that for this state of affairs to exist it is necessary that:

$$S = I.$$

Determination of an equilibrium level of Y is shown graphically in Figure 7–4. The diagram contains one new feature—the level of investment. We assume that business expectations and the interest rate are such that businesses want to invest OI dollars per year. This level of investment is shown as the II curve in Figure 7–4(B). In Figure 7–4(A) it is added vertically

Figure 7–4
The equilibrium level of Y

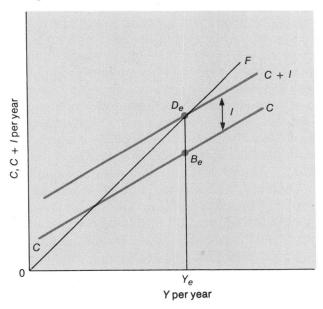

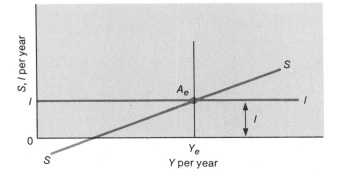

to the *CC* curve to determine the $C + I$ curve. At income level Y_e investment spending exactly equals savings, as Figure 7–4(B) shows. Figure 7–4(A) provides additional information. Suppose that income OY_e is available to be spent. From that amount of income Y_eB_e will be spent on consumption and B_eD_e will be saved. The level of investment is also B_eD_e so all savings are invested. Further, the total amount earned from the production and sale of Y_eB_e of consumption goods and B_eD_e of investment goods is Y_eD_e. This amount of income earned by resource owners is equal to the amount OY_e that was originally assumed to be available for spending. So total income initially available to be spent is equal to total spending which in turn generates an equal amount of income which is now available to be spent. As long as S equals I, total earning and total spending will be equal and Y will be in equilibrium.

Disequilibrium levels of *Y.*   What happens if national income is not in equilibrium? What happens if people want to spend less than they are currently earning? Or more? Whenever Y is in disequilibrium, forces are set in motion to bring it into equilibrium. This will occur if Y is above its equilibrium level and it will also occur if Y is below its equilibrium level.

Suppose that for some reason Y is above its equilibrium level. People do not want to spend as much on C and I as they are currently earning. In Table 7–4, for example, let income earned in Period I be $1,500 billion. In Period II suppose that $1,200 billion is spent on C leaving S equal to $300 billion. But suppose businesses desire to invest in only $200 billion worth of new capital. Total spending in Period II will be $1,400 billion generating income of a like amount in that period.

Income earned in Period II and available to be spent in Period III is $100 billion less than the amount earned in Period

Table 7–4
Period analysis—*NNP* falling ($ billions)

	\multicolumn{7}{c}{*Period*}
	I	*II*	*III*	*IV*		*N*	*N + 1*
Y	1,500	1,400	1,320	1,256	—	1,000	1,000
C	—	1,200	1,120	1,056	—	800	800
S	—	300	280	264	—	—	200
I	—	200	200	200	—	200	200
MPC = 4/5							

I and available to be spent in Period II. If the *MPC* is ⅘, the drop in the amount available to be spent in Period III will cause a decrease in consumption of $100 billion times ⅘, or $80 billion. Consequently, *C* in Period III will be $1,120 billion and *S* will be $280 billion. If businesses continue investing only $200 billion per period, then total spending and total income earned in Period III will be only $1,320 billion.

Income will continue to decrease as long as *S* is greater than *I*. But note that as we move from Period II to Period III to Period IV, *S* is decreasing. Eventually it will decrease enough so that *S* again equals *I* and income will again be in equilibrium. This will occur at some Period *N* where we show $1,000 billion as the equilibrium level of *Y*.

Diagrammatically, income Y_4 in Figure 7–5 is above the equilibrium level. Consumption is Y_4A_4. Saving is A_4B_4. But investment is only A_4G_4, leaving G_4B_4 of savings unspent or hoarded. The income level will fall, causing *S* to be less and less until at income level Y_e savings and investment are equal at level A_eG_e. All that is being earned is being spent and *Y* is in equilibrium.

Suppose now that *Y* is below the equilibrium level. This

Figure 7–5
Y above the equilibrium level

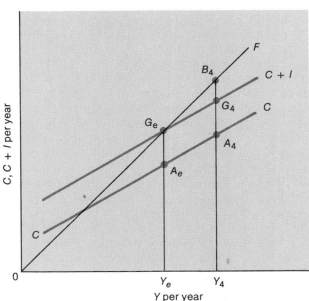

Table 7–5
Period analysis—*NNP* rising ($ billions)

				Period			
	I	*II*	*III*	*IV*		*N*	*N+1*
Y	500	600	680	744	—	1,000	1,000
C	—	400	480	544	—	800	800
S	—	100	120	136	—	—	200
I	—	200	200	200	—	200	200
MPC = 4/5							

means that people want to spend more than they are currently
earning. They are able to do this by drawing on past stocks
of hoarded funds or on money newly created by the banking
system. The movement of *Y* toward equilibrium is illustrated
by Table 7–5. Income earned in Period I, available for spending
in Period II, is $500 billion. Let $400 billion be spent on consumption in Period II with $100 billion saved. But suppose
investors want to invest in $200 billion worth of new capital
goods. The value of goods sold and income earned in Period
II will be $600 billion, and this amount is available to be spent

Figure 7–6
Y below the equilibrium level

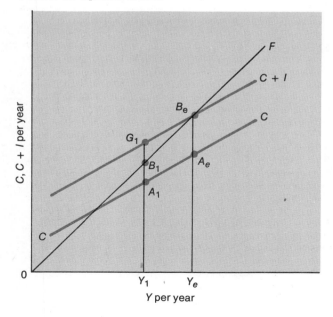

in Period III. If the *MPC* is ⅘ and people have $100 billion more to spend in Period III than in Period II, their expenditures on *C* will rise by $80 billion to $480 billion. Savings will be $120 billion. Assuming that investment remains constant at $200 billion, income earned in Period III is $680 billion. As long as *S* is less than *I*, *Y* will continue to increase period by period with the increases becoming smaller and smaller. Eventually income will reach the level at which $S = I$ and will be in equilibrium. We show $1,000 billion as the equilibrium level of *Y*.

The movement upward toward an equilibrium *Y* is illustrated graphically in Figure 7–6. Let the initial level of *Y* be Y_1. The consumption level is Y_1A_1 and savings are A_1B_1. Investment is A_1G_1 and is greater than savings. More is being spent than is being earned currently and *Y* increases. As *Y* increases, *S* increases also until at income level Y_e savings and investment are equal and income is in equilibrium.

Income determination—the public sector included

Expansion of the income determination model to include the public sector of the economy is easily accomplished. The basic principle is not changed—income will be in equilibrium when all of the income earned in the economy is just being spent. The additional elements introduced into the model are total tax collections, or *T*, of the government and the government goods and services, or *G*, component of *NNP*.

The effects of adding in *T* and *G* are shown in Table 7–6. Let total earnings of Period I be $1,200 billion. Now suppose that the government takes $200 billion in taxes from income

Table 7–6
Period analysis—the government included

	Period				
	I	*II*	*III*	*IV*	*V*
Y	1,200	1,200	1,200	1,200	1,200
T	—	200	200	200	200
C	—	800	800	800	800
S	—	200	200	200	200
I	—	200	200	150	150
G	—	200	200	250	250

earners. The income of private parties available to be spent in Period II is $1,000 billion, or income earned in Period I minus taxes collected in Period II. Assume that $800 billion is spent on C. Savings in Period II will be $200 billion—what is left after T and C have been removed in Period II from the income earned in Period I. Suppose now that businesses decide in Period II to invest $200 billion dollars in new capital—all savings are absorbed into investment. Suppose also that the government provides $200 billion worth of government goods and services—the tax collections withdrawn from the public's earnings are used to provide the public with an equivalent value of G. Income earned in Period II is, as we have learned already, equal to the value of products produced and sold in Period II; that is,

$$Y_{II} = C_{II} + I_{II} + G_{II}.$$

In dollar amounts, income earned in Period II is $1,200 billion—the same amount that was earned in Period I.

Carrying the analysis through Period III, $1,200 billion are available for disposal in Period III. Again let T be $200 billion and C be $800 billion. Savings are $200 billion. If I and G remain at the $200 billion level, income earned in Period III is again $1,200 billion and Y is in equilibrium. But in order for Y to be in equilibrium note carefully that it is necessary for

$$S + T = I + G.$$

It is not necessary, however, that $S = I$ and $T = G$ in order for income to be in equilibrium. Consider Period IV. Suppose that I drops to $150 billion and at the same time G rises to $250 billion. Income earned in Period IV will still be $1,200 billion and will be in equilibrium. If increases in G are offset by decreases in I, or if increases in I are offset by decreases in G, total spending does not change.

The expanded model is illustrated graphically by Figure 7–7. As we noted in the period analysis above, savings are what is left after T and C have been subtracted from the income earned during the preceding period. Viewing the same thing in a different way, we can say that if C is subtracted from income earned in the preceding period, then $S + T$

Figure 7–7
Equilibrium Y—the government included

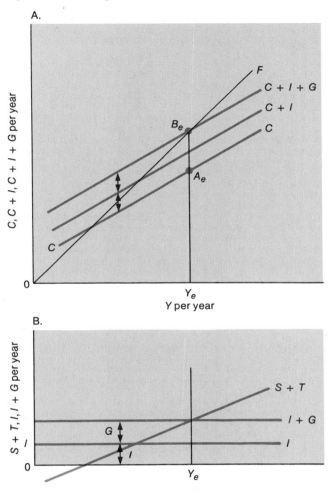

remains. Translating this analysis into graphic terms, consider income level Y_e in Figure 7–7(A). Consumption at that level is $Y_e A_e$. Thus $A_e B_e$ measures $S + T$ at income level Y_e. Point D_e in Figure 7–7(B) is set accordingly so that $Y_e D_e = A_e B_e$. Other points on the $S + T$ curve are determined in the same way. The $S + T$ curve is obtained by subtracting the CC curve vertically from the $0F$ line.

Government goods and services are easily incorporated into Figure 7–7. The level of G is added vertically to the II curve of Figure 7–7(B) to obtain the $I + G$ curve. In Figure 7–7(A) the level of G is added vertically to the $C + I$ curve to obtain the $C + I + G$ curve. The $C + I + G$ curve shows the value of all products that will be produced and sold at each of various levels of Y.

Income will be in equilibrium at Y_e. At that income level $S + T$ will be $A_e B_e$ in Figure 7–7(A) or $Y_e D_e$ in Figure 7–7(B). Investment plus government goods and services will also be $A_e B_e$ and $Y_e D_e$, respectively. All that is being earned by the public is being spent. Withdrawals from the spending stream in the form of tax collections and savings are being reinjected into the spending stream through investment and the provision of government goods and services.

Any deviations of Y from level Y_e will set forces in motion to bring it back to that level. At a higher income level $S + T$ will exceed $I + G$. All that is being earned is not being spent and Y will contract to level Y_e. At a lower income level $I + G$ will exceed $S + T$. More is being spent than is being earned and Y will rise until it reaches Y_e.

SUMMARY

The models for the determination of national income that we develop in this chapter will make it possible for us to probe further into the problems of how well the economy performs over time than we have been able to do on the basis of the analysis in previous chapters. To understand how the level of Y is determined, it is necessary that we view it from two vantage points: (1) the value of the products comprising it, and (2) the income generated in its production. For income to be in equilibrium over time the income generated in producing consumption goods and services, investment goods, and government goods and services must just be spent in purchasing them. When the public wants to spend more than it earns, Y will rise. When it wants to spend less than it earns Y will fall.

The key to whether or not all that is earned is just being spent is the relationship between $S + T$ and $I + G$. If $S + T > I + G$, Y will fall. If $S + T < I + G$, Y will rise. If $S + T = I + G$, all that is being earned is being spent and Y is in equilibrium.

QUESTIONS AND PROBLEMS

1. To avoid double counting which of the following should *not* be included as a part of *NNP?* Explain in each case.

    a. The value of a bushel of wheat used to make flour.

    b. The value of an automobile used by Ms. Green for personal purposes.

    c. The value of an automobile used by a traveling salesman solely for business purposes.

    d. A diamond sold to Elizabeth Taylor.

    e. A diamond sold to make an industrial cutting tool.

2. What is the relationship between the next value of goods and services sold in final form during a year and the income earned by resource owners? Explain carefully, ignoring indirect business taxes.

3. Assuming that there is no public sector in the economy, why is national income in equilibrium when $S = I$?

4. Show with a set of diagrams the relationship between consumption and savings at alternative levels of national income. Why must $MPC + MPS = 1$?

5. With the public sector of the economy included, show and explain the determination of the equilibrium level of national income:

    a. by means of period analysis.

    b. with a diagram.

Chapter 8

Government control of the national income level

Over time the level of national income undergoes changes. These changes show up as periods of recession or economic slack and periods of inflation. In this chapter we attempt to determine the causes of changes in the level of national income and to show how monetary and fiscal policies may be used to control them.

PROBLEMS IN THE ECONOMY'S PERFORMANCE

Even though an economy's national income is drawn back toward an equilibrium level when for some reason it deviates above or below that level, there is nothing inherently desirable about the equilibrium position. Two basic problems may occur with respect to equilibrium levels of Y. First, the absolute level at which Y is in equilibrium at any given time may be an undesirable level—it may be at recession levels and/or it may be at levels that generate inflation. Second, the equilibrium level itself may be unstable over time, contracting and expanding, expanding and contracting.

The absolute level of Y

National income is in equilibrium when total spending in the economy is the same as the total amount of income being earned. It is the income level at which the amount that the public wants to save, added to the amount that the government withdraws from earnings in the form of taxes, is just equal to the amount that businesses want to invest, together with the amount that the government wants to spend in providing government goods and services. It is the level at which $S + T = I + G$. But this level need not be a full employment level of Y—it may be below or above the full employment level.

Recession levels. An equilibrium level of Y that is below the full-employment level, tending toward recession, is illustrated in Figure 8–1. Let Y_f be the level of Y at which the economy's resources would be fully employed. In the situation that we show, the amount that businesses want to invest, coupled with government spending, falls short of absorbing all of the savings and tax collections that occur at that income level. At Y_f, savings plus taxes would be $A_f D_f$ while, government spending plus investment are $A_f B_f$. There would be an $I + G$ shortfall of $B_f D_f$ dollars, so Y_f cannot be the equilibrium level of income. Income will fall, causing S to decrease, thus

Figure 8–1
Less than full-employment equilibrium

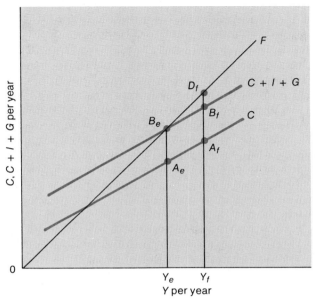

reducing $S + T$. At Y_e both $S + T$ and $I + G$ are equal to $A_e B_e$ dollars and income is in equilibrium. But that level of income is insufficient to support full employment and may even be a recession level.

The fundamental reason why the equilibrium level of Y need not be the full employment level is that savings decisions and investment decisions are made by different groups of decision makers. Government tax and expenditure decisions are, of course, made by the government. Once these are made, savings decisions are made by the general public, which includes everyone who has income to spend. Investment decisions are made largely by the business community, a relatively small segment of the general public. The forces that determine how much businesses will invest are not the same as those that determine how much the general public will save. Thus there is no reason to expect that at a full employment level of income such as Y_f savers will want to save and investors will want to invest precisely those amounts at which $S + T = I + G$. This would happen only by chance or at random. However, at a level of income such as Y_f, the fact that $S + T > I + G$ will cause income to fall, reducing S, until income reaches a

Figure 8–2
Greater than full-employment equilibrium

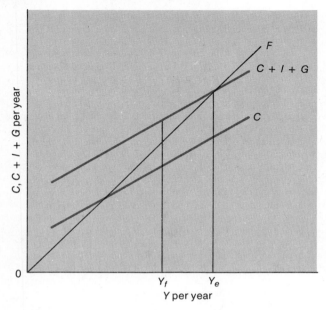

level such as Y_e at which $S + T = I + G$. National income itself adjusts to the level at which savings and investment are brought into line so that $S + T = I + G$.

Inflation levels. The equilibrium level of Y can just as well occur above the full-employment level as below—and for the same reasons. In Figure 8–2, let the full employment level of Y be Y_f but suppose that investment decisions and savings decisions at Y_f are such that $S + T < I + G$; that is, at the full employment level of Y people want to spend more than they are currently earning. Since the excess spending cannot be met by output increases, prices must rise. Rising prices increase Y, which is expressed in current dollars, until it reaches Y_e where $S + T = I + G$. Again, we see that when savings and investment decisions are such that $S + T \neq I + G$, adjustments in income occur until the equality is once more restored between the withdrawals from the earnings stream and the injections into the income stream.

The instability of Y

Over time the equilibrium level of Y itself may be quite volatile. At one point in time it may be slightly below the full employment level. Shortly thereafter it may move downward to a recession level. Then it may move back toward a full employment level. An inflationary level may follow. Then it may decrease again. The immediate causes of instability in the equilibrium level of Y are changes in one or more of the elements in $S + T = I + G$. We shall consider changes in investment, government spending, and in consumption (which operates through S in the foregoing equality), and we shall develop a concept called the national income multiplier.

Changes in investment. Of the elements in $S + T = I + G$, investment is thought to be the most unstable. Business decision makers are a sensitive lot with an ear and an eye continually cocked to pick up sounds and sign from the economy. What they pick up affects their expectations and, consequently, the amount of investing they want to do in new plant, equipment, inventories, and the like. Changes in the interest rate can also affect their investment decisions.

In Figure 8–3, let Y_1 be the initial equilibrium level of Y. The consumption function is initially C_1C_1 while $C_1 + I_1 + G_1$ shows the initial relationship between the income level and total spending. Savings plus taxes are A_1B_1. Investment and government spending are also A_1B_1.

Figure 8–3
Effects of a change in investment

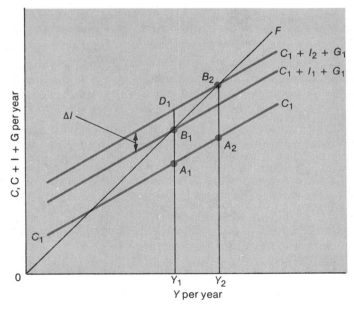

Now suppose that the prospects of peace in the Middle East and possible expansion of world trading relationships improves the expectations of business decision makers. They decide to increase the annual level of investment from I_1 to I_2. In Figure 8–3 the increase in investment ΔI will shift the $C + I + G$ curve upward to $C_1 + I_2 + G_1$. At the old level of income Y_1, investment plus government spending is now A_1D_1 and it exceeds the savings plus taxes level of A_1B_1. National income will increase to Y_2, increasing savings and raising $S + T$ to A_2B_2. The new level of investment plus savings is also A_2B_2 so national income is in equilibrium at the higher level.

The process can and does work in reverse. Both domestic and world events and occurrences can depress business expectations causing the level of new investment to fall. The result would be a downward shift of the $C + I + G$ curve and a lower equilibrium level of Y.

Changes in government spending. Changes in government spending, not matched by changes in tax collections, have the same kind of impact on Y as do changes in investment. Suppose, for example, that the government increases its military outlays as it did in the latter half of the 1960s during the Vietnam escalation. Suppose further that it does not increase its tax collections. The effects are those illustrated in Figure 8–4. The initial equilibrium level of Y is Y_1 with $S + T = I + G$ at A_1B_1 dollars. The increase in government expenditures from G_1 to G_2 shifts the $C + I + G$ curve upward by ΔG to $C_1 + I_1 + G_2$, raising the equilibrium level of Y to Y_2. At Y_2, $S + T = I + G = A_2B_2$ dollars. A decrease in government spending instead of an increase would shift the $C + I + G$ curve downward, reducing the equilibrium level of Y.

Changes in consumption. The propensity of the economy's population to consume is thought to be much more stable than the level of investment. Consumption patterns and consumption levels of households become habitual, tending to become more or less adjusted to household income levels. Autonomous or spontaneous changes in consumption are not as likely to occur as rapidly or to be of as great a magnitude as changes in investment. Nevertheless, they can and do occur and their effects must be taken into account.

In Figure 8–5 the initial equilibrium level of income is Y_1 with $S + T = I + G = A_1B_1$ dollars. An increase in consumption

Figure 8–4
Effects of a change in government spending

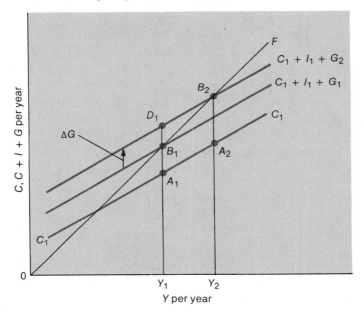

Figure 8–5
Effects of an increase in consumption

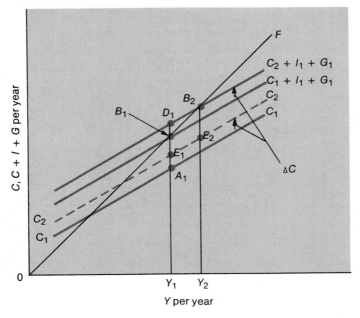

shifts the consumption function C_1C_1 upward by ΔC to C_2C_2. The upward shift in the consumption function must also shift the $C + I + G$ curve upward by ΔC to $C_2 + I_1 + G_1$. The increase in consumption at the Y_1 income level is A_1E_1, so savings plus taxes are reduced from A_1B_1 to E_1B_1. Investment plus government spending are assumed to have remained constant; that is, $E_1D_1 = A_1B_1$. So $S + T$ is now less than $I + G$; that is, $E_1B_1 < E_1D_1$. More is being spent than is being earned at income level Y_1 so income will rise. When it reaches Y_2, $S + T = I + G = E_2B_2$ and it is again in equilibrium. A decrease in consumption would have the opposite effect of that described. A decrease in consumption would result in an increase in S, an increase in $S + T$, $S + T > I + G$ and a decrease in Y to the level at which $S + T = I + G$.

The multiplier. Intuitively one would expect changes in investment, or in government spending, or in consumption to result in approximately equal changes in national income in the same direction. However, this is not the case. They will bring about changes in Y that are greater than the initial changes in any one of the foregoing components of *NNP* through so-called multiplier effects.

The nature of the national income multiplier and multiplier effects is illustrated in Table 8–1. From Period I to Period II national income is in equilibrium. In Period III an increase in I occurs, raising I from \$200 to \$300 billion. The \$100 billion increase in I increases income earned in Period III by \$100 billion. Assuming that the *MPC* is ⅘, the extra \$100 billion available to be spent in Period IV will increase C in Period IV by \$80 billion to \$880 billion, which in turn increases income

Table 8–1
Multiplier effects of a change in investment (\$ billions)

	Period							
	I	*II*	*III*	*IV*	*V*		*N*	*N + 1*
Y	1,200	1,200	1,300	1,380	1,444	—	1,700	1,700
T	—	200	200	200	200	—	200	200
C	—	800	800	880	944	—	1,200	1,200
S	—	200	200	220	236	—	300	300
I	—	200	300	300	300	—	300	300
G	—	200	200	200	200	—	200	200

$MPC = 4/5$
$m = 5$

earned in Period IV by $80 billion. Of the extra $80 billion available to be spent in Period V, $64 billion will be spent on C, raising C in Period V to $944 billion and increasing income in Period V by $64 billion to $1,444 billion. Increases in C and corresponding increases in Y, each equal to $\frac{4}{5}$ of the increase in the immediately preceding period will continue until in some Period N they are so close to zero that they become negligible. National income will again be in equilibrium, now at a level of $1,700 billion. And, as we show in moving from Period N to Period $N + 1$, $S + T = I + G$.

The total increase in Y from Period II to Period N is determined by summing the increases that occur period by period. In Period III the increase is $100 billion. In Period IV, it is $100(\frac{4}{5})$ or $80 billion. In Period V it is $100(\frac{4}{5})^2$ or $64 billion. And so on until the increases approach zero in Period N. These increases form a convergent geometric series:

$$100 + 100(\tfrac{4}{5}) + 100(\tfrac{4}{5})^2 + 100(\tfrac{4}{5})^3 + \cdots + 100(\tfrac{4}{5})^n$$

$$= 100 \, \frac{1}{1 - \tfrac{4}{5}} = 100 \cdot 5 = \$500 \text{ billion.}$$

The multiplier m is the term $\dfrac{1}{1 - \tfrac{4}{5}}$ or 5 in this case. Its magnitude depends on the *MPC*. if the *MPC* were $\frac{3}{4}$ instead of $\frac{4}{5}$, the multiplier would be 4 instead of 5. If the *MPC* were $\frac{1}{2}$, the multiplier would be 2. The multiplier shows how much an initial change in investment will change national income; that is, it shows:

$$\frac{\Delta Y}{\Delta I} = \frac{1}{1 - \text{MPC}} = m$$

or:

$$\Delta I \cdot m = \Delta Y$$

The multiplier also operates when a change occurs in either G or C. In Table 8–1 we could have substituted a $100 billion increase in G in place of the increase in I. Investment would continue through successive periods at $200 billion and G would continue at $300 billion. Savings would grow period by period until in Period N they would be $300 billion. At that point $S + T = I + G$ and Y would be in equilibrium at $1,700 billion. The initial $100 billion increase in G would have generated a $500 billion increase in Y.

The same kind of reasoning will show us that a $100 billion increase in C in Period III will yield a $500 billion increase in Y if the MPC is $\frac{4}{5}$. In Period III if C increases to $900 billion, S decreases to $100 billion and income of Period III would be $1,300 billion. Consumption of Period IV would be $980 billion and S would be $120 billion. Following through to Period N, C rises eventually to $1,300 billion, S returns to the $200 billion level and the other magnitudes, T, I, and G are each $200 billion—$S + T = I + G$ and the equilibrium level of income is $1,700 billion.

The multiplier thus exerts a leverage effect on Y when changes occur in I, C, or G. The tendency of Y to be unstable because of instability in these three components of NNP—particularly because of instability in I—is accentuated by the operation of the multiplier.

CONTROL OF THE ECONOMY'S PERFORMANCE

Government authorities can exercise some degree of control over the level of national income through the use of monetary and fiscal policies. We have discussed the nature of monetary policies already—we need only to show their impacts in terms of the national income analysis framework. Fiscal policies refer to the tax collection and expenditure policies of the federal government. Their importance as components of the $S + T$ and $I + G$ relationships is self-evident. We will show how they are used in this section, but a detailed discussion of the impact of the governmental presence on the economy will be reserved for the next chapter.

Via the investment level

If the equilibrium level of Y is below the full-employment level, it would appear that government policies to stimulate or increase the level of investment would be in order. Easy monetary policies to increase the rate of growth of the money supply would seem to be in order. The FRB could engage in open-market purchases of government securities which would tend to raise the prices of those securities and, in turn, lower interest rates. In addition to decreasing interest rates directly, open-market purchases put additional reserves into the banking system. The banking system, to encourage additional borrowing by businesses, will tend to lower the interest rates they charge to borrowers. Interest is the price paid by businesses for funds to invest in new capital. Decreases in the interest rate mean lower costs of investment and should tend to cause increases in investment. The effects of an increase in investment of ΔI dollars on the equilibrium level of income was illustrated in Figure 8–3.

Events of the 1970s tell us that the use of easy money policies to increase the level of I or Y, and to decrease unemployment may encounter snags along the way. While generally expansionary throughout the decade of the 1970s, the FRB has applied the monetary brakes hard a few times—notably in 1969 and 1970, in 1974, and again in late 1978 and early 1979— either triggering or raising fears of recession. Business uncertainty, or unfavorable business expectations may well offset any favorable effects that expansionary monetary policies may have had on interest rates. As a matter of fact, nominal or current interest rates have not decreased in the 1970s. High average rates of expansion of the money supply have contributed to inflation and inflation itself has held current interest rates well above the annual rates of inflation.[1] Generating increases in I through easy money policies on the part of the government may be difficult to accomplish.

If the equilibrium level of Y is above the full-employment level, I can be reduced through tight money policies and the equilibrium level of income will also fall. Tight money policies, primarily open-market sales of government securities by the FRB, will tend to decrease the prices of government securities and raise interest rates. Banking system reserves will be reduced and banks will tighten up their lending policies—primarily by raising interest rates. Higher interest rates mean higher costs of investing and businesses would tend to reduce the amount of new capital resources that they purchase. A lower level of I means a shift downward in the $C + I + G$ curve and a lower equilibrium level of Y.

---

1. Consider, for example, that you are lending $100 to someone on January 1 of a given year at 10 percent interest to be repaid December 31 of that year. At the end of the year you would receive $110 from the borrower. Suppose that the inflation rate for the year is 10 percent. The $110 that you receive will now purchase only the same amount of goods and services as the $100 that you loaned at the beginning of the year. The nominal or current interest rate of 10 percent does not really allow you as a lender to receive any *real* return on your loan. To obtain a positive *real interest rate*—purchasing power in addition to the purchasing power you loan out— you must charge a current interest rate that is greater than the rate of inflation.

A major risk when the government tightens monetary policies is the possibility that the tightening may be overdone, triggering recession and unemployment. Forecasting the extent to which investors will react to decreases in or to lower rates of increase in the money supply can easily miss the mark. Businesses can easily develop unfavorable expectations and decrease I by more than the monetary authorities intended. Monetary managers—the Federal Reserve Board of Governors—must move cautiously along a very thin line.

Via the consumption level

The government may also be able to affect the level of national income by nudging the level of consumption up a little or down a little as the need to do so arises. Both monetary policies and fiscal policies may be used to attempt to change consumption. But as we noted earlier, consumption patterns and levels are more likely to be habitual and ingrained than are investment patterns and levels and, hence, are likely to be more difficult to influence. In this section we shall confine our discussion to the effects of monetary policies, leaving the effects of fiscal policies on C for the next section.

To the extent that monetary policies influence C they would reinforce the influence that they would have on I. An easing of monetary policy—an increase in the rate of growth of the money supply—would be expected to increase the level of C by placing more purchasing power in the hands of the general public. A tightening of monetary policy—a decrease in the rate of growth of the money supply—would be expected to have the opposite effect if it were carried far enough. An induced increase in consumption in the amount ΔC dollars would shift the $C + I + G$ curve upward as Figure 8–5 shows, bringing about an increase in Y that is a multiple of ΔC. A decrease in C would reduce the equilibrium level of Y.

Via fiscal policy

Most economists believe that fiscal policy—the manipulation of tax collections and government spending—has a strong effect on the level of national income. In fact, fiscal policies are usually put on a par with monetary policies in the federal government's arsenal of weapons for combatting economic instability. How fiscal policy fits into the national income model is the subject matter of this section. A detailed examination of the role of the government in the economy is made in the following chapter.

Full employment and inflation. During periods of full employment, if aggregate demand is increasing faster than aggregate supply, demand-pull inflation occurs. In the national income context this situation is one in which the equilibrium level of Y is above the full employment level. At the full employment level of Y, $S + T < I + G$, thus creating inflationary pressure.

The appropriate fiscal policy for this situation is a reduction of government expenditures, an increase in tax collections, or both of these combined. Reductions in G and/or increases in T can be carried far enough so that $S + T = I + G$ at the current level of Y, thus making the current level the equilibrium level of Y. If, in Figure 8–4, the full employment level of Y were Y_1 while the equilibrium level is Y_2, a reduction in G of ΔG will reduce the equilibrium level to the full employment level of Y, thus removing the inflationary pressure. The same result could be achieved by raising T or by simultaneously lowering G while increasing T.

Increases in T will have repercussions on both the level of investment and the level of consumption. Taxes are costs to business firms. Increases in the taxes levied on businesses and their products mean decreased net income for businesses and decreases in the level of investment that they are willing to undertake. Tax increases on households will lower their disposable incomes and will shift the consumption function downward. These effects will augment those stemming directly from decreases in G.

Recession. During recession the equilibrium level of Y is below the full-employment level and the problem is that of moving the equilibrium level upward. The appropriate fiscal policy would be increases in G, decreases in T, or both of these at the same time. Such a fiscal policy would make $S + T < I + G$, thus stimulating an expansion of Y and a reduction in unemployment. Again the increases in G would operate directly to increase Y. The decreases in T would stimulate higher levels of investment and consumption thus augmenting the direct effects of the increases in G.

Problems with fiscal policy. Fiscal policy seems straighforward enough; however, certain problems arise in using it for stabilization purposes. These problems may not loom large when fiscal policy is used on a small scale to help control the level of Y. They increase in magnitude as the scale on which fiscal policy is used is stepped up.

One problem that surfaces in the use of fiscal policy is the appropriate timing for expenditure or tax changes. Expenditure changes and tax changes require advance planning, Congressional hearings, passage by the Congress, and the president's signature. This is a time-consuming process. Once approval is gained even more time is required to put the changes into effect. In total one to three years may be needed from the time that the need for a change is perceived and the time when a change is actually put into effect. Since it is difficult to forecast precisely when a recession or a period of inflation will occur or when they will end, we may find that when fiscal changes are actually put into effect the need for them is over. Or worse yet, the need may have changed so that the fiscal policy actually put into effect makes matters worse rather than better. Suppose for example that inflation is the problem and that tax increases along with expenditure decreases are fed into the Congressional mill. Now suppose that by the time these changes are enacted into law the state of the economy has changed to a problem of recession. The fiscal policy being put into effect would augment the recession.

Another problem is that for political reasons fiscal policies tend to have an inflationary bias, making the use of fiscal policy to control inflation extremely difficult. Voters seem to like having the government increase its expenditures in their areas for their special interests. They also prefer less taxes to more. Politicians running for office or for re-election are not unaware of these desires and many take actions to fulfill them. The results, as the record of the last 20 years shows, are deficits and inflationary pressures.

Stabilization of the economy at a level near the full-employment level by means of monetary and fiscal policies will be easier the more quickly deviations from stability can be detected and the sooner corrective measures are put into effect. Our analysis indicates that monetary policy is more flexible and can be initiated more quickly than can fiscal policy. In fact since 1965 a good argument can be made that fiscal policy, rather than contributing to greater economic stability, has actually had a destabilizing effect, contributing heavily to the inflation of the late 1960s and the 1970s.

The time required to put monetary policy into effect is minimal. Open-market purchases or sales as needed can begin immediately. Discount rates can be changed quickly and so can required reserve ratios. The response of the banking system will soon thereafter be relfected by changes in the rate of growth of the money supply.

There is much current discussion of neutralizing the effects of the federal budget on the level of economic activity by requiring the government to bring it into balance and keep it there. If this were done, the burden of stabilizing the economy would rest on the Federal Reserve Board of Governors. Can monetary policy alone be sufficient to prevent recessions and inflation from occurring? Opinion is divided. We have no generally accepted answers.

Some economists—notable among them is Milton Friedman—maintain that monetary policies too often operate in a destabilizing way and that they, too, should be subjected to a given rule rather than being left to the discretion of the Federal Reserve Board of Governors. Such a rule would prescribe that the money supply be controlled so that it exhibits slow steady growth over time. A 4 percent growth rate—approximately in line with the average rate of growth of the economy's output—is frequently suggested. Coupled with an approximately balanced federal budget, it is argued that a monetary rule of this sort would prevent fiscal and monetary policies from being destabilizing. It is recognized that changes in investment and consumption over time could bring about periods of mild inflation or mild recession; however, it is thought that if the proposed fiscal and monetary rules are strictly adhered to, these would tend to be self-correcting.

SUMMARY

Over time the equilibrium level of national income tends to exhibit instability—periods of declining economic activity and rising unemployment, periods of robust economic activity, and periods of inflation. Whenever total spending in the economy becomes less than total earnings, the equilibrium level of Y will fall. Whenever total spending rises above total earnings, the equilibrium level of Y will increase.

Changes in Y over time are triggered by changes in investment, in consumption, and in government spending together with tax collections. Investment seems to be the most volatile of the three. Changes in any of the components of *NNP* lead to amplified changes in *Y* because of multiplier effects.

The judicious use of monetary policy and fiscal policy by the federal government can bring economic fluctuations under control. Monetary policy can be used to influence the levels of investment and consumption. Fiscal policy acts directly on the levels of government spending and taxation. Together they can counteract adverse autonomous changes in investment and consumption.

There is some recent evidence that fiscal and monetary policies, rather than counteracting economic instability, have actually augmented it because of timing problems and because of political considerations. To avoid these problems some economists argue that fixed rules regarding fiscal policy and monetary policy should be adhered to by the government. One rule would be an approximate balance in the federal budget. Another would be slow steady growth of the money supply over time. It is argued that while observance of these rules would not completely eliminate economic fluctuations, it would keep them within tolerable bounds.

QUESTIONS AND PROBLEMS

1. Suppose the federal government has a balanced budget and, at the full employment level of national income, businesses are not willing to invest as much as the public wants to save. Explain with the aid of a diagram what the result will be.

2. Define the national income multiplier. What is the magnitude of the multiplier if
   a. the $MPC = \frac{3}{4}$?
   b. the $MPC = \frac{9}{10}$?
   c. the $MPC = 1$?
   d. the $MPS = \frac{1}{6}$?

3. Suppose that national income is in equilibrium at a level of $2,000 billion. $I = \$200$ billion. $G = \$300$ billion. $MPC = \frac{2}{3}$.
   a. What is the level of C?
   b. Must $S = \$200$ billion and $T = \$300$ billion? Explain.
   c. If I increases by $100 billion, what will be the new equilibrium level of Y?

4. In what ways can the government control the level of
    a. consumption?
    b. investment?

5. What are the major problems in using fiscal policy as a device to stabilize the economy?

6. What advice would you give the president, the Congress, and the Federal Reserve Board of Governors on how to keep the economy stable over time?

Chapter 9

Government economic activities

Through the ages one government or another has engaged in almost any economic activity one can name. At the present time, the governments in countries such as Cuba, the Peoples Republic of China, and the Soviet Union, dominate almost all economic activities. In others, such as the United States or West Germany, the scope of government economic activity is much more restricted. What are the bases for determining which activities governments should perform, to what extent they should perform them, and how the costs of the activities should be met? These are the questions that are addressed in this chapter.

APPROPRIATE GOVERNMENT ECONOMIC ACTIVITIES

In thinking logically about which economic activities a government should perform it is useful to ask first why a government should engage in any economic activities at all. The answer to the question is that by acting through governments, people can obtain certain net benefits collectively that they either cannot obtain at all or would obtain less efficiently by acting as individuals.

Government economic activity is worthwhile to the community to the extent that it can make resources yield greater benefits to the community than those resources could yield if they were used by private producers. But, in what areas can government economic activity bring about more efficient resource use? In the analysis of this problem, it will be useful first to establish a classification scheme for the goods and services produced by an economic system and, second, to use the scheme in laying out possible areas in which government activity may yield greater efficiency than private activity.

Classification of goods and services

The goods and services produced by an economic system are frequently classified according to the way in which the public benefits from their consumption. The classification includes: (1) individually consumed items, (2) collectively consumed items, and (3) semicollectively consumed items. We shall look at these in turn.

Individually consumed items. Goods and services that yield satisfaction only to the person that consumes them are said to be individually consumed. Hamburgers are a case in point. Only the consumer of a hamburger reaps the benefit of its consumption. The joys associated with the act of consumption are not extended to others. Most consumer goods and services fall in this category—food, clothing, housing, appliances, and the like.

Collectively consumed items.   Goods and services that are jointly consumed by a group of people rather than by any one individual make up the collectively consumed category. An important characteristic of a collectively consumed item is that it is *nondivisible*—it cannot be divided up among individuals so the amount of it each individual consumes cannot be determined. Another important characteristic is that of *nonexclusion*—if the item is provided for group consumption no member of the group can be excluded from its benefits. National defense provides an example of such a service. The amount of national defense that any individual consumes per year cannot be determined. Additionally, if national defense services are provided, there is no way that any one person living in the country can be denied its benefits.

Semicollectively consumed items.   There are some goods and services consumed that not only yield benefits directly to the ones who consume them but, in addition, may yield benefits to others. The benefits yielded to nonconsumers are called *spillover benefits*. Primary education provides an example. The principal beneficiary of a primary education is the person who receives it—who learns to read, write, and do arithmetic. But others in the community gain. The quality of life will be higher in a community that is literate than it would be if the community were not literate. Many other examples can be cited. It is also possible that the consumption of a good may benefit the consumer directly, but may impose *spillover costs* on others. The transportation services of your automobile may be an item of this kind. Though it yields satisfaction to you when you drive it, it pollutes the air and reduces the well being of others.

Areas of government economic activity

Government economic activities are often grouped into four areas. Boundaries between areas need not be hard and fast—overlapping may occur. The areas are: (1) the production of goods and services; (2) the provision of rules for the economic game; (3) the prevention of force and fraud; and (4) the accomplishment of social goals. What criteria are important in determining the extent to which the government should operate in each of these areas?

Production of goods and services. Governmental units are usually in a better position to produce collectively consumed goods than are private groups. Consider, for example, a neighborhood that decides to provide its police protection privately, sharing the costs of the service among the residents of the community. If the service is provided, no one person in the group can be denied the benefits of a crime-free neighborhood. But, suppose one person decides not to pay a share of the costs. The group has no way of compelling the person to do so and the person becomes a *free rider*. When private groups attempt to provide collectively consumed goods and services they are often plagued with the free-rider problem. Governments on the other hand, are coercive institutions. With their powers of taxation they can coerce *all* members of a group to pay a share for any collectively consumed item. For those collectively consumed goods and services that the public desires more urgently than it desires other goods and services, production by the government seems to be warranted in order to avoid the free rider problem.

Individually consumed goods and services are another matter. Governments have at one time or another, or in one place or another, engaged in the production of almost every kind of individually consumed item. One of the important issues of modern times is that of socialism versus private enterprise, or the extent to which governments should enter into the production of individually consumed items. Most socialists will argue that the government is the most efficient producer. Private enterprise advocates will argue that the private sector produces more efficiently than the government can. A great deal more information is needed on comparative efficiencies of the public sector of the economy versus the private sector in order to resolve the issue; however, available evidence seems to indicate that most individually consumed goods and services are best left to the private sector. Governmental units are not noted for the efficiency of their operations.

Semicollectively consumed goods that yield spillover benefits tend to be underproduced by the private sector of the economy and some government encouragement of their production may be in order. The private sector of the economy will expand the production of such an item to the point at which the direct primary benefits to the consumer of an additional unit of it just equal the addition to the producer's costs of producing it. But at this level of consumption and production the additional unit yields spillover benefits to the society as well as primary benefits to the consumer. The total additional or *marginal benefits* of consumption—primary plus spillover—thus would exceed the additional or *marginal costs* of production of a unit of the good. As we shall see more clearly later, when the marginal benefits from a one unit addition to the consumption of an item exceed the marginal costs of its production, its output and consumption levels are too low relative to those of other items. Some government production of additional output or some government subsidization of private producers can bring the desired expansion about.

Semicollectively consumed goods that incur spillover costs tend to be overproduced by the private sector and some government discouragement of production may be needed. Again, the private sector of the economy tends to provide that level of output of an item at which its marginal *primary* benefit to consumers equals the *private* marginal costs of producing it. The *private* marginal costs of production are the direct addition to the output level. But this additional unit of output reduces the satisfaction level of nonconsumers of the product, thereby imposing a *spillover* marginal cost on the society. The *true* marginal cost of the item is thus the *private* marginal cost plus the *spillover* marginal cost. The *true* marginal costs of producing the item will exceed the marginal benefits of consuming it, indicating that its output is too large relative to the outputs of other goods and services. Through taxes and/or through imposing additional "clean-up" costs on producers or consumers of the good, the government can reduce the output and consumption level of it.

Prevention of force and fraud. In order for the scarce resources and the limited technology of an economy to produce the largest possible output of want-satisfying goods and services, people must be prevented from preying on one another. Governments with their coercive powers are in a unique position to provide the necessary law and order, although they often fall far short of perfection in this function.

First, people must be prevented from stealing one another's property or from intimidating one another in a coercive way. As we learned earlier, both parties to a voluntary exchange gain. But in an exchange in which one person is coerced by another to give up property, or in which the person's property is stolen, the party that is coerced must necessarily lose from the exchange.

Second, people must be prevented from taking advantage of others by fraudulent means; that is, by misrepresenting the terms of the exchange. Where fraud is involved the party on whom the fraud is perpetrated is at first made to believe that the exchange will be beneficial; but the exchange, when consummated, turns out differently than it was represented, causing the party to lose.

Provision of rules of the game.   The people of a society find that they can obtain economic benefits if certain rules of the economic game are established and enforced by some objective—and coercive—agency apart from those who are playing the game. The government can be such an agency. Among the important rules for a private enterprise system are: (1) the maintenance of stability in the economy, (2) the enforcement of workable competition in buying and selling, and (3) the regulation of natural monopoly.

Economic stability implies the absence of sharp or prolonged periods of inflation and/or unemployment. The government plays a unique and stragetic role in stabilizing the economy. It controls the economy's money supply. Further, its expenditures and its tax collections are large enough relative to the size of the private sector of the economy to have a significant influence on the overall level of economic activity. No private agency has the means available to carry out the function of stabilizing the economy. Nor would any private agency have the requisite objectivity or the lack of self-interest that we attribute to an ideal government.

A price system used to guide and direct economic activity in a private enterprise economy functions best when competition exists among sellers and among buyers of product. *Workable competition* means that there are enough buyers and enough sellers of any given kind of product or service so that no one can unduly affect the total supply of, the demand for, or the price of the item. Competition is the antithesis of monopoly, so we expect that an ideal government would be concerned with keeping monopoly at the minimum possible level and with encouragement of the maximum possible degree of competition. Antitrust laws and their enforcement are an important part of the rules of the game. In some product markets, however, competition among sellers is not possible. Public utilities typically sell in such markets. A city cannot have several suppliers of water, or electricity, or natural gas, or telephone service. Distribution networks are such that consumers cannot switch from one possible seller to another. They tend to be locked into the distribution system of a single seller, and a single-seller monopoly usually provides the most efficient means of supplying each of these goods or services to consumers. To prevent such monopolistic sellers from taking advantage of consumers, regulation of their activities—particularly their prices—is in order as a part of the rules of the economic game. Again, government with its coercive powers is in a unique position to make and enforce the rules.

Accomplishment of social goals. Governments engage in many economic activities in order to accomplish desired social ends. Some of these have been discussed already—encouraging the expansion of outputs of goods that yield spillover benefits to the public and inducing the contraction of outputs of those that entail spillover costs. But the major social goal that governments are expected to accomplish is of a different character—it is income redistribution. Whether or not income redistribution yields *economic benefits* to the society as a whole is difficult if not impossible to determine. However, no one can dispute that it is a function that the society believes to be desirable and that it expects the government to perform.

The almost universally approved method of income redistribution is that of income transfers from taxpayers to the poor. Most people believe that voluntary transfers by private individuals who are well off to those at the bottom of the income distribution scale will be insufficient to make sizable inroads on poverty problems. Most believe that transfers must be coerced through taxation and subsidization and that the government is the appropriate agency to accomplish them. Transfers are not always in the form of money, although a large part of them are. Some consist of such things as government subsidized housing, food stamps, free medical care, and the like.

GOVERNMENT EXPENDITURES

We have discussed the major economic reasons for governments to engage in economic activities. What do their actual expenditure patterns look like? We shall consider first current U.S. government expenditures. Second, trends in government expenditure since 1960 will be reviewed.

Current types of expenditures. We show a current cross section of U.S. government expenditures by function for the fiscal year ending September 30, 1978, in Table 9–1. Two items tower head and shoulders above the rest: (1) National Defense and (2) Income Security.

National defense is a part of the *G* portion of *GNP* and *NNP*. It is a collectively consumed service. Since government goods and services produced for the general public are not usually sold in markets at market prices, it is assumed that

Table 9–1
Federal government expenditures*, fiscal year ending September 30, 1978 ($ billions)

National defense	105.2
Human resources	235.4
Income security	146.2
Health	43.7
Education, training, employment, and social services	26.5
Veterans' benefits and services	19.0
Other nondefense	110.2
International affairs	5.9
General science, space, and technology	4.7
Energy	5.9
Natural resources and environment	10.9
Agriculture	7.7
Commerce and housing credit	3.3
Transportation	15.4
Community and regional development	11.0
Administration of justice	3.8
General government	3.8
General purpose fiscal assistance	9.6
Interest on federal debt	44.0
Undistributed offsetting receipts	−15.8
Total outlays	450.8

* Unified budget.

Source: *The Budget of the United States, Fiscal Year 1980.*

their total value to the public is equal approximately to what they cost. So the value of government goods and services provided us is thus considered to be equal to what the government spends in order to provide them. Thus we value the national defense provided us for 1978 at $105.2 billion. Many nondefense goods and services also appear in the budget. These include a large part of most of the expenditure categories listed with the exception of Income Security; Veterans Benefits and Services; Interest on the Federal Debt; Education, Training, Employment, and Social Services; and Agriculture.

Items such as Income Security and Interest on the Federal Debt are government transfer expenditures. They represent transfers of purchasing power from the general public to those who receive the government expenditure with the government acting as the collecting and disbursing agency. The government produces no goods and services in the process of making the transfers. Consequently, the transfer payments are *not* a part of the *G* component of *GNP* and *NNP*. The major part of the Income Security item is made up of old age, survivors, and disability insurance payments, along with Medicare and the federal government's part of Medicaid. It also includes federal government outlays for federal employee retirement and disability, unemployment compensation, and public assistance. Interest on the Federal Debt is a straight transfer of purchasing power from taxpayers to those parties who own the government bonds representing the amount of federal debt outstanding.

Items such as Veterans' Benefits and Services; Education, Training, Employment, and Social Services; and Agriculture are a mixture of goods and services produced by the government and government transfer payments. Thus some part of them is included in *G* and the rest is not. Under the Veterans' Benefits and Services classification, some government expenditures are used to provide governmentally produced health care, primarily through veterans' hospitals. The transfer part of the expenditures under this classification consist of pensions, disability allowances, insurance payments, and the like. Similarly, in the Education, Training, Employment, and Social Services classification, some training, educational, and social services are provided directly by the government to recipients and thus is a part of *G*. A very large part of the expenditures under this classification is of a transfer nature simply shifting purchasing power from the general public to certain individuals with the government specifying how the transferred funds are to be used. In the Agriculture classification most of the amount paid is in the form of transfers from the general public to the receivers of agricultural subsidies. A small part of it generates research services which are a part of *GNP*.

Government expenditures under several of the classifications represent in part attempts by the government to encourage or expand semicollectively consumed outputs of the economy where social spillover benefits are presumed to occur and to discourage outputs or restrict outputs where social spillover costs are presumed to exist. Expenditures in the health field typify the former. So do transportation expenditures. Expenditures to protect the environment and to conserve natural resources are examples of the latter.

Expenditure trends

How have federal government expenditures changed over time? In Table 9–2 we trace the patterns of selected government expenditures from 1960 through 1968. In order to obtain a better overview of the relative importance over time of each expenditure category, we express each of them as a percentage of *GNP* for each of the years listed.

Total government expenditures exhibit an enormous abso-

Table 9–2
Trends in U.S. government expenditures and *GNP* ($ billions)

Fiscal year†	All expenditures*		National defense		Income security		Interest on debt		
	Total	% of GNP	Total	% of GNP	Total	% of GNP	Total	% of GNP	GNP
1960	92.4	18.5	45.2	9.1	18.3	3.7	6.9	1.4	497.3
1965	118.4	18.0	47.5	7.2	25.7	3.9	8.6	1.3	657.1
1970	196.6	20.5	78.6	8.2	43.1	4.5	18.3	1.9	959.0
1975	326.2	22.4	85.6	5.9	108.6	7.5	30.9	2.1	1,457.3
1976	366.4	22.6	89.4	5.5	127.4	7.9	34.5	2.1	1,621.7
1977	402.7	22.0	97.5	5.3	137.9	7.5	38.0	2.1	1,834.0
1978	450.8	22.1	105.2	5.1	146.2	7.2	44.0	2.2	2,043.4
1979E ...	493.4	21.6	114.5	5.0	158.9	6.9	52.8	2.3	2,289.4

* Unified budget.
† Transition quarter, July–September, 1976, omitted.

Source: *The Budget of the United States, Fiscal Year 1980.*

lute increase in dollar terms from 1960 to 1979. But *GNP* has increased rapidly, too. As a percent of *GNP,* total government expenditures have also increased but the increase is much less striking when viewed in these terms. Nevertheless, we can note some relative increase in the public sector and some relative decrease in the private sector of the economy over the two decades.

Defense expenditures are thought by many to be the major contributor to rising government expenditures over time, but the table does not indicate that this is so. Relative to *GNP,* defense expenditures have shrunk from 9.1 percent in 1960 to 5.1 percent in 1978. The trend reflects partly the very large growth in *GNP.* It also reflects termination of the Vietnam War, and the absence of any major U.S. military activities since the withdrawal from Vietnam.

Income security transfers show a huge increase in both absolute and relative terms. Whereas in 1960 defense expenditures were relatively much larger than income security payments, by 1975 the situation was reversed. After peaking in relative terms in 1976, income security payments have declined slightly as a proportion of *GNP.* The increasing level of income security payments results from larger government commitments to social programs—Social Security, Medicare, Medicaid, Food Stamps, and the like. Many questions are being raised about how effective these expenditure increases are in alleviating poverty. A large proportion of the increases in transfers appear to be going to persons who are *not* living in poverty.

GOVERNMENT REVENUES

How do we pay for the government goods and services provided us and the transfer payments that government makes? All of us know well the major source of government revenue. It is, of course, the proceeds of taxation. When tax receipts are insufficient to cover government expenditures the government borrows by issuing and selling government bonds to cover the deficit. In the present section we shall concentrate on taxes, leaving borrowing to be discussed later. First, we examine the current tax structure. Second, we review trends in tax collections since 1960.

Current types of revenues

In reviewing the component parts of federal tax receipts in Table 9–3 we note that individual income taxes comprise about 45 percent of the total. Personal income tax rates are graduated according to income level. For an individual or family some amount of income—determined by personal exemptions—is not taxed at all. Successive increments in one's income level are taxed at successively higher rates, each higher tax rate being applicable only to that increment in income for which it is specified with the rest of the income taxed at lower rates. The tax rate ranges from 14 to 70 percent of taxable income at the time of the present writing.

Estate and gift taxes are not very important in the total tax structure. They account for less than 2 percent of total tax receipts. They are intended to impede intergeneration transfers of capital resources but they do not really succeed in accomplishing this end.

Social security taxes have become the second largest component of federal tax receipts. These are payroll taxes and are used to pay social security benefits to persons over 65 and to eligible dependents of persons who have worked in employments covered by old age, survivors, and dependents insurance. They also finance a large part of the Medicare program for those persons over 65 who are eligible for social security benefits. In addition, a part of the social security taxes collected by the federal government are earmarked to finance unemployment benefit programs operated by individual states.

Taxes on corporate net income, or corporation income taxes, provide almost 15 percent of the federal government's total tax receipts. Like personal income tax rates, corpora-

Table 9–3
Federal government receipts, fiscal year ending September 30, 1978
($ billions)

Individual income taxes	181.0
Corporation income taxes	59.9
Social insurance taxes and contributions	123.4
Excise taxes	18.4
Customs deposits	6.6
Estate and gift taxes	5.3
Miscellaneous receipts	7.4
Total receipts	402.0

Source: *The Budget of the United States, Fiscal Year 1980.*

tion income taxes are graduated; however, the set of rates is a much simpler one. At the present time the first $25,000 of annual corporation net income is taxed at a rate of 17 percent; the second $25,000 at 20 percent; the third $25,000 at 30 percent; the fourth $25,000 at 40 percent; and all over $100,000 is taxed at 46 percent. The part of a corporation's income that is paid out as dividends to corporation stockholders is then taxed a second time as the personal income of those stockholders.

Sales or excise taxes are indirect business taxes. Some, like the federal gasoline tax, are levied on physical units of goods, gallons for example. Others are levied as a percent of the value of a good or service and thus depend on the selling price of the item taxed. In total, excise taxes account for almost 5 percent of the federal government's tax receipts.

Trends in revenues

Tax collections, like government expenditures, have exhibited a strong upward trend over the years in terms of absolute dollar amounts. Tax collections as a percent of *GNP*, however, have remained remarkably steady since 1960 as Table 9–4 shows. Over the years recorded in the table they have amounted to roughly one fifth of *GNP*. The federal government's total tax collections have been increasing at about the same rate as *GNP*.

Individual income taxes, the largest component of total tax receipts, show the same set of trends. Absolute dollar amounts have risen at about the same rate as *GNP*. They have varied slightly above and below 8.5 percent of *GNP* Social security taxes have shown dramatic increases in both absolute terms and as a percent of *GNP*. In absolute terms they have increased to almost 10 times their 1960 level. As a percent of *GNP* they have about doubled. An increasing labor force size, rising wage payments, expanded coverage of social security programs, and the need for funds to cover larger and larger individual and family benefits account for the trend.

Excise taxes have been shrinking as a part of the total tax package. While *GNP* has quadrupled in dollar amounts from 1960 to 1978, indirect business taxes have not even doubled. They have declined relatively from 2.4 to less than 1 percent of GNP.

Table 9–4
Trends in U.S. government receipts and *GNP* 1960–1976 ($ billions)

Fiscal year*	All receipts		Individual income taxes		Corporation income taxes		Social insurance taxes and contributions		Excise taxes		GNP
	Total	% of GNP	Total	% of GNP	Total	% of GNP	Total	% of GNP	Total	% of GNP	GNP
1960	92.5	18.6	40.7	8.2	21.5	4.3	14.7	3.0	11.7	2.4	497.3
1965	116.8	17.8	53.9	8.2	28.9	4.4	25.0	3.8	14.6	2.2	657.1
1970	193.7	20.2	90.4	9.4	32.8	3.4	45.3	4.7	15.7	1.6	959.0
1975	281.0	19.3	122.4	8.4	40.6	2.8	86.4	5.9	16.6	1.1	1,457.3
1976	300.0	18.5	131.6	8.1	41.4	2.6	92.7	5.7	17.0	1.0	1,621.7
1977	357.8	19.5	157.6	8.6	54.9	3.0	108.7	5.9	17.5	1.0	1,834.0
1978	402.0	19.7	181.0	8.9	60.0	2.9	123.4	6.0	18.4	0.9	2,043.4
1979E	456.0	19.9	203.6	8.9	70.3	3.1	141.8	6.2	18.4	0.8	2,289.4

* Transition quarter, July–September, 1976, omitted.

Source: *The Budget of the United States, Fiscal Year 1980.*

Philosophies of taxation

The variety of taxes levied by government reveals three general philosophies of taxation. One of these is the *ability-to-pay* philosophy. Another is the *benefits-received* philosophy. The third, if it can be dignified by the word "philosophy," is the *expediency* philosophy.

The *ability-to-pay* philosophy is straightforward in principle—it simply says that those with greater ability to pay should pay more than those with lesser ability to pay. Two problems arise. The first is that of determining what constitutes ability to pay. Is it comparative incomes or comparative accumulations of wealth? Or is it some combination of the two? The second problem is that of how much more those of greater ability should pay than those of lesser ability.

With regard to the first problem, wealth and income are closely related. The possessions that we call wealth have value because of their capacities for producing income. Thus, for the most part, if comparative incomes are used as the measure of ability to pay they will reflect comparative wealth positions also. The heavy reliance of the federal government on the personal income tax recognizes this basic relationship as well as the importance of the ability-to-pay philosophy. Gift and estate taxes, however, are essentially taxes on comparative wealth positions.

With regard to the second problem, the choices open to a society are whether to make taxes proportional, progressive, or regressive. A *proportional* tax is one that takes a constant proportion of everyone's income—say 20 percent—regardless of the size of individual incomes. A *progressive* tax is one that takes a larger pecent of higher incomes than it does of lower incomes. If persons who earn $20,000 per year pay 30 percent of their incomes in taxes while those who earn $10,000 per year pay 20 percent of their incomes in taxes, the tax structure is said to be progressive. The federal personal income tax thus has a progressive rate structure. A *regressive* tax is one that takes a larger percent of lower incomes than it does of higher incomes. Suppose, for example, that a 10 percent tax is paid on incomes of $10,000 per year and an 8 percent tax is paid on incomes of $15,000 per year. The rate is regressive. Note, however, that it is possible—although not necessary—for the absolute amount of the tax collected from a person at the higher income level to be higher than that collected from a person at the lower income level even though the tax is regressive. Social security taxes, which take a given percent of a person's income up to a maximum level and exempt the amount of income earned above that level, are regressive.

The *benefits-received* philosophy supports the view that those who receive the most benefits from government expenditures should bear the greatest tax cost for them. Federal gasoline taxes earmarked for the federal highway system provide an example. So do social security taxes. This philosophy has a ring of *quid-pro-quo* equity to it; however, if it were used exclusively, government programs to help the poor would be wiped out since the poor would be expected to provide the tax revenues for the programs designed to help them.

Some taxes are levied according to the philosophy of *expediency*—taxes are levied wherever revenue can be raised and the distribution of the tax load among taxpayers is forgotten. Many excise taxes fall partly in this category. So does the corporation income tax. The primary shortcoming of this philosophy is that it ignores equity in the tax structure.

GOVERNMENT BORROWING AND THE FEDERAL DEBT

In only one of the fiscal years since 1960 has the U.S. government collected enough tax receipts to meet its expenditures. In 1960 itself there was a small budget surplus of $269 million as Table 9–5 indicates. In 1969 the first Nixon administration ran a surplus of $3.2 billion. In every other year since 1960 the federal budget has been in deficit. How are deficits, or the amount by which government spending exceeds tax collections, financed? The usual method employed by the U.S. Treasury is to borrow; that is to issue and sell enough new government bonds and Treasury bills to meet the deficit. Each year's deficit adds to the total federal debt. In this section we discuss the economic effects of government borrowing to finance expenditures and the economic effects of the federal debt.

The economic effects of borrowing

When the federal government runs a budget deficit it is injecting more purchasing power into the economy's spending stream with its spending than it is withdrawing with its tax

Table 9–5
Total U.S. budget receipts and outlays and the federal debt, 1960–1979 ($ billions)

Fiscal year*	Total receipts	Total outlays	Surplus (+) or deficit (−)	Federal debt Total	% of GNP
1960	92.5	92.2	+ 0.3	290.9	58.5
1961	94.4	97.8	− 3.4	292.9	57.6
1962	99.7	106.8	− 7.1	303.3	55.5
1963	106.6	111.3	− 4.7	310.8	53.9
1964	112.7	118.6	− 5.9	316.8	51.4
1965	116.8	118.4	− 1.6	323.2	49.2
1966	130.9	134.7	− 3.8	329.5	45.7
1967	149.6	158.3	− 8.7	341.3	44.1
1968	153.7	178.8	−25.1	369.8	44.6
1969	187.8	184.6	+ 3.2	367.1	40.6
1970	193.7	196.6	− 2.9	382.6	39.9
1971	188.4	211.4	−23.0	409.5	40.2
1972	208.7	232.0	−23.3	437.3	49.4
1973	232.2	247.1	−14.9	468.4	37.9
1974	264.9	269.6	− 4.7	486.2	35.8
1975	281.0	326.2	−45.2	544.1	37.3
1976	300.0	266.4	−66.4	631.9	39.0
1977	357.8	402.7	−44.9	709.1	38.7
1978	402.0	450.8	−48.8	780.4	38.2
1979E	456.0	493.4	−37.4	839.2	36.7

* Transition quarter, July–September, 1976, omitted.

Source: *The Budget of the United States Government, Fiscal Year 1980.*

collections. The net effects of the deficit depend, however, upon who it is that buys the bonds and the circumstances under which they are purchased. We shall identify two groups of purchasers: (1) nonbank persons, businesses and institutions and (2) commercial banks.

From the nonbank public. If the Treasury sells new government bonds and Treasury bills to nonbank buyers who would otherwise have used their purchasing power to buy consumer goods and services or capital goods, the effects on economic activity are similar to those resulting from financing government spending through taxation. Private spending is reduced by the amount of the securities sold and the reduction approximately offsets the government spending that brought on the deficit. A deficit financed in this way would not increase total spending in the economy.

Suppose, however, that a deficit is financed by the sale of government securities to nonbank buyers who would otherwise have held idle money. There will be no direct increase

in the money supply, but government borrowing and spending
puts idle money to work increasing the velocity of circulation.
Thus government spending is not offset by a reduction in private spending. Consequently, total spending in the economy
will increase.

Ordinarily we would expect borrowing through the sale of
new government securities to the nonbank public to result
in some combination of the foregoing possibilities. Some are
purchased with money that would have been spent in some
other way. Some are purchased with money that would have
been hoarded or left idle. On balance total spending will be
increased but by less than the amount borrowed. Some of
the borrowing will have the effect of "crowding out" private
investment and consumption.

From commercial banks. If the government finances a deficit by selling securities to commercial banks—or to parties
who in turn sell them to commercial banks—total spending
in the economy will be increased under some circumstances
while under other circumstances it will not. The effects depend
upon whether or not the banking system is holding excess
reserves.

Suppose that the banking system has excess reserves when
it is sold new government securities by the Treasury. Banks
will pay the government for the securities by establishing
checking accounts for the government. As the government
spends the amounts borrowed, these checking accounts are
transferred to the private parties to whom the government
makes payments. The net effect of financing government
spending in this way is thus an increase in the money supply
and there is no reduction in private spending to offset the
government spending that generated the deficit. Total spending
in the economy is increased.

If the banking system has no excess reserves it cannot create
new money. Purchases of new government securities from the
Treasury can occur only as old bank loans to private parties
fall due or as other bank investments are liquidated. When
old bank loans are repaid, those who make the repayments
use their existing deposits to buy them. Purchases of new government securities by banks and the establishment of corresponding amounts of deposits for the government at the banks
can be accomplished only to the extent that they replace those
deposit reductions of private parties. No net increase in banks'

deposits are possible. Since government borrowing from banks under these circumstances essentially just replaces private borrowing, government spending of what is borrowed is approximately offset by a reduction in private spending (because of the reduction in private borrowing) and there is no increase in total spending in the economy. The effects of financing government spending in this way is similar to the effects of financing the spending through taxation.

To summarize, financing government expenditures through borrowing may or may not increase total spending in the economy. Total spending will be increased if the government borrows from private parties that would otherwise have held idle money, and if it borrows from banks when banks have excess reserves. Total spending will not be increased if the borrowing is from private parties who would otherwise have spent the money they loan to the government, and if the borrowing is from banks when banks have no excess reserves.

The economic effects of the federal debt

A federal debt of $800 billion or more worries a great many people. Are their fears supported by economic analysis or are they to a large extent groundless? Three commonly expressed concerns are: (1) that the magnitude of the debt is too great; (2) that future generations are being asked to pay for current generation extravagances; and (3) that a large debt is inflationary. We shall consider each in turn.

Magnitude of the debt.   The federal debt does indeed look large in absolute terms and it has almost tripled since 1960 as Table 9–5 indicates. But is the absolute size of the debt a cause for concern? If so, why? At least two major points seem to worry the general public. First, how can such a tremendous debt—one that is likely to grow even more—ever be repaid? Second, paying interest on the debt is an ever increasing burden.

Actually the federal debt does not need to be repaid. Individuals who have loaned the government money by buying government bonds must be repaid, of course, when their bonds fall due. But in order to pay off maturing bonds the Treasury needs only to sell new ones, using the proceeds of the new issue to pay off the maturing issue. The purchasers of the new bonds may or may not be different parties from those whose maturing bonds are paid. Thus the debt can be a debt in perpetuity, with new bonds replacing old ones and with the possibility of a changing composition of bondholders or government creditors.

If it were desirable for some reason for the government to pay off the debt, the process of collecting taxes to do so would simply take purchasing power out of the hands of those who pay the taxes and put it in the hands of those whose bonds are maturing. What if a taxpayer is also a bondholder and by some quirk of fate pays in taxes precisely the amount that the government would need to redeem his maturing bond? Money simply passes from his taxpaying pocket into his receipts-from-bond-sales pocket. If bondholders in general spend smaller proportions of their dollars of purchasing power than taxpayers in general, the process of taxing and paying off maturing bonds would slow total spending in the economy. This could be offset by expansionary monetary policies on the part of the Federal Reserve authorities. Only to the extent that bondholders are foreigners would the U.S. economy necessarily suffer from paying off the federal debt. U.S. taxpayers would be transferring purchasing power over U.S. goods and services to foreign bondholders and the use of that purchasing power to buy U.S. goods and services would reduce the total amount of goods and services that U.S. residents have to consume.

Despite the large increase in the magnitude of the debt since 1960, the proportion of their incomes that taxpayers would have to pay in order to retire the debt was smaller in 1978 than it was in 1960. In 1960 the federal debt in dollar terms was 58.5 percent of *GNP*. In 1978 it was only 38.2 percent of *GNP*.

The existence of a federal debt requires that interest on the debt be paid. Annual expenditures of the federal government contain an interest item that has grown along with the magnitude of the debt. If the government were operating on a balanced budget, a corresponding amount of tax collections would be used to pay interest on the debt. Purchasing power of taxpayers would be reduced and that of bondholders would be increased by the amount of interest paid. Since no net goods or services are generated by the payment of interest, the process is a government transfer payment. No burden to the economy as a whole is engendered by these annual transfers unless for some reason they cause dislocations and inefficiencies in resource use and/or the consumption of goods and services.

Burden on future generations. Does the debt mean that costs of what the present generation is consuming in government goods must be borne by future generations? We learned in Chapter 1 that the upper limits to *GNP* or *NNP* are set by the quantities and qualities of resources available to the economy together with the economy's techniques of production. The present generation can consume no more than that although it may increase present *G* at the expense of *C* or *I*. Similarly, future generations have available to consume whatever *GNP* or *NNP* resources and techniques available at that time can produce. Only if the process of adding to the federal debt by the present generation somehow inhibits the accumulation of resources between now and the time of future generations can the federal debt transfer an economic cost from the present to future generations.

Inflation. The size of the federal debt is not a factor that by itself causes inflation. It is the process of *accumulating* federal debt that may be inflationary. The size of the debt is increased by a federal government deficit and that deficit may be inflationary. So, rather than the absolute size of the debt, it is the change in debt from a smaller to a larger absolute size and the rapidity with which that change is accomplished that should cause concern about inflation.

Economic effects in summary. When we look at the economy as a whole in terms of the size of *GNP* and *NNP* it is not at all certain that the magnitude of the federal debt is of any real significance. To be of significance from the overall point of view it must adversely affect the size of the economy's output from year to year and it would be exceedingly hard to demonstrate that this is the case.

The primary impact of the debt appears to be its *transfer* effects—the transfers of purchasing power from taxpayers to bondholders that occur as interest on the debt is paid. These transfers increase in absolute terms along with the size of the debt. They also increase whenever inflation causes interest rates to rise. The importance we attach to any absolute size of the debt will depend upon our views regarding the desirability or undesirability of the transfers that occur. If we dislike the direction of the transfers, then we dislike a large federal debt.

SUMMARY

Different governments at different points in time have engaged in almost every conceivable kind of economic activity. In attempting to determine appropriate areas of government economic activities it is useful to classify goods and services as (1) individually consumed, (2) collectively consumed, and (3) semicollectively consumed. Actual areas of government economic activities include (1) the production of goods and services; (2) the prevention of force and fraud; (3) the provision of rules of the game; and (4) the accomplishment of social goals.

In performing its economic activities the government of the United States spends large amounts of money. The largest group of its expenditures is in the transfer category. In the production of goods and services, national defense is the largest item. Over time expenditures to provide income security have risen dramatically in both absolute amounts and as a proportion of *GNP*. Defense expenditures have risen in absolute amounts but have fallen substantially as a proportion of *GNP*.

Tax collections are the primary source of revenue for meeting government expenditures. The individual income tax provides the largest amount followed by social insurance taxes, corporation income taxes, and excise taxes, in that order. The most notable trends over the last 20 years have been a virtual explosion of social insurance taxes in both absolute and relative terms, a modest relative decline in corporation income taxes and a substantial relative decline in excise taxes. The principles or philosophies underlying the distribution of the tax load among taxpayers are (1) ability to pay, (2) benefits received, and (3) expediency.

Borrowing has been used to some extent to finance government expenditures—particularly over the last 20 years. At the extremes borrowing may (1) have the same effects as taxation or (2) generate additional purchasing power through increases in V and M. Generally, the effects fall somewhere between the extremes. Large-scale borrowing within the span of a few years is likely to be inflationary.

Borrowing leads to the accumulation of a federal debt represented by government bonds and Treasury bills outstanding. The debt has grown rapidly in absolute terms since 1960 but has been decreasing as a percent of *GNP*. It appears that there has been no impairment as yet in the capacity of the economy to carry the debt. Contrary to prevailing public opinion the accumulation of debt does not burden future generations with the fruits of present generation extravagance—unless it somehow causes future *GNP* to be lower than it would otherwise be. The size of the debt itself is not a force contributing to inflation; however, the debt accumulation process is often inflationary.

QUESTIONS AND PROBLEMS

1. Place each of the following goods in its appropriate classification as collectively consumed, individually consumed, or semicollectively consumed, giving your reasons in each case:
   a. A lighthouse on a reef.
   b. Water from a municipal water works.
   c. Polio booster shots.
   d. An automobile.

2. What is meant by the statement that government should provide "rules of the game" for economic activity?

3. Make a list of the goods and services produced by your municipal government. Which of these are collectively consumed? Which are individually consumed?

4. What is the nature of the "free rider problem?" How would you suggest solving it?

5. What major changes have occurred in the pattern of federal government spending since 1960? The pattern of taxation?

6. By running large federal budget deficits in the 1970s, have we transferred costs of "high" living to future generations? Explain.

PART THREE

MICROECONOMICS: HOW THE PARTS HANG TOGETHER

The microeconomic part of the analytical framework provides a systematic way of studying the relationships among the economic units that engage in economic activity. Its major objective is to examine how economic activity is organized. What motivates economic units? What constitutes efficient organization of economic activity? Can the economic system provide acceptable measures of justice or equity as among economic units? We may not have all the answers but we can most certainly raise the questions.

Chapter 10

The foundations of demand

In any economy the wants and the desires of consumers, as individuals and as groups, are the prime movers of economic activity. But how are the many and varied wants of thousands of persons projected into the web of economic activity? It all starts with individual consumer behavior. Demands for goods and services like beef and gasoline originate with individual consumer units—families and/or unattached individuals.

Consumer units face a continuing and sometimes frustrating economic problem. They want more than they can afford. We can break the problem down into two parts: (1) tastes and preferences—what each consumer would like to do, and (2) budget constraints—what each consumer is able to do. From these parts we can fashion individual consumer demands that can be added together to form market demands for each of the goods and services that an economy produces.

TASTES AND PREFERENCES

Every consumer unit has its equivalent of the Sears or the Neiman-Marcus catalogue, which it thumbs through with wistful eyes. The consumer's wants and desires are many and varied as we indicated in Chapter 1. We need not concern ourselves at this point with how they come into being—whether they spring full-blown from the consumer's own psychological and physiolgical makeup or whether they are developed as the consumer is exposed over time to various social forces including advertising. The important point is that consumer units have developed over time want patterns or sets of want priorities. These we call consumers' *tastes and preferences* or consumers' *preference patterns*.

Underlying postulates

Most people behave in a consistent rational way in their roles as consumers. Some, of course, do not, and we can say little of an analytical nature about the exceptions. What constitutes consistent rational behavior on the part of the overwhelming majority? We characterize it as requiring the fulfillment of three basic postulates.

First, we postulate that a consumer *prefers more* of any one good *to less* of it. The consumer would rather have four pairs than three pairs of shoes per year. Three hundred lunches per year are preferred to 250. And so on. There is an implication in this postulate that the consumer does not become satiated with any good. In fact, as we shall see later, satiation with any good implies irrational behavior.

Second, we postulate that the many *choices* of goods and combinations of goods available in the economy *can be ranked* by the consumer. The consumer, confronted by basket of goods and services *A, B, C,* and *D* can put the baskets in a rank order with, say, *B* preferred to *A, A* preferred to *C,* and *C* equivalent to *D.* This postulate simply amounts to saying that the consuming unit knows its own tastes and preferences.

Third, we postulate that the consumer's ranking is *transitive.* This means that if the consumer tells us basket *A* is preferred to basket *B,* and basket *B* is preferred to basket *C,* then basket *A* is also preferred to basket *C.* Or, if the consumer is indifferent between basket *A* and basket *B,* and is indifferent between basket *B* and basket *C,* then indifference between basket *A* and basket *C* follows. The transitivity postulate is really a consistency postulate.

The indifference map

The foregoing postulates enable us to construct a graphic picture of the consumer's tastes and preferences—what the consumer would like to do. To simplify matters suppose we limit the economy to two goods, apples *(A)* and fig leaves *(F).* In Figure 10–1 we measure apples in bushels per month on the vertical axis and fig leaves in units per month on the horizontal axis. Every point on the diagram represents some combination of bushels of apples and number of fig leaves. Point *C,* for example, represents fives bushels of apples and three fig leaves per month. If the axes of the diagram are extended sufficiently, the space within the axes contains an infinite number of combinations.

We can locate other combinations equivalent to *C* by questioning the consumer. If we ask how combination *B* compares with combination *C,* the answer must be that *B* is preferred to *C* since it contains more apples and the same number of fig leaves as *C.* Suppose that when combination *A* is compared with *C* we find that it would make no difference which combination the consumer has. This is reasonable, since *A* contains

Figure 10–1
A consumer's indifference map

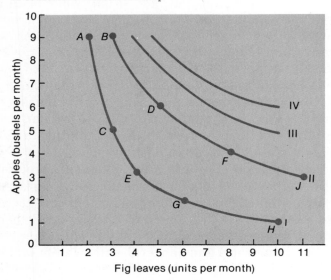

fewer fig leaves and more apples than *C*. Suppose that in the course of the questioning we establish that combinations *A*, *E*, *G*, and *H* are all equivalent to combination *C*. The consumer is indifferent among these combinations. These combinations, together with all other combinations that are equivalent to *C* in the consumer's mind, trace out *indifference curve* I.

Turning now to combination *B* we can find the whole set of combinations that are equivalent to *B*. These include such combinations as *D*, *F*, and *J*, and they trace out indifference curve II. Any combination on indifference curve II is preferred to any combination on indifference curve I. This will be so because the consumer's preferences are transitive. All combinations on indifference curve I are equivalent to *C* in the consumer's preference rankings. All combinations on indifference curve II are equivalent to *B*. Since *B* is preferred to *C*, the consumer must also prefer any other combination on II to any other combination on I.

A whole set of indifference curves—I, II, III, IV, and many others—can be drawn for a consumer, giving us a graphic picture of the consumer's tastes and preferences. There are as many curves in the set as we care to draw. Two important points must be kept in mind: (1) each curve shows the combinations that yield a given level of satisfaction to the consumer; that is, the consumer is indifferent among the combinations represented by any one indifference curve, and (2) the consumer prefers combinations on higher indifference curves (those farther from the origin of the diagram) to combinations on lower indifference curves. The complete set of indifference curves is called the consumer's *indifference map.*

Indifference map characteristics

The indifference curves making up a consumer's indifference map have three basic characteristics. First, each indifference curve slopes downward to the right. Second, no two indifference curves intersect. Third, indifference curves are convex to the origin of the diagram.

The downward slope of each indifference curve simply reflects the postulate that the consumer prefers more to less of anything. In Figure 10–2 the line *AB* is horizontal; that is, it does *not* slope downward to the right. For *AB* to be an indifference curve, combinations *A* and *B* must each yield the same satisfaction level to the consumer. But since *B* contains

Figure 10–2
Indifference curve characteristic

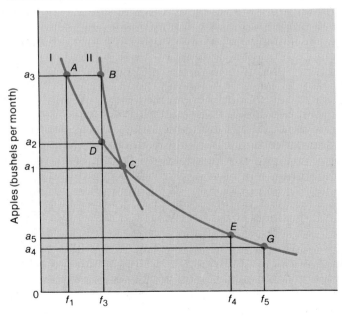

more fig leaves than A and the same amount of apples, indifference between the two combinations would violate the postulate that the consumer prefers more to less. For the consumer to be indifferent between two combinations when one contains more fig leaves than the other, the combination that contains more fig leaves must also contain fewer apples. Combination D provides a possible example. It may be equivalent to A. It will be equivalent if, and only if, the additional satisfaction the consumer gets from f_1f_3 more fig leaves is just offset by the decrease in satisfaction the consumer would experience in giving up a_2a_3 of apples. For this to be the case the indifference curve must slope downward to the right.

An intersection of two indifference curves as shown by I and II in Figure 10–2 violates the postulate of transitivity of the consumer's preferences. Combination A is equivalent to combination C in the consumer's mind. Combination B is also equivalent to C if I and II intersect. But if B is preferred to A, both A and B *cannot* be equivalent to C. So I and II *cannot* intersect. We have drawn either I or II incorrectly in Figure 10–2.

In order to see that indifference curves are convex to the origin we rely on common sense. Consider points A and E in Figure 10–2. At A the consumer would have relatively many apples and relatively few fig leaves as compared with those comprising combination E. Consequently, we would expect that at combination A the consumer would be willing to give up more apples to get an additional fig leaf than would be the case at point E. At point A apples would be less valuable relative to fig leaves than they would be at point E. Convexity of the indifference curve to the origin reflects this expectation. At A the consumer would be willing to give up a_2a_3 bushels of apples to get f_1f_3 fig leaves. At point E, letting $f_4f_6 = f_1f_3$, the consumer would be willing to give up only a_4a_5 bushels of apples to get the same additional quantity of fig leaves.

The amount of one product a consumer is just willing to give up to get an additional unit of another is called the *marginal rate of substitution* of the second for the first. In Figure 10–3 suppose the consumer is considering combination A which contains five bushels of apples and one fig leaf. To obtain an additional fig leaf the consumer would be willing to give up two bushels of apples, moving to combination B on the same indifference curve. The marginal rate of substitution of fig leaves for apples, or MRS_{fa}, is two. Between B

Figure 10–3
The marginal rate of substitution of fig leaves for apples

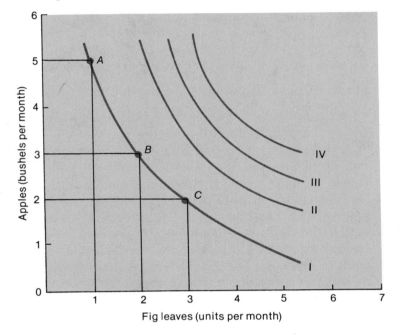

Fig leaves (units per month)

and *C* the MRS_{fa} drops to one. A decreasing MRS_{fa} as the consumer moves down to the right around an indifference curve, giving up apples and obtaining additional fig leaves, means the same thing as convexity to the origin.

THE BUDGET CONSTRAINT

A consumer's indifference map depicts all levels of satisfaction that a consumer could possibly experience between zero and levels approaching absolute bliss. The consumer is constrained, however, in the satisfaction level that can actually be attained by income and the prices of the products available. The budget limitation on the consumer is shown graphically with a budget line on the same type of diagram as the one used for the indifference map.

The budget line

Consider a consumer with a disposable income of $64 per month. Let the price of apples be $16 per bushel while fig leaves are priced at $8 each. In Figure 10–4, if the consumer's entire income is spent on apples, four bushels can be purchased. The consumer would not be able to purchase any fig leaves and would be at point A. Note that point A is determined by dividing the consumer's disposable income I by the price per bushel of apples p_a. At the opposite extreme if the entire disposable income is spent on fig leaves, $\dfrac{I}{p_f} = 8$; that is, eight fig leaves could be purchased. Point B denotes eight fig leaves and no apples.

A straight line from A to B shows the combinations of apples and fig leaves that are available to the consumer. If the consumer were at point A, purchasing four bushles of apples, a fig leaf could be obtained by giving up one half bushel of apples. The sacrifice of apples would release four dollars which the consumer could use to purchase the fig leaf. By giving up another one half bushel of apples, the consumer could purchase a second fig leaf per month and would be at point C with three bushels of apples and two fig leaves. The consumer can move to any combination on AB by sacrificing

Figure 10–4
The consumer's budget line

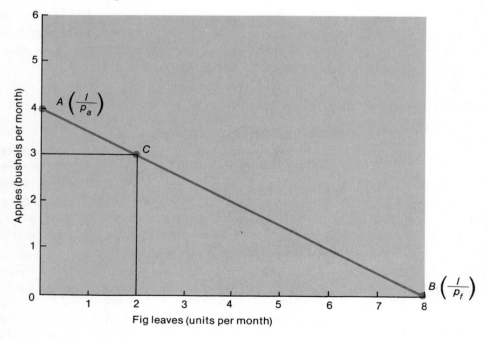

apples for fig leaves or fig leaves for apples. An additional
fig leaf can always be obtained by giving up a half bushel
of apples. An additional bushel of apples can always be obtained by giving up two fig leaves. The line *AB* showing what
the consumer is able to do in the market for apples and fig
leaves is the consumer's *budget line* or budget constraint.

Note that the *slope* of the budget line is determined by the
ratio of the price of fig leaves to the price of apples. The slope
of the line shows the number of units that the line drops for
each one unit movement in the horizontal direction. In Figure
10–4 it is:

$$\frac{\dfrac{I}{p_a}}{\dfrac{I}{p_f}} = \frac{I}{p_a} \cdot \frac{p_f}{I} = \frac{p_f}{p_a}$$

Since $p_f = \$4$ and $p_a = \$8$, the slope of *AB* is:

$$\frac{p_f}{p_a} = \frac{\$4}{\$8} = \frac{1}{2}$$

Changes in the budget's line

Changes in the consumer's income, with the prices of the
products purchased remaining constant, will shift the budget
line parallel to itself. Suppose, for example, that in Figure
10–5 the consumer's income is cut from $64 to $32 per month.
The consumer can now buy two bushels of apples, or four
fig leaves, or any combination of apples and fig leaves on
the straight line *EF*. A reduction in income thus shifts the
budget line inward, parallel to itself, toward the origin of the
diagram. By the same token an increase in income, with product prices constant, shifts it outward, parallel to itself, away
from the origin. Since the prices of food and clothing are not
changed, the slopes of the budget lines are all equal to ½.

An increase in the price of one product, with income and
the price of the other product remaining constant, will pull
the corresponding end of the budget line toward the origin.
Suppose that the price of fig leaves rises from $8 to $16 each.
The $64 income level will now buy only four fig leaves if only
fig leaves were purchased and the budget line becomes *AG*

Figure 10–5
Effects of an income change on the budget line

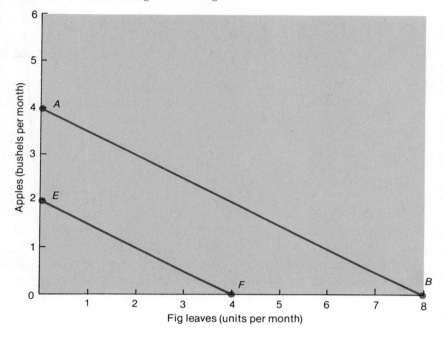

Figure 10–6
The effects of a change in product price on the budget line

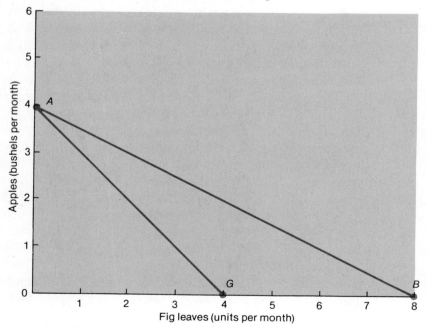

in Figure 10–6. Note that the slope of the new budget line is $16/$16, or one. Similarly, a decrease in the price of one product will shift the corresponding end of the budget line outward away from the origin.

MAXIMIZATION OF SATISFACTION

By superimposing the consumer's budget line on the consumer's indifference map we can show graphically the combination of apples and fig leaves that maximizes the consumer's satisfaction within the limits of the budget constraint.

The budget line of Figure 10–7 shows what the consumer is able to do. If all income were spent on fig leaves the consumer would be at point B taking quantity $0B$ fig leaves and no apples. Or if all incomes were spent on apples the consumer would be at point A taking $0A$ bushels of apples and no fig leaves. Combination C, containing a_5 bushels of apples and f_1 fig leaves is also possible. So are combinations D and E on the budget line. It is even possible for the consumer to take a combination below and to the left of the budget line,

Figure 10–7
Maximization of satisfaction by the consumer

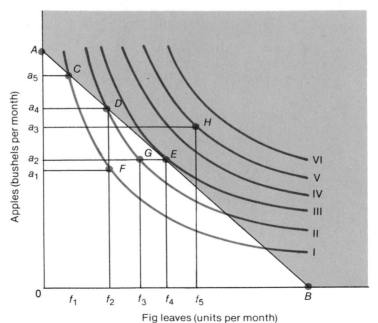

Fig leaves (units per month)

like combination *F*. In fact any combination represented by a point in the shaded area is available.

The indifference map in Figure 10–7 shows what the consumer would like to do. The combinations on any one indifference curve yield the same level of satisfaction to the consumer. Thus, the consumer is indifferent between combinations such as *C* and *F,* or *D* and *G*. Combinations on higher indifference curves are preferred to those on lower ones so either *D* or *G* would be preferred to *C* or *F*. Combinations on VI are preferred to those on V and those on V are preferred to those on IV. Similarly, those on IV yield higher satisfaction than those on III. Combinations on II and I rank in that order below those on III.

That part of the indifference map lying in the shaded area shows the consumer's preference ranking of those combinations of goods that the budget constraint will allow. Combination *D* is preferred to *C*. Combination *G* is preferred to *F*. Combination *E* is preferred to *D* or *G*. Combination *H* is preferred to any of the foregoing combinations but is beyond the reach of the consumer's budget.

Of all the combinations available, combination *E,* containing f_4 fig leaves and a_2 bushels of apples yields the highest level of satisfaction available to the consumer. Any other combination on or below the budget line is on a lower indifference curve. Indifference curve III is the highest indifference curve the consumer can reach and it can be reached only if the consumer takes combination *E*. No other combination on indifference curve III is available, given the consumer's income and the prices of fig leaves and apples that determine budget line *AB*.

Note that combination *E* is the one at which the consumer's budget line is just tangent to an indifference curve. Thus, indifference curve III and the budget line have the same slope at *E*. The slope of the indifference curve measures the consumer's marginal rate of substitution of fig leaves for apples while that of the budget line measures the ratio of the price of fig leaves to the price of apples. Thus, at point *E*

$$MRS_{fa} = \frac{p_f}{p_a};$$

that is, the rate at which the consumer *is just willing* to substitute fig leaves for apples is equal to the rate at which it *would be necessary* in the markets to give up apples to obtain fig leaves. The analysis can be extended to as many goods and services as consumers purchase. To maximize satisfaction any one consumer must purchase that combination of goods and services at which his or her marginal rate of substitution between any two of them is equal to the price ratio between them.

THE CONSUMER'S DEMAND FOR ONE PRODUCT

The step from the determination of the combination of goods that maximizes a consumer's satisfaction to the determination of the consumer's demand for one good is not very great. It will be easier to understand if we stick to the highly simplified two-commodity world. The results can then be generalized to a multicommodity world.

The consumer's demand curve for one good—say, fig leaves—should show the quantities per unit of time that will be taken at alternative possible prices, other things being equal. The "other things" that must remain constant are: (1) the consumer's tastes and preferences, that is, the indifference map; (2) the consumer's money income; and (3) the prices of other goods—in this case the price of apples.

An increase in the price of fig leaves, with the consumer's income and the price of apples held constant, will shift the budget line in Figure 10–8(A) from AB_1 to AB_2. The change in the price of fig leaves has no impact on the A end of the budget line. If we denote the consumer's income as I_1 dollars and the initial price of fig leaves as p_{f1}, the B_1 end of the budget line is located by I_1/p_{f1}. If the price of fig leaves *increases* to p_{f2}, this end of the budget line shifts inward to B_2, located by I_1/p_{f2}. Thus for each different price of fig leaves the B end of the budget line is located at a different fig leaf quantity—smaller and closer to the origin for higher prices; larger and farther from the origin for lower prices.

At each different price of fig leaves the consumer maximizes satisfaction with the combination of fig leaves and apples at which the appropriate budget line is tangent to an indifference curve. When the price of fig leaves is p_{f1} the budget line is AB_1 and is tangent to indifference curve IV at point E. The quantity of fig leaves taken is f_1 bushel. In Figure 10–8(B) we plot price p_{f1} on the vertical axis and quantity f_1 on the hori-

Figure 10–8
Determination of the consumer's demand curve for fig leaves

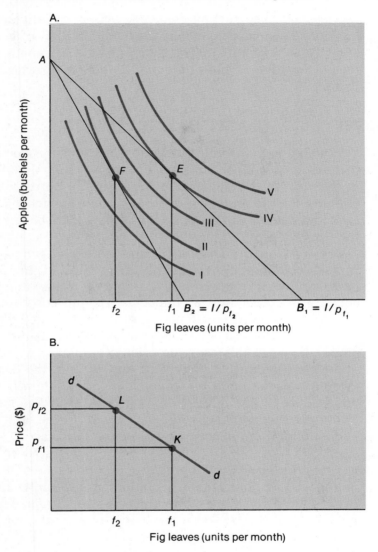

A.

Apples (bushels per month)

A

F E

V

III

IV

II

I

f_2 f_1 $B_2 = I/p_{f_2}$ $B_1 = I/p_{f_1}$

Fig leaves (units per month)

B.

Price ($)

d

p_{f2} L

p_{f1} K

d

f_2 f_1

Fig leaves (units per month)

zontal axis, determining point K. Point K is a point on the consumer's demand curve for fig leaves. It shows how many fig leaves the consumer will take at that price. If the price of fig leaves rises to p_{f2} the budget line becomes AB_2, which is tangent to indifference curve II at point F. The quantity of fig leaves taken when the consumer maximizes satisfaction

f_2. In Figure 10–8(B), plotting p_{f2} and f_2 we obtain point L, a second point on the consumer's demand curve for fig leaves. At other fig leaf prices we can obtain additional budget lines and the corresponding quantities of fig leaves at which the consumer maximizes satisfaction. These pairs of prices and quantities trace out the demand curve dd of Figure 10–8(B).

The demand curve of an individual consumer for any other good or service is determined conceptually in the same way as that for fig leaves. To determine a consumer's demand curve for gasoline, or corn flakes, or pairs of socks, or anything else we must hold the "other things" listed above constant. Then we confront the consumer with one price of the item for which the demand curve is to be determined. The consumer maximizes satisfaction—moves to a combination of goods at which the budget constraint is tangent to the highest possible indifference curve. We observe the quantity of the item in question and we have the price-quantity coordinates for one point on the demand curve for the item. To obtain the coordinates of another point on the demand curve we confront the consumer with another price of the item, holding the "other things" as they were before. Again, the consumer maximizes satisfaction. We observe the quantity taken and we have the second set of coordinates. The process can be repeated to obtain as many points on the demand curve for the item as we desire. But each time we change the price of the item we must let the consumer maximize satisfaction at the new price before making the quantity observation.

The individual consumer's demand curve for a product would be expected to slope downward to the right; that is, an inverse relationship would exist between the price and quantity taken. There are two reasons why this would be so. First, an increase in the price of the good pulls the budget line for that item in toward the origin of the consumer's indifference curve diagram, forcing the consumer to a lower indifference curve. This means that the consumer's purchasing power or *real income* has been decreased. We would expect ordinarily that the decrease in real income would decrease the consumer's purchases of the item that has increased in price. This is the *income effect* of a price change. In addition, the increase in the price of the good relative to the prices of other goods makes the consumer want to substitute some of the other goods that are now relatively cheaper for some of the items for which the price has risen. This is the *substitution effect* of a price change. The income effect and the substitution effect combine to reduce the quantity purchased when the price of an item rises or to increase the quantity purchased when the price falls.

THE MARKET DEMAND CURVE

The market demand curve for a product—like the one we discussed and used in Chapter 2—is a composite of the individual consumer demand curves for the item. As we stated at that point, it shows the quantities per unit of time that all consumers together will purchase at alternative prices, other things being equal.

In constructing the market demand curve from individual consumer demand curves for a product, we add the latter horizontally. Suppose, for example, that in Figure 10–9 Brown and Jones are the only consumers of pizzas. Their respective demand curves are shown in Figures 10–9(A) and 10–9(B). To obtain the market demand curve we sum the quantities they will take at each possible price and plot the sums in Figure 10–9(C). At prices of $4 and above, Jones will not enter the market so Brown's demand curve is the market demand curve. At $4 each, 5 pizzas per week will be taken and point *A* on the market demand curve is determined. At a price of $2 per pizza Brown will take 10 and Jones will take 5 per week. Together they take 15, locating point *B* on the market demand curve. Other points comprising the market demand curve can be located in a similar way. The procedure is perfectly general

Figure 10–9
The market demand for pizzas

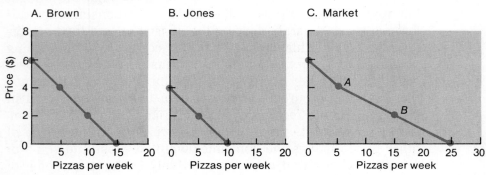

and can be extended to as many consumers as a market contains. It is applicable to any product.

As we noted in Chapter 2 the market demand curves for the many goods and services produced and sold in the economy will also, with rare exceptions, slope downward to the right. This almost universal *law of demand* occurs for two reasons. First, the individual consumer demand curves for any given product slope downward to the right. Second, as the price of an item rises some consumers who would use it at lower prices are not willing to buy it at all at higher prices. Conversely, at lower prices some consumers who would not buy at higher prices become purchasers at lower prices.

Many noneconomists either do not recognize or do not really understand the law of demand. We often see news media accounts or hear rhetoric to the effect that increases in the price of an item—gasoline, for example—does *not* decrease the quantity that consumers will take. Some of those who make such assertions seem to believe that consumers demand some fixed quantity of an item regardless of its price. But can this really be the case for *all* of the consumers in the economy? Others neglect the fact that in an economy experiencing inflation the prices of other goods are rising along with the price of the item in question, say gasoline. It may be that the *relative* price of the item is not rising at all; incomes, demand curves, and supply curves are all shifting upward and there is no decrease in the quantity purchased of any one good. It may be, too, that in some cases noneconomists, observing that both the price *and* the quantity purchased of an item are increasing, do not recognize the distinction between an increase in demand and a movement along a demand curve. The demand for an item may be increasing; that is, the demand curve is shifting to the right. The result will be an increase in *both* price and quantity exchanged. However, these results when observed tell us nothing about the slope of the demand curve when it is in any one position.

PRICE ELASTICITY OF DEMAND

Even though we expect the demand curves for virtually all goods and services to slope downward to the right, the responsiveness of the quantity taken to a price change differs a great deal from product to product. It is important to sellers and it is important to policy makers to know how responsive quantities taken of different goods are to changes in their respective prices. We call the responsiveness concept the *price elasticity of demand*. It can be applied to both individual consumer demand curves and market demand curves.

Elasticity measurement

Price elasticity of demand for a good is determined by dividing the percentage change in quantity by the percentage change in price when there is a small change in the price of a product. In Figure 10–10 let the initial demand and supply curves for bicycles be *DD* and *SS*, respectively. The price is $80 and the quantity purchased is 3,000 per year. Now suppose that supply increases to S_1S_1. The price decreases to $70 and the quantity purchased increases to 4,000 per year. The percentage change in quantity is 1,000/3,000, or 33.3 percent. The percent-

Figure 10–10
Elasticity of demand

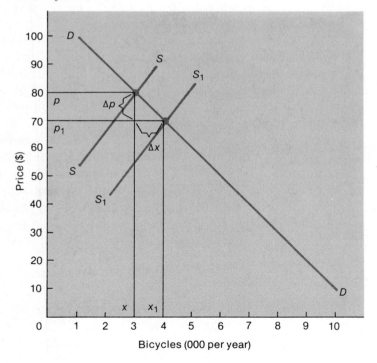

Bicycles (000 per year)

age change in price is −$10/$80, or −12.5 percent. Thus, the elasticity coefficient ϵ is determined as follows:

$$\epsilon = \frac{\dfrac{1{,}000}{3{,}000}}{\dfrac{-\$10}{\$80}} = \frac{33.3\%}{-12.5\%} - -2.67$$

It means that for a small price change in the neighborhood of $70 to $80 a one percent price change leads to a 2.7 percent change in quantity purchased. Since the quantity changes are in the opposite direction from the price changes, the elasticity coefficient is a negative number. For our purposes we can ignore the sign, using only its absolute value.

A different coefficient results if *DD* and $S_1 S_1$ are the original demand and supply curves and if supply then decreases to *SS*. Quantity purchased decreases from 4,000 to 3,000 bicycles in response to a price increase from $70 to $80. The elasticity coefficient becomes:

$$\epsilon = \frac{\dfrac{-1{,}000}{4{,}000}}{\dfrac{\$\ 10}{\$\ 70}} = \frac{-25\%}{14.3\%} = -1.75$$

The discrepancy between the coefficients is not a matter of great concern. It occurs because we are measuring elasticity between number intervals that are fairly large for both price and quantity. If the number intervals were smaller, the discrepancy would also be smaller. If the price change and the quantity change were infinitesimal, there would be no discrepancy at all. We would be measuring elasticity at a single point on the demand curve. Actually the elasticity of demand changes as we move down or up the demand curve for a product. To obtain completely accurate elasticity coefficients we should measure elasticity at the $80 price, at the $70 price, and at all possible prices between $80 and $70. Such a procedure would be very cumbersome so we settle for something less than complete accuracy. It would not be unreasonable to use either the 2.67 coefficient or the 1.75 coefficient.

It is even better to use some sort of an average of the two

coefficients. A very easy way of computing such an average is provided by the use of the following formula:

$$\epsilon = \frac{\dfrac{\Delta p}{p_1}}{\dfrac{\Delta x}{x}}$$

where p_1 is the lower of the two prices and x is the lower of the two quantities. Referring to Figure 10–10, the elasticity coefficient for the changes indicated in price and quantity thus becomes:

$$\epsilon = \frac{\dfrac{1,000}{3,000}}{\dfrac{-\$10}{\$70}} = \frac{33\frac{1}{3}\%}{-14\frac{2}{7}\%} = -2.33,$$

which lies between the other two coefficients that we computed for this same price change.

In Table 10–1 the set of elasticity coefficients between points on the demand curve of Figure 10–10 is shown. Column (3) lists the coefficients for $10 price intervals working down the

Table 10–1
Elasticity of demand and total expenditures

(1) Price	(2) Quantity per year	(3) Elasticity (p↓)	(4) Elasticity (p↑)	(5) Elasticity (average)	(6) Total expenditure
$100	1,000				$100,000
		10.00	4.50	9.00	
90	2,000				180,000
		4.50	2.67	4.00	
80	3,000				240,000
		2.67	1.75	2.33	
70	4,000				280,000
		1.75	1.20	1.50	
60	5,000				300,000
		1.20	0.83	1.00	
50	6,000				300,000
		0.83	0.57	0.67	
40	7,000				280,000
		0.57	0.37	0.43	
30	8,000				240,000
		0.37	0.22	0.25	
20	9,000				180,000
		0.22	0.10	0.11	
10	10,000				100,000

demand curve as we did in our first computation. Column (4) lists the coefficients working up the demand curve as we did in our second computation. Column (5) is the set of average elasticities that results from use of the averaging formula. This is the set that we shall use.

Elasticity coefficients are classified into three groups. First, where coefficients have an absolute value greater than one [1], demand is said to be *elastic*. Second, where coefficients are less than one in absolute value, demand is *inelastic*. Third, where coefficients have an absolute value of one, demand is of *unitary elasticity*.

Elasticity, price changes, and total expenditures

The magnitude of the elasticity coefficient is directly related to what happens to total consumer expenditures on a product (or total receipts of sellers) when the price of the product changes. A decrease in price when demand is elastic will increase total consumer expenditures (sellers' receipts) for the product. This relationship is demonstrated in Table 10–1. Every price decrease where $\epsilon > 1$ results in an increase in total consumer expenditures (sellers' receipts) for bicycles. The mathematical common sense of the relationship is that if $\epsilon > 1$ and price decreases, the *percentage increase* in quantity is greater than the percentage decrease in price. Since total expenditures (receipts) are equal to price times quantity purchased, the result will be an increase in those total expenditures (receipts). Similarly, a decrease in price when elasticity is unitary leaves total expenditures (receipts) unaffected. If demand is inelastic, a price decrease will decrease total expenditures (receipts). For price increases the effects on total expenditures will be reversed. These relationships are tabulated in Table 10–2.

Table 10–2
Elasticity, price changes, and total receipts

Elasticity of demand	Price increase	Price decrease
$\epsilon > 1$	TE and TR decrease	TE and TR increase
$\epsilon = 1$	TE and TR unchanged	TE and TR unchanged
$\epsilon < 1$	TE and TR increase	TE and TR decrease

As an illustration of the importance of demand elasticity for the decisions of sellers, consider the possibility that you are the only wine merchant in a university town. If you raise the price per bottle and demand is elastic, what will happen to your total receipts? If demand is inelastic, what will happen to your total receipts? Would you definitely increase the price if $\epsilon < 1$?

Sound government policy making may also turn on elasticity considerations. Suppose, for example, that the elasticity of demand for wheat is greater than one. If the objective of government policy is to increase the total receipts of wheat farmers as a group, would you recommend that acreage controls sufficiently restrictive to reduce supply to be employed? Why or why not?

Determinants of elasticity

What factors determine how responsive the quantity that consumers will take of a product is to changes in its price? The three most important ones are: (1) the availability of substitutes for it, (2) the importance of it in consumer's budgets, and (3) whether the price changes under observation are relatively high or relatively low for the product.

If good substitutes are available for a product, demand will be more elastic than it would be if they were not. Consider Coors beer, for example. Since there are many other brands available a small price change in Coors, with the prices of other brands remaining constant, will likely result in a relatively large quantity response. If the price of Coors rises, many consumers will switch to other brands which are now relatively less expensive. If the price of Coors decreases, many consumers will switch from other brands which are now relatively more expensive. Suppose we lump all brands of beer together. Quantity taken will be much less responsive to price changes for all beer than it would be for any one brand.

Items that are insignificant in consumers' budgets tend to have less elastic demand than those that occupy an important place. The quantities of spices such as pepper and allspice are not very responsive to price changes. Quantities of automobiles purchased are likely to be much more responsive.

The mathematics of elasticity computations show that demand tends to be more elastic at relatively high than at relatively low prices. Look at Table 10–1 and Figure 10–10 again. At the high price and low quantity levels the percentage change in quantity will be relatively high because of the low base by which the change in quantity is divided while the percentage change in price will be relatively low because of the high base price by which the change in price is divided. At low price and high quantity levels the situation is reversed. The percentage change in quantity is relatively much lower and the percentage change in price is relatively much greater. For most demand curves these conditions will hold.

In general, then, demand tends to be more elastic for goods that have good substitutes, are important in consumer budgets, and where the price changes considered occur on the upper part of the demand curve. Demand tends to be least elastic for goods that have no good substitutes, are insignificant in consumers' budgets, and where price changes occur on the lower part of the demand curve.

SUMMARY

Demand, which provides the motivating force for economic activity, originates with individual consumers. An individual consumer has unlimited wants but, because of budget considerations, is limited in the extent to which those wants can be satisfied. Indifference curve techniques show how the consumer's resolution of this problem generates the consumer's demand curves for goods and services.

An individual consumer usually will choose to allocate available income among different goods and services in a way such that the consumer's satisfaction level is as high as possible. The consumer's preference pattern, or tastes and preferences, are represented graphically by an indifference map. The budget constraint is depicted as the budget line. The consumer maximizes satisfaction by choosing the combination of goods and services on the budget line at which the budget line is just tangent to an indifference curve. The combinations of goods and services comprising that indifference curve yield the highest level of satisfaction that the consumer's budget will permit.

The consumer's demand curve for one good is derived by changing the price of the good, holding "other things" constant, and observing the quantities of it that will be taken at the different prices. At each different price of the good the consumer must be purchasing the satisfaction-maximizing quantities of *all* goods and services at the time we observe the quantity of the one. The resulting set of quantities and prices for the good under consideration constitutes the consumer's demand schedule for it and can be plotted as the demand curve.

The market demand curve for a product is the horizontal summation of individual consumer demand curves for it. To obtain it we simply add together the quantities per unit of time that all consumers together will take at each possible price.

Virtually all demand schedules and demand curves conform to the law of demand, exhibiting an inverse relationship between price and quantity that will be purchased per unit of time. However, the responsiveness of quantity purchased to price changes will differ from product to product. Price elasticity of demand for any one good measures the responsiveness of its quantity to small changes in its price. Elasticity of demand has important implications for pricing decisions of business firms and for economic policy making because of its relationship to the total expenditures that consumers will make on a product.

QUESTIONS AND PROBLEMS

1. Draw and explain the nature of a consumer's indifference map for hot dogs and gasoline.
2. What happens to a consumer's budget line for hot dogs and gasoline if the consumer's income increases? Show with a diagram and explain.
3. State and explain the conditions under which a consumer maximizes satisfaction.
4. Using indifference curve techniques to aid you in your answer, what impact would you expect rising gasoline prices (relative to other prices) to have on gasoline consumption?
5. Given the market demand curve for toothpaste, if a one percent decrease in price leads a one percent increase in the quantity purchased, what can we say about
   a. elasticity of demand for the price change?
   b. the effect of the price change on the total receipts of sellers of toothpaste?

Chapter 11

The foundations of supply

In much the same way that demand originates with individual consumers, supply originates with individual production units or business firms. Thousands of firms make decisions with regard to what goods and services to supply and how much of each to supply. These decisions depend upon the demand for the various products and on what it costs to produce them. In this chapter we develop the cost side of the picture. First, we examine a typical firm's production function. Second, we discuss the firm's cost outlays. Third, we observe how a firm determines its least-cost combination of resources. Fourth, we establish the various cost curves for the firm.

THE FIRM'S PRODUCTION FUNCTION

Production activity is carried on by individual firms that vary greatly in size and in the nature of their production activities. Some are engaged in extracting minerals from the ground. Others take semi-produced or semifinished materials and process them into forms closer to that in which they are sold to consumers. Still others, like grocery stores, buy products that appear to be in finished form and sell them to consumers. But the production process for an item is not really complete until it reaches the hands of its ultimate user. Thus inventories of groceries in the supermarket are really semifinished goods—production is completed as the buyer walks away from the check stand with the sack of groceries.

Figure 11–1
The production process for a firm

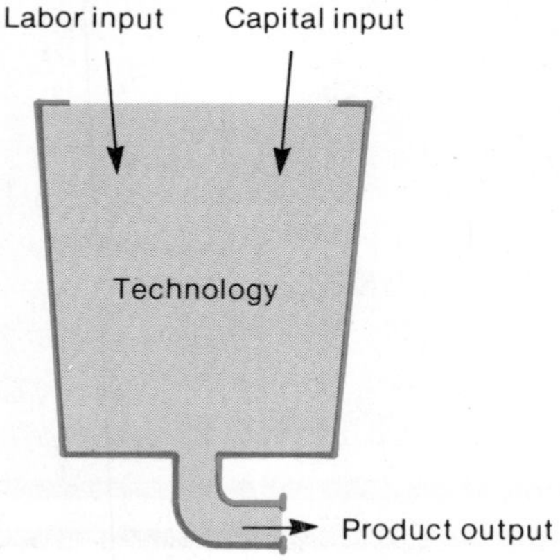

Conceptually, the production process is essentially the same for all firms. Schematically, as in Figure 11–1, a firm obtains labor and capital resource inputs, stirs them with stick in a particular technological manner, and products outputs of processed items. The relationship between the input quantities per unit of time and the output quantities per unit of time is called the firm's *production function,* the term function being used in a mathematical sense to denote the dependency relation of outputs to inputs. A firm's production function is influenced greatly by the law of diminishing returns. The production function is usually depicted diagrammatically by economists as an isoquant map. We shall look at each of these in turn.

The law of diminishing returns

Many happenings are blamed on the law of diminishing returns—usually erroneously so. If over the years a wife's love for her husband diminishes, this development is laid at the door of the law of diminishing returns. But the use of the term in economics is much more specific than that; it is used to describe an important feature of a firm's production. The *law of diminishing returns* states that if the firm increases its inputs of one resource by equal increments, holding the quantities of other resource inputs constant, the resulting increments in product output will eventually become smaller and smaller.

Ordinarily we would expect that, with a given level of technology, increases in *both* labor and capital inputs will increase a firm's output. We expect also that if *only one* input is increased, output will increase. A little reflection, together with everyday observations, will indicate that there is a limit to how much output quantities can rise from increases in the quantities of one resource input only. The existence of such a limit, determined by the fixed quantities of the other resource inputs, means that the law of diminishing returns must operate.

Suppose, for example, that a piece of land is planted with a given quantity of seed corn and that labor as an input is variable in quantity. The more labor that is used per year on the given complex of land and seed corn, the smaller will be the increment in product output from a one-unit increment in labor. In Table 11–1 the labor column and the output column illustrate the law of diminishing returns. Note that with nine

Table 11–1
The law of diminishing returns

Land (acres)	Seed corn (bushels)	Labor (person-hours per year)	Output (bushels per year)	Marginal physical product of labor (bu. per person-hour)
1	1	1	15	15
1	1	2	29	14
1	1	3	42	13
1	1	4	54	12
1	1	5	64	10
1	1	6	72	8
1	1	7	78	6
1	1	8	82	4
1	1	9	84	2
1	1	10	84	0

or ten units of labor we show the land and seed corn complex reaching its maximum output capacity.

The law of diminishing returns for one resource operates because there is an absolute maximum output quantity that a given complex of other resources can produce. A given amount of capital with which variable quantities of labor can be used has finite limits on the total output level that it can sustain. And the more labor that is used on the capital the less capital each worker has to work with and the less will be the contribution of an additional worker to the firm's total output.

The increase in a firm's output resulting from a one-unit increment in the input of one resource, holding the quantities of other resource inputs constant, is called the *marginal physical product* of the variable resource. In Table 11–1 the output level when four units of labor per year are used is 54 bushels of corn. If the quantity of labor used were five instead of four the output level would be 64 bushels. So the marginal physical product of labor for the fifth unit of labor used is 10 bushels of corn. The law of diminishing returns can be restated in terms of the marginal physical product of the variable resource. Equal increments in the variable resource, hold ing other resources constant in quantity, eventually result in diminishing marginal physical product of the variable resource. The last column of Table 11–1 illustrates the computation of the marginal physical product of labor, MPP_L, and the operation of the law of diminishing returns.

The firm's isoquant map

Graphically, a firm's production function is plotted as an isoquant map. An isoquant map is similar in concept to a consumer's indifference map, except that it related quantities of resource inputs to quantities of product output. Suppose that a firm uses two resources, capital and labor, to produce shirts.

Any one *isoquant* shows the different combinations of the two resources that will produce a given quantity of the product per unit of time (the word "isoquant" means "equal quantities"). In Figure 11–2, suppose that ten shirts can be produced by using seven units of capital and one unit of labor per unit of time. Point *A* locates that capital-labor combination. Suppose also that four units of capital and two units of labor will produce ten shirts. This combination is represented by point *B*. Similarly, suppose that either two units of capital and three units of labor or one unit of capital and four units of labor will produce ten shirts. Point *C* and *D*, respectively, are determined. Altogether such points as *A*, *B*, *C*, and *D* form the ten-shirt isoquant. But note that there is no actual geometric measurement of shirts in the diagram.

It appears reasonable that if combination *B* produces 10 shirts, combination *F* will produce a larger quantity, say, 15

Figure 11–2
An isoquant map for a firm

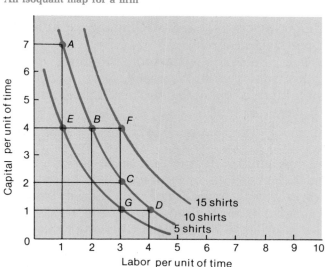

shirts. Combination F contains more labor and the same amount of capital as does B. All combinations that will produce 15 shirts trace out the 15-shirt isoquant. Similarly all combinations of labor and capital that will produce five shirts locate the five-shirt isoquant. Many more isoquants could be drawn in Figure 11–2; in fact, one could be drawn for every conceivable level of production. Altogether they constitute the firm's *isoquant map.*

Isoquants exhibit the same characteristics as indifference curves. First, they are downward sloping to the right. Second, they are non-intersecting. Third, they are convex toward the origin of the diagram.

The downward slope of an isoquant indicates that the marginal physical product of each resource is positive, or greater than zero. In Figure 11–2 suppose the firm is using combination C initially. If the firm gives up a unit of capital without changing the quantity of labor, total output will fall, unless the isoquant is vertical from C to G. In fact total output will fall by an amount equal to the change in the quantity of capital of Δk multiplied by the MPP_K. In this particular case the decrease in output is:

$$\Delta k \cdot MPP_K = 1 \times 5 \text{ shirts} = 5 \text{ shirts.}$$

We know that MPP_K is 5 shirts because the one-unit decrease in the quantity of capital employed reduces total output from 15 to 10 shirts. But the same reasoning will hold whatever the MPP_K happens to be—as long as it is positive, a reduction in the quantity capital used, holding the quantity of labor constant, will decrease output.

In order to hold output constant at 15 shirts when the amount of capital employed is decreased, labor must be substituted for capital in the production process. Enough additional labor must be used so that:

$$-\Delta k \cdot MPP_K = \Delta l \cdot MPP_L = 5 \text{ shirts;}$$

that is, the addition to output from the additional labor used must just compensate for the decrease in output resulting from the decrease in the quantity of capital used. Since an increase in one resource is required to compensate for a decrease in another in order to hold output constant, an isoquant for the two resources will necessarily slope downward to the right.

An intersection of two isoquants would mean that the combination of labor and capital at the intersection yields two different output levels. This is not reasonable if the firm always uses the most efficient technology available. One would expect that if a firm uses the most efficient technology available, higher output levels will require the use of greater quantities of one or more of the resource inputs.

Convexity of isoquants to the origin means that the larger the ratio of one resource to another, say labor to capital, the less of the second the firm can give up to get an additional unit of the first if output is to be kept constant. Consider combination *A* in Figure 11–3. If the firm is to hold output constant at ten shirts per unit of time, it could give up three units of capital to obtain an additional unit of labor. It would then be using combination *B*—more labor and less capital than before. If the firm moves from point *B* to point *C,* increasing the ratio of labor to capital, we show that only two units of capital would be given up for the additional unit of labor. From *C* and *D* only one unit of capital would be given up to get the additional unit of labor. The firm's decreasing capability of giving up capital to obtain additional units of labor is reflected by convexity to the origin of the isoquant.

But is convexity of an isoquant to be expected? The rate at which a firm can give up one resource to obtain an additional unit of another, holding the output level constant, is called

Figure 11–3
The marginal rate of technical substitution of labor for capital

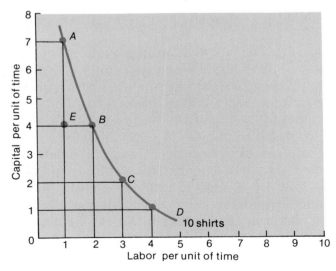

the *marginal rate of technical substitution* of the latter for
the first. In Figure 11–3, the marginal rate of technical substitution of labor for capital, or the $MRTS_{LK}$, between points A
and B is 3. Three units of capital can be given up to obtain
the additional unit of labor. Letting the change in capital be
Δk and the change in labor be Δl, then

$$MRTS_{LK} = -\frac{\Delta k}{\Delta l} = -\frac{3}{1} = -3,$$

which is the slope of the isoquant between points A and B.
We can ignore the sign and concern ourselves only with the
absolute value of the number. Between A and B we know
that:

$$-\Delta k \cdot MPP_K = \Delta l \cdot MPP_L$$

or:

$$-\frac{\Delta k}{\Delta l} = \frac{MPP_L}{MPP_K}.$$

Consequently:

$$MRTS_{LK} = -\frac{\Delta k}{\Delta l} = \frac{MPP_L}{MPP_K} = \text{the slope of the isoquant.}$$

Convexity to the origin occurs if as we move from A to B to
C to D:

$$MRTS_{LK} = -\frac{\Delta k}{\Delta l} = \frac{MPP_L}{MPP_K}$$

is decreasing. The law of diminishing returns assures that this
will be so. As the ratio of labor to capital is increased—more
and more labor per unit of capital is used—the MPP_L will
decline and the MPP_K will increase. The MPP_K increases because less and less capital is being used per unit of labor.

The firm's isoquant map thus provide a fairly complete picture of what it takes to convert resource inputs into outputs
of product. Any one isoquant shows the combinations of resources that are needed to produce a given level of output.
A complete set of isoquants shows all possible output levels
and the resource combinations that can be used to produce
them.

THE FIRM'S COST OUTLAYS

The amounts and the combinations of resources that a firm can use are limited by its total cost outlays and the prices it must pay for resources. Suppose the firm's cost outlay T is eight dollars per unit of time, the price of capital p_K is two dollars per unit, and the price of labor p_L is one dollar per unit. In Figure 11–4 if the entire cost outlay is made for capital, the firm can purchase T/p_K or four units of capital. On the other hand if it spends the entire amount for labor it can purchase T/p_L or eight units of labor. The line AB joining these two points shows the limits to the combinations of labor and capital that the firm can purchase and is called an *isocost* (meaning equal cost) curve. Note at each combination of capital and labor shown by the line, like that at point D, the total cost outlay is eight dollars.

The *slope* of the isocost curve shows the rate at which the firm is able to trade capital for labor in resource markets, given the prices of the resources. If the firm were initially purchasing combination E with its eight dollar total cost oulay and wanted to move to combination D, it must give up one unit of capital to obtain the additional two units of labor; that is, the slope of the line is one half. The slope of the isocost

Figure 11–4
The firm's isocost curves

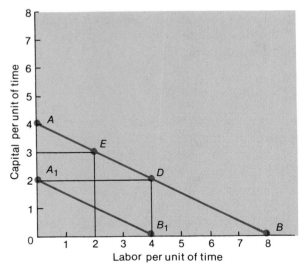

curve is determined by the ratio of the price of labor to the price of capital. It is measured by:

$$\frac{\dfrac{T}{p_K}}{\dfrac{T}{p_L}} = \frac{T}{p_K} \cdot \frac{p_L}{T} = \frac{p_L}{p_K}.$$

If the price of labor is one dollar per unit and the price of capital is two dollars per unit, then the firm must give up one unit of capital to obtain two units of labor, or \$1/\$2 determines that the isocost slope is one half.

The *position* of the isocost curve is determined by the firm's total cost outlay. If the total cost outlay were cut in half to four dollars with p_K and p_L remaining constant at two dollars and one dollar, respectively, the isocost curve would be shifted inward to $A_1 B_1$. An increase in the firm's total cost outlay would shift the isocost curve outward parallel to itself.

EFFICIENT RESOURCE COMBINATIONS

The manager of a firm would ordinarily be expected to seek efficiency in the operation of its production facilities. Efficiency is measured in terms of the relationship of output to input. Under most circumstances we would expect the firm to move toward obtaining the maximum output possible for any given cost outlay. We shall consider the conditions that must be met in order for this objective to be met. Then we shall develop the firm's expansion path.

Maximum output for a given cost outlay

The isoquant map and the isocost curve of Figure 11–5 illustrate the determination of the firm's most efficient combination of resources, given its cost outlay. The isocost curve $K_t L_t$ is determined by the firm's cost outlay and by the prices of labor and capital. The firm can obtain any combination of labor and capital on or below the curve. If the name of the game is efficiency, the firm will use the resource combination that will produce the maximum possible output; that is, the combination that will put it on the highest possible isoquant. Combination A containing k_1 units of capital and l_1 units of labor

Figure 11–5
Maximum output resource combination

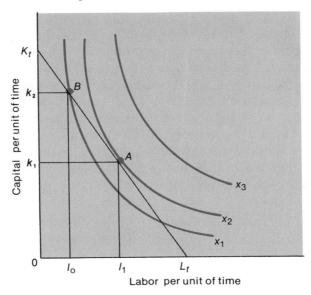

is the appropriate one, and quantity x_2 of shirts is the maximum possible output. Combination B containing k_2 units of capital and l_0 units of labor could have been chosen but note that a smaller amount of product, x_1, would have been produced. A larger amount of product like x_3 is not attainable with the given cost outlay.

Combination A of capital and labor is the combination at which the firm's given isocost curve is tangent to an isoquant. That isoquant is the highest one the firm can reach. Note that at point A the slope of the isoquant, MPP_L/MPP_K, is the same as the slope of the isocost, p_L/p_K; that is

$$\frac{MPP_L}{MPP_K} = \frac{p_L}{p_K}$$

or:

$$\frac{MPP_L}{p_L} = \frac{MPP_K}{p_K}$$

This last equality means the firm is spending its cost outlay to purchase the combination of labor and capital at which a dollar's worth of labor contributes the same increment to the firm's output as does a dollar's worth of capital. Or, to put it another way, the combination is such that the marginal physical product of a dollar's worth of labor is the same as the marginal physical product of a dollar's worth of capital. No dollar of cost outlay could contribute more to the firm's output if switched from its present use to the purchase of an additional dollar's worth of another resource. These are the conditions that must be met if a firm is to produce efficiently.

The common sense of the efficiency conditions can be seen more clearly if we consider combination B. At point B the firm is producing an output of x_1 shirts. The slope of the isoquant at that point is determined by MPP_L/MPP_K and it is greater than the slope of the isocost, p_L/p_K.

If:

$$\frac{MPP_L}{MPP_K} > \frac{p_L}{p_K},$$

then:

$$\frac{MPP_L}{p_L} > \frac{MPP_K}{p_K}.$$

This means the marginal physical product of a dollar's worth of labor is greater than the marginal physical product of a dollar's worth of capital at point B. The marginal physical product of a dollar's worth of capital tells us how many shirts the firm would lose by giving up a dollar's worth of capital. The marginal physical product of a dollar's worth of labor is the number of shirts the firm would gain by adding a dollar's worth of labor. So if:

$$\frac{MPP_L}{p_L} > \frac{MPP_K}{p_K},$$

the firm can increase its output by transferring dollars away from capital resources toward labor resources with *no change* in its total cost outlay. Thus, it would move down the isocost curve from B toward A getting on higher and higher isoquants until it reaches an output level of x_2 shirts at point A.

The expansion path and costs of production

The firm—unlike a consumer—is not confined to a given cost outlay, but is relatively free to increase it or decrease

Figure 11–6
The expansion path

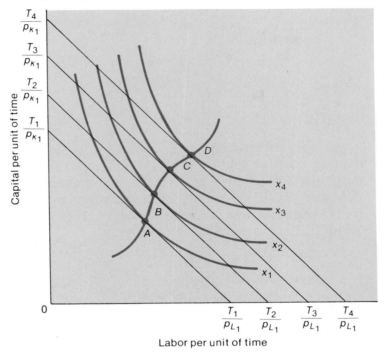

Labor per unit of time

it as its managers may desire. Instead of a given isocost curve, the typical firm has a family of isocost curves like those of Figure 11–6. Total expenditures on captial and labor are increased from T_1 to T_2 to T_3 to T_4 while the prices of capital and labor are held constant at p_{K1} and p_{L1}, respectively. For each possible level of expenditure on resources for each isocost curve there is a most efficient combination of labor and capital. These are indicated by points A, B, C, and D. Points like A, B, C, and D trace out the firm's *expansion path* showing all of the efficient combination of capital and labor as the firm increases its cost outlays and its level of production. Note that at point A the total cost outlay is T, and the product output is x_1. At point B the total cost outlay is T_2 and the output is x_2. Points C and D show the maximum outputs obtainable with cost outlays T_3 and T_4. Table 11–2 shows the relationship between outputs and costs—$x_1 < x_2 < x_3 < x_4$ and $T_1 < T_2 < T_3 < T_4$.

Table 11–2
Relation between output level and costs

Output	Cost
x_1	T_1
x_2	T_2
x_3	T_3
x_4	T_4

COSTS OF PRODUCTION

The firm's expansion path is the bridge between its production function and its costs. But as we cross it we should make certain that we understand the economic meaning of the term "costs." We consider first the fundamental cost concepts. Then we turn to the firm's cost curves.

Fundamental cost concepts

Alternative costs.   The principle of *alternative costs,* or opportunity costs as they are often called, is fundamental to economic analysis. We met this concept in Chapter 1, but it is so important that it bears reemphasis at this point. The cost to the economy of a firm's output is the values of other outputs that could have been produced if the resources the firm uses had been used instead to produce those other outputs. Thus, the cost of producing a bushel of wheat is the value of the farm products that must be given up in order to produce it. Or, looking at the concept from a slightly different viewpoint, the cost of the resources used by a firm is the value of what those resources could produce in their best alternative uses.

Explicit costs.   Most of a firm's costs of production are paid out directly to hire or buy the resources it needs to produce its product output. Such expenditures are called *explicit costs.* They include the costs of hiring labor, leasing land, purchasing raw and semifinished materials, and the like. Sometimes we refer to them as out-of-the-pocket expenses. Usually they coincide fairly well with accounting costs.

Implicit costs.   Some of a firm's costs are the costs of firm-owned or self-employed resources. These are called *implicit costs* because they frequently do not show up on the firm's books of account or are not paid out directly to hire or buy resources. A family business provides a common example. The proprietor of a small grocery store pays out money to rent and equip part of a building and also purchases stocks of groceries. These are explicit costs. But the labor of the proprietor's family is frequently not taken into account as a cost. The labor expended in operating the business could have been hired out to someone else and used to produce other products. Suppose that the family members could have earned $30,000 per year if they had worked for someone else. The value of the labor in its best alternative use is clearly a cost of production in the business—$30,000 in this case—whether it is so recorded in books of account or not. It is an implicit cost.

For corporations the average earnings of stockholders are an important implicit cost of production. The stockholders of a corporation own its assets and that part of the corporation's net earnings necessary to provide an average rate of return to stockholders on their investment is an implicit cost of production. It is what corporations must yield to stockholders to induce them to maintain their investment in the plant and equipment that corporations (i.e., their stockholders) own. Accounting procedures do not consider average yields to stockholders in the form of dividends and/or appreciation of the value of stock as costs; however, from the point of view of economics they must be treated as such.

The cost curves of a firm

In order to determine how much product it should produce a firm must be able to estimate what the production costs of each of various alternative output levels will be. The total cost or *TC* of alternative output levels is of greatest importance, but there are several components of total cost that are useful analytically. We shall look at these in turn for a firm that has estimated what its daily costs of production will be.

Total costs.   In the first four columns of Table 11–3 we list the firm's best estimates of what its total costs will be for various output levels per day. Column (2) lists *total fixed costs,* or *TFC.* These are the costs that are associated with the firm's size—costs of its plant, heavy equipment, and key management personnel. They are incurred whether or not the firm produces anything, and they do not change as the output level is in-

Table 11–3
Costs of production per day for a firm

(1) Output (X)	(2) Total fixed costs (TFC)	(3) Total variable costs (TVC)	(4) Total costs (TC)	(5) Average fixed costs (AFC)	(6) Average variable costs (AVC)	(7) Average costs (AC)	(8) Marginal costs (MC)
1	$10	2	$12	$10.00	$2.00	$12.00	2
2	10	4	14	5.00	2.00	7.00	2
3	10	7	17	3.33	2.33	5.67	3
4	10	11	21	2.15	2.75	5.25	4
5	10	16	26	2.00	3.20	5.20	5
6	10	22	32	1.67	3.67	5.34	6
7	10	29	39	1.43	4.14	5.57	7
8	10	37	47	1.25	4.62	5.87	8
9	10	46	56	1.11	5.11	6.22	9
10	10	56	66	1.00	5.60	6.60	10

creased or decreased. In order to exist a firm must incur certain minimum total *fixed costs* for *fixed resources,* such as those listed above. Suppose that total fixed costs are $10 per day. They are plotted as the *TFC* curve in Figure 11–7.

There are many resources that the firm runs through its plant in order to produce its product output. It must purchase raw and semifinished materials, labor, power, transportation services, and the like. These are the firm's *variable resources.*

Figure 11–7
Total cost curves for a firm

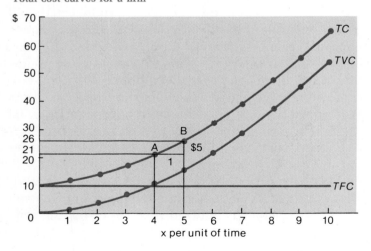

If it produces no output it does not need to purchase any of them. The more output it produces, the larger the quantities of variable resources needed. The costs incurred by the firm for variable resources are its *total variable costs* or *TVC*. Obviously the greater the desired output level of the firm, the greater will be its total variable costs. The T values in Figure 11–6 and Table 11–2 are total variable cost concepts.

The total variable cost associated with each possible output level must be the *minimum* variable cost of producing each one. At each possible output level a least-cost combination of variable resources must be used as we indicated in Figure 11–6. In Figure 11–6 and Table 11–2, T_1, T_2, T_3, and T_4 are the minimum total variable costs of producing outputs x_1, x_2, x_3, and x_4, respectively. Numerical content is given to them in columns (1) and (3) of Table 11–3. They are plotted in Figure 11–7 as the *TVC* curve.

Column (4) of Table 11–3 is the *total cost* or *TC*, column. It is computed simply by adding together the *TFC* and the *TVC* at each output level. The relationship between *TC* and the output level is represented graphically by *TC* in Figure 11–7.

Per unit costs. Columns (5) through (8) of Table 11–3 are derived from the total cost columns. The relationships of average cost, or *AC*, to the level of output is shown by column (7) with columns (5) and (6) providing a breakdown of average cost into its component parts. Column (8) lists marginal costs— a new concept that we will examine shortly.

When we divide *TFC* by output at each of the possible output levels we obtain *average fixed costs*, or *AFC*. Since *TFC* is constant for all output levels, *AFC* as recorded in column (5) must decline as output increases. In Figure 11–8, column (5) is plotted as the *AFC* curve.

In a similar way *AVC* of column (6) is determined by dividing *TVC* by output, and *AC* of column (7) results from dividing *TC* by output at each of the various output levels. Columns (6) and (7) are plotted as *AVC* and *AC*, respectively, in Figure 11–8.

Marginal cost, or *MC*, is a different concept. It is defined as the change in total costs per unit change in the firm's output; that is, as TC/x. Thus in column (4) if output is increased from one to two units per day, *TC* increases from \$12 to \$14

Figure 11–8
Per unit cost curves for a firm

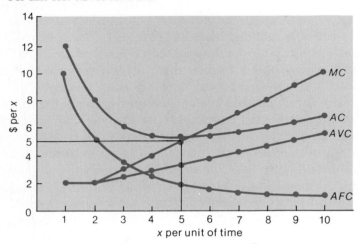

and *MC* is $2. When output is increased from 6 to 7 units per day *TC* increases from $32 to $39 and *MC* is $7. The *MC* schedule for output levels of two through ten units is recorded in column (8) and is plotted as *MC* in Figure 11–8.

Relationships of *MC* to *TC* and *AC*. Marginal cost and the slope of the firm's total cost curve at any given output level are the same thing. In Figure 11–7 note that at an output level of four units, *TC* is $21; and that at an output level of five units, *TC* is $26. Marginal cost of the fifth unit is $5, which is the slope of the *AB* segment of *TC* if the *AB* segment is considered to be a straight line. In Figure 11–8, *MC* at the five-unit output level is thus plotted as $5—five $1 units above the base line. The same relationship can be established for every other output level. We can reason that the increasing slope of the *TC* curve in Figure 11–7, beginning with the two-unit output level, and the increasing *MC* curve in Figure 11–8, beginning with the two-unit output level, give us exactly the same information.

The relationships between *MC* and *AC* for a firm are illustrated in Figure 11–8. They are also indicated numerically in Table 11–3. When *MC* is less than *AC, MC* is pulling *AC* down; that is the *MC* curve *always* lies below the *AC* curve when *AC* is decreasing. When *MC* is greater than *AC, MC* is pulling *AC* up; that is, when *AC* is rising *MC* is greater than *AC*. It follows that the MC curve cuts the AC curve at the output level where AC is minimum—changing from decreasing to increasing.

SUMMARY

The quantities per unit of time of a product that will be supplied at various possible prices depend upon what it costs individual firms to produce them. Production costs depend in turn on the production functions of firms and on the costs of resource inputs. We have examined production functions, cost outlays, efficiency in production, and costs of production in some detail in order to better understand the mechanism of supply.

The production function of a firm relates its product output to its resource inputs and is shown graphically as an isoquant map. The operation of the law of diminishing returns for any one variable resource input is an important and distinguishing characteristic of a firm's production function. Cost outlays of a firm, together with resource prices, determine the firm's isocost curves.

At any given level of cost outlay the most efficient combination of resources the firm can use is that at which the isocost is just tangent to an isoquant. The isoquant represents the highest output level that the given cost outlay can achieve. Or the isocost shows the least possible cost of producing the output level represented by the isoquant. The most efficient combination of resources is that at which the marginal physical product of a dollar's worth of one resource equals that of any other resource used. The tangency points of isoquants to a family of isocost curves, given the prices of the resources used, trace out the firm's expansion path.

A firm's costs include implicit as well as explicit costs of resources used. The true economic costs of resources used by the firm are alternative or opportunity costs. A firm's total costs of production can be subdivided into total fixed costs and total variable costs. Data for the latter come from isocost-isoquant analysis and the expansion path of the firm. From the total cost concepts, per unit costs at various output levels are derived. These are overall average costs which can be separated into average fixed costs and average variable costs. Marginal costs also are obtained from the total cost curve.

QUESTIONS AND PROBLEMS

1. Is a firm's production function a concept involving relationships among money values or is it concerned with physical relationships, only? Explain.

2. Explain the law of diminishing returns using land areas of uniform size and quality as the variable resource.

3. Suppose that a farm firm's daily marginal physical product schedules for labor and fertilizer used in producing wheat are those listed below. The price of fertilizer is $2 per pound. The price of labor is $10 per unit. If the firm makes a cost outlay of $36 per day on these two resources, how much of each should it use?

	Labor		Fertilizer	
Quantity	MPP_L		*Quantity*	MPP_F
1	28 bu.		1	10 bu.
2	24 bu.		2	8 bu.
3	20 bu.		3	6 bu.
4	16 bu.		4	4 bu.
5	12 bu.		5	2 bu.

4. Explain the relationship between a firm's expansion path and its total cost curve.

5. Draw and explain a complete set of total cost curves for a firm. Do the same for its per unit cost curves.

6. How is *MC* related to *TC?* to *AC?*

Chapter 12

Adjustments of supply and demand in competitive markets

CHECKLIST OF ECONOMIC CONCEPTS

Competitive markets
Mobility
Demand curve facing the firm
Total revenue curve
Marginal revenue
Profit maximization
Total cost curve
Marginal cost
Loss minimization
Supply curve of the firm
Economic profits
Economic losses
Long run
Entry into an industry
Exit from an industry

H uman wants are the prime movers in economic activity. Over time, the pattern of wants changes, responding to changing cultural, social, technological, and economic developments. As demand patterns change how can supply patterns be altered to meet them? In turn how do changes in potential supply patterns evolving from the development of new techniques, the discovery of new resource supplies, and the exhaustion of existing resource supplies affect the demand patterns? In this chapter we address ourselves to the forces that bring about adjustments in quantities produced and quantities demanded in a competitive market economy. First, we define competitive market structures. Second, we study the behavior of single producing and selling unit or firm. Third, we expand the analysis to encompass a set of competitive markets.

COMPETITIVE MARKET STRUCTURES

The processes adjusting supply to demand patterns are most easily seen in market structures that are *competitive*. Although there is much *imperfect competition* and some *monopoly* in our economy we shall assume for the present that competition prevails. In the following chapter we introduce monopoly and imperfect competition into the analysis to see how they affect the operation of the economy.

If the market for a specific good or service is to be considered competitive, several conditions must prevail. First, there must be *many sellers and buyers* of the product. Second, there must be *no price fixing*. Third, buyers and sellers must be *mobile*. Fourth, buyers and sellers must be *knowledgeable* as to what is available where and at what price.

Many sellers and many buyers of a product means that any one individual buyer or seller is insignificant in the market as a whole. One seller does not place a large enough part of the total supply of the product on the market to be able to affect its price. Consider, for example, a farmer who sells wheat. No one farmer is able to influence the market price. Similarly, in the market for oranges, how much influence do you as an individual buyer have?

If there is no price fixing in a market, the price of the product is free to move up and down in response to changes in demand and supply. If markets are to be truly competitive, the government must not set price ceilings or price flows. Neither can groups of buyers or groups of sellers acting in collusion.

Mobility implies that sellers are free to sell wherever they can find buyers and buyers are free to buy from any seller of the product. Ordinarily we would expect sellers to sell to whomever will pay them the highest price for the product. Similarly buyers will buy from whomever will sell to them at the lowest price. In essence mobility means that in the market for the product a single price will prevail.

However, if mobility of buyers and sellers is to have meaning and is to be exercised in a rational, logical way, buyers and sellers must have knowledge of economic data. They must know what goods and services and what resources are available, who is selling or buying them, and the prices that are being asked or offered for them.

Competitive markets in which the foregoing conditions are largely met furnish a useful approximation to how a private enterprise economy works. Once the set of principles underlying the operation of a competitive economy are firmly grasped, they can be appropriately modified to take into account the effects of monopoly, imperfect competition, governmental intervention, and the like.

A COMPETITIVE FIRM

On the supply side of the market for an item the individual firm is the basic economic unit. From the point of view of business organization the firm may be a single proprietorship, a partnership, or a corporation. Which form it takes is more important for purposes of description than for purposes of analysis. We shall consider in turn the objectives of a firm; the conditions that must be met for it to maximize profits; and the firm's supply curve for the product.

Objectives

Ask the manager of any firm why the firm is in business and the reply will be "to serve the public." This answer has a socially acceptable sound to it, but from the point of view of economics a more useful and usually more accurate answer would be "to make a profit." These two answers, as we shall see later, are not quite as divergent as they may appear to be at first glance.

Profit maximization seems to be a good first approximation to what firms try to achieve. The managers of firms are like most of the rest of us—they prefer more to less. If a firm is confronted with two alternative courses of action, one of which will yield more profit than the other, ordinarily it will choose the more profitable one, if the circumstances in which the actions are to be carried out are more or less the same. Followed to its logical conclusion choices of this type lead a firm toward activity that maximizes profits.

Firms may have additional objectives, of course. They may desire to obtain the goodwill of their customers. Managers may seek the approval of their fellow citizens. Some managers are empire builders. But in most instances such other objectives are not necessarily incompatible with profit maximization.

Profit maximization by a firm operating in a competitive market requires that the firm make choices among alternative output levels. Profit is the difference between the firm's total receipts or revenue and its total costs at each possible output level, so the managers of the firm must determine the paths of its revenues and its costs as the output level is increased or decreased.

Revenues

The competitive firm is too small relative to the entire product market in which it sells to be able to influence the price of the product. It can sell as much or as little as it desires at the price determined by the market as a whole. Suppose that the market price of phonograph records is seven dollars. At a higher price the individual firm can sell nothing. Buyers will purchase the product from other sellers who charge the market price of seven dollars. The individual firm does not need to accept a lower price since it can sell all that it wants to place on the market at that price.

The demand schedule for the individual firm's sales consists of the first two columns of Table 12–1. It shows how much the firm can sell at alternative price levels. Plotted in Figure 12–1, it is the horizontal line *dd*.

Once the market price of the product is known, the total

Table 12–1
Revenues of a firm

(1) Price (p)	(2) Quantity per u.t. (x)	(3) Total revenue (TR)	(4) Marginal revenue (MR)
$7	1	$ 7	$7
7	2	14	7
7	3	21	7
7	4	28	7
7	5	35	7
7	6	42	7
7	7	49	7
7	8	56	7
7	9	63	7
7	10	70	7

revenue of the firm at alternative sales levels is easily determined. At each output level the price is multiplied by the output
to obtain total revenue. The result is listed as column (3) in
Table 12–1. Plotted in Figure 12–2 the firm's total revenue curve,
TR, shows the relationship between its sales levels and its
total revenue.

Figure 12–1
The demand curve facing a competitive firm

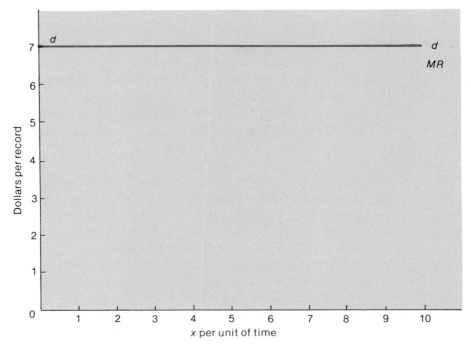

Figure 12–2
Total revenue curve of a competitive firm

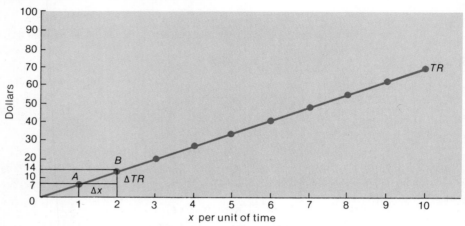

x per unit of time

The *TR* curve increases at a constant rate; that is, it is an upward sloping straight line from the origin of the diagram. In common sense terms, as Table 12–1 indicates, each one unit addition to output and sales adds seven dollars, or the price of the product, to the firm's total receipts. Each such *addition* to total receipts is called the *marginal revenue* or *MR* of the firm. In the example of Table 12–1 marginal revenue is seven dollars at each and every output level. Graphically it coincides with the *dd* curve of Figure 12–1.

In Figure 12–2, marginal revenue is measured by the slope of the *TR* curve. Note for example that if sales increase from one to two units, ΔTR or the change in total revenue is \$7 and Δx, the change in output is one unit. Marginal revenue is $\frac{\Delta TR}{\Delta x}$ or $\frac{\$7}{1}$ which is the slope of the *TR* curve between points A and B. Using the same reasoning we can easily verify that the slope of the *TR* curve between any other two output levels is $\frac{\$7}{1}$ which is *MR*.

Profit maximization and loss minimization

As discussed in the last chapter, the competitive firm's revenues combined with its costs determine the output of maximum profit for the firm. The total cost and the total revenue sched-

ules for a seller of phonograph records are listed in columns
(2) and (3) of Table 12–2. Marginal revenue and marginal cost
are listed in columns (4) and (5). Profits, the difference between
total revenue and total cost at each sales or output level, are
listed in column (6). Profits are maximum at a sales level of
either six or seven records. It will be convenient (and correct)
to consider the seven-unit output level to be the true maximum.

Note that profits are maximum at the output at which marginal revenue and marginal cost are equal. At outputs smaller
than six units *MR* exceeds *MC,* meaning that an increase in
output and sales will increase total receipts more than it increases total costs. Such an output increase raises the firm's
profits. Moving from six to seven units adds the same amount
to total cost that is added to total receipts and therefore adds
nothing more to profits. If the output is increased beyond the
seven-unit level, *MC* is greater than *MR.* This means that the
increase in total costs for such an expansion is greater than
the increase that it yields in total revenue. It causes profits
to decline. The basic condition, then, for profit maximization
by the firm is that it must choose the output level at which
its *MR* equals its *MC.* At that output its total receipts exceed
its total costs by the greatest possible amount.

Profit maximization by the firm is shown graphically in Figure 12–3. In Figure 12–3 (A) profit is measured by the vertical
distance between the *TR* and the *TC* curves. Output level *x*
is the one at which the spread is greatest; that is, it is the
output of maximum profit. At output *x* the slope of the *TR*

Table 12–2
Profit maximization by a firm

(1) Quantity per u.t. (x)	(2) Total revenue (TR)	(3) Total cost (TC)	(4) Marginal revenue (MR)	(5) Marginal cost (MC)	Profit (¶)
1	$ 7	$12	$7	—	(−)$ 5
2	14	14	7	$ 2	0
3	21	17	7	3	4
4	28	21	7	4	7
5	35	26	7	5	9
6	42	32	7	6	10
7	49	39	7	7	10
8	56	47	7	8	9
9	63	56	7	9	7
10	70	66	7	10	4

Figure 12–3
Profit maximization by a competitive firm

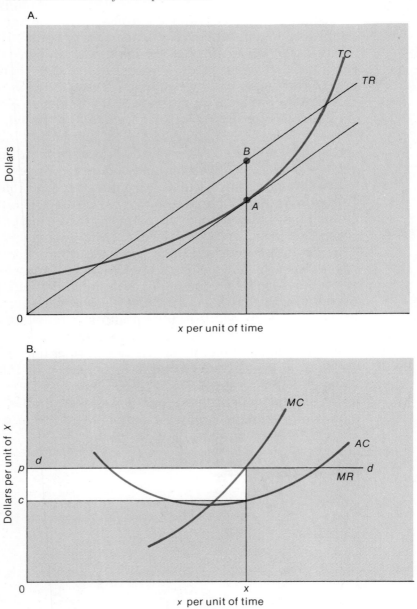

curve, or *MR,* is the same as the slope of the *TC* curve, or *MC.* Total profit at that output is *AB* dollars.

The same information is shown in per unit form in Figure 12–3(B). Output *x* is the one at which *MR* equals *MC.* At lower outputs *MR* is greater than *MC* so profits are increased by output expansion. Any output increase beyond *x* will increase total costs more than it will increase total receipts—that is, *MC* is greater than *MR* for the increase—which will cause profits to decrease. Profit per unit of sales at output *x* is measured by *cp,* price minus average cost at that output. Total profits, which are maximum at output *x,* are *cp* times *ox,* or the area of the shaded rectangle.

Individual firms do not always make profits. The market price of a product may be too low to cover the firm's average costs. If the firm expects the low price to be a temporary phenomenon, it may accept losses for a time and stay in business. If it expects that the low price will be permanent, the firm will accept losses only for the time that it takes to liquidate its plant and get out of the industry.

Minimization of losses is shown in Figure 12–4. The product price and *dd* are below the *AC* curve of Figure 12–4(B) at all output levels. This means that in Figure 12–4(A) the *TR* curve is below the *TC* curve at all output levels. The firm must incur losses no matter what output it produces; the problem is to find the output level at which total losses are least. In Figure 12–4(A) losses are measured at each output by the vertical distance between the *TC* curve and the *TR* curve, and they are minimum at output *x.* At output *x* the slope of the *TR* curve equals the slope of the *TC* curve; that is, *MR* equals *MC.* Consequently, in Figure 12–4(B) the loss minimizing output is also depicted as output *x.* Losses are *BA* in Figure 12–4(A). In Figure 12–4(B) they are *pc* times *ox* or the shaded area. Loss minimization like profit maximization occurs at the output level at which *MC* equals *MR.*

The firm's supply curve

How much product per unit of time will a firm supply at various possible price levels? Consider Figure 12–5. The firm faces the market price for its product and the demand curve facing the firm is horizontal at that price level. Since *MR* for the firm is the same as the product price, the *MR* curve of

Figure 12–4
Loss minimization by a competitive firm

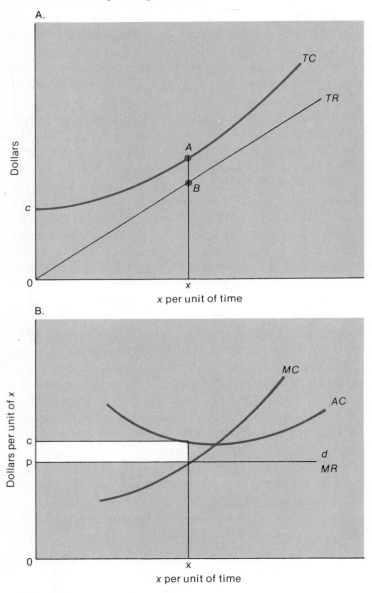

A.

B.

the firm coincides with the demand curve that it faces. If the
market price is p_1, the demand curve facing the firm is d_1d_1
and the marginal revenue curve is MR_1. Profits are maximum
at x_1, the output level at which $MC = MR_1$. So at price p_1
the firm will supply quantity x_1 per unit of time. Using the

Figure 12–5
The supply curve of a competitive firm

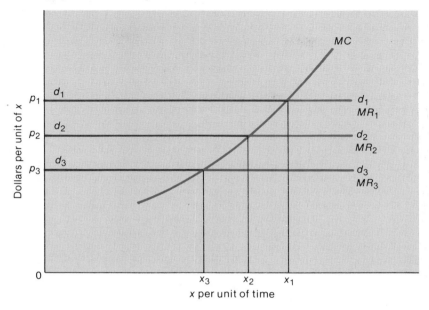

same reasoning, if the price were p_2 the firm would supply quantity x_2. If the price were p_3 the quantity placed on the market by the firm would be x_3. It becomes apparent that the firm's marginal cost curve is its supply curve for the product.

COMPETITIVE MARKETS

The pieces of the puzzle are almost in place. In Chapter 9 we learned that individual consumer demand is the basis for market demand and that the market demand curve for any given product is the horizontal summation of individual consumer demand curves for it. From the supply curves of individual firms the market supply curve for a product can be constructed. We can then determine the market price, individual firm output, and market output for the product.

The market supply curve

The market supply curve for a product is obtained from individual firm supply or marginal cost curves. Suppose in

Figure 12–6
The market supply curve

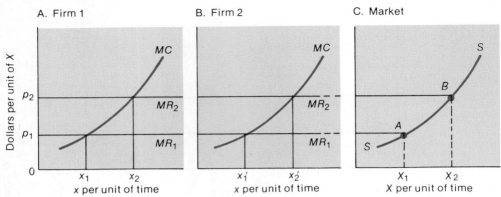

Figure 12–6 that Firm 1 and Firm 2 are two of many firms selling records. For all three diagrams the price-axis scales are identical. The quantity-axis scale for the market diagram is greatly compressed relative to those of the individual firm diagrams. At price p_1, Firm 1 maximizes profits by placing quantity x_1 on the market. Similarly, Firm 2 maximizes profits with quantity x_1'. Each of the many firms in the market produces the quantity at which its MC equals MR_1 and p_1. Adding together all the individual firm quantities that will be produced at price p_1 we obtain quantity X_1 for the market as a whole. This price and quantity determines point A on the market supply curve. Point B is determined by adding the quantities that all firms will supply at price p_2. Other points making up the market supply curve are established in the same way. The market supply curve SS is thus the horizontal summation of individual firm marginal cost or supply curves.

Price and outputs

The simultaneous determination of the market price, the individual firm output, and the market output of a product is illustrated in Figure 12–7. The market demand curve is the horizontal summation of individual consumer demand curves. The market supply curve is the horizontal summation of individual firm supply curves. Price p is the equilibrium price.

The representative firm is confronted with market price p, and demand curve dd for its own output. Its marginal revenue

Figure 12–7

A. Representative firm

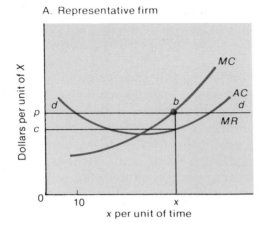

B. Market

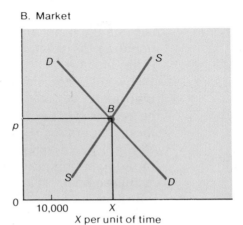

curve *MR* coincides with *dd*. The profit maximizing output is *x* at which *MC* equals *MR*. Profits of the firm are *cp* times *Ox*.

The market output level is *OX* and is obtained by adding together the outputs of all firms in the industry. (Note: How did we obtain point *B* on the market supply curve)? Again, quantity scale of the market diagram must be considerably compressed in comparison with that of the representative firm if we are to get both diagrams on the same page. We obtain approximately the right perspective if we let the same distance that measures 10 units of the product on the firm's diagram represent 10,000 units on the market diagram.

Profits and losses

We have used the terms *profits* and *losses* to indicate positive and negative differences between the total revenues and the total costs of a firm. These terms can be ambiguous. They do not have the same meaning to a student of economics that they have to the general public.

The "profits" of a firm are understood ordinarily by the general public to mean the net income of the firm as net income is defined by usual accounting procedures. But a problem arises because the definition of costs from an accounting point of view is not the same as the definition of costs from an economics point of view. In accounting procedures the return

that accrue to investors in the firm—that is, to its owners—
are not costs of production. But students of economics consider
as costs the costs of *all* resources used to produce the product
including the costs of the resources furnished by the owners
of the business.

The net income figure—"profit" to the general public—ar-
rived at for an accounting period by a firm's accountants is
the return that is available for the owners of the business.
These owners are the stockholders of the corporation, the part-
ners in a partnership, or the proprietor of a single proprietorship, depending upon the legal form of the firm. Owners of a
business expect at least an average return on their investment
in it. Such an average return is the cost to the firm of holding
the owner's resources in the business—the cost of preventing
those resources from going elsewhere into other productive
endeavors in the economy. *This cost is built into the cost
curves of the firm.* If the net income of the firm is just sufficient
to yield an average return on investment to its owners the
economic profit of the firm is zero. Its average cost curve is
just tangent to the demand curve it faces as we show in Figure
12–8. The firm is not in trouble. Zero profit means that the
firm is doing as well as the average firm in the economy. (Have
you shifted your mental gears yet from the "profit" concept

Figure 12–8

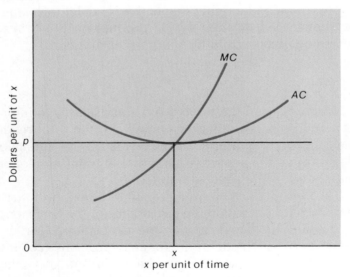

held by the general public to the concept of *economic profit?)* If net income is greater than the total amount necessary to yield an average return on investment to the firm's owners, *economic profit* exists. If net income is less than the amount that would provide an average yield, the firm is incurring *economic losses.* We use the terms *profits* and *losses* in this book in the economic sense only.

Entry and exit of firms

Over an extended period of time it is possible for potential firms to enter or for existing firms to leave a competitive industry. In the competitive world, shifts in the productive capacity of the economy from any one line of production to others would occur in this way. The length of the time period necessary for entry and/or exit will vary, depending upon the industries involved. Some, like hot dog stands, may be easily and quickly entered. Others, like textile mill, will require a longer planning and construction period. Whatever the time span necessary for firms to enter or exit a given industry we refer to that period as the *long run* for that industry. For different industries the long run will encompass different time spans.

The force that motivates the entry of new firms into an industry is profit possibilities. When the firms in an industry are making profits they provide the investors in those firms with higher than average returns on their investments. Higher than average returns seldom go unnoticed. In the long run they attract new investment and new firms in.

On the other hand losses provide the incentive for firms in an industry to leave it. Losses mean that returns to investors in the industry are below the average for investors economy wide; however, they do not necessarily signify that the net income of the firm is negative. It may or it may not be. But investors will want to withdraw their investments from the loss-incurring industry and reinvest other industries where the returns will be greater.

The cause and the effects of entry into a competitive industry are illustrated in Figure 12–9. Let the initial demand and supply curves for calculators be *DD* and *SS.* Suppose that the average cost and marginal cost curves of a representative firm selling them are *AC* and *MC.* The product price is *p;* the individual

Figure 12–9
Entry into a competitive industry

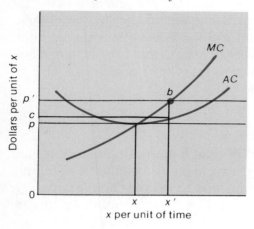

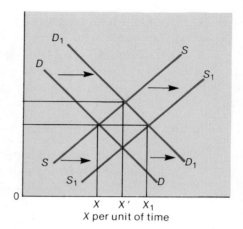

firm output is x; and the market output level is X. No profits or losses are being made so there is no incentive for new firms to enter or for existing firms to exit.

Now suppose that consumer preferences in the economy shift away from slide rules and toward calculators. The demand curve shifts to the right from DD to D_1D_1, raising the product to price p'. Firms in the calculator industry now make profits; those of the representative firm of Figure 12–9 are cp' times Ox'.

In the long run the greater than average rate of return on investment in this industry attracts new investment in. With the entry of new firms there are more MC curves to add horizontally to obtain the industry supply curve; consequently, it shifts to the right toward S_1S_1. The increasing supply presses the market price down, decreasing the profits of individual firms. However, as long as profits can be made by entering firms, the industry is a good one in which to invest. Entry will stop when enough firms have entered to cause the price of the produce to be equal to the minimum average costs of production of the representative firm; that is, when profits have been reduced to zero. In Figure 12–9 this occurs when the supply curve reaches position S_1S_1; price is p; individual firm output is x; and total market output is X_1. In response to the increase in demand the total productive capacity and the total output of the industry has been increased by the entrance of new firms.

Now consider the slide rule industry. In Figure 12–10 let the initial demand and supply curves for slide rules be *DD* and *SS*, resulting in a market price of *p* and creating zero profit situation. Now suppose that consumer preferences shift away from slide rules toward calculators, causing the demand for slide rules to decrease to D_1D_1. The market price will fall to *p'* and the market output will fall to *Y'*. Individual firm output will decrease to *y'* and losses equal to *p'c* times *Oy'* will occur.

In the long run the losses induce firms to leave the industry since they yield a less than average return on investment. As firms exist the market supply curve shifts to the left toward S_1S_1 because of the reduction in the number of *MC* curves that are added horizontally to get the market supply curve. The product price rises from *p'* as supply decreases, but as long as the price is below the minimum points of individual firm *AC* curves, losses are incurred and exit continues. When enough firms have left to bring price up to the level of the minimum *AC's* of individual firms losses become zero, the rate of return on investment is equal to the economy-wide average, and the exodus of firms stops. Industry output has decreased to Y_1 because of the reduction in the productive capacity of the industry.

Profits and losses operate continually to redirect productive capacity in an economy characterized by competition. Where profits exist, returns on investment are above average. Where

Figure 12–10
Exit from a competitive industry

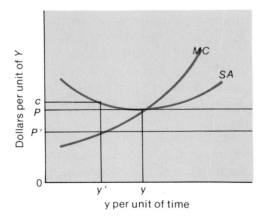
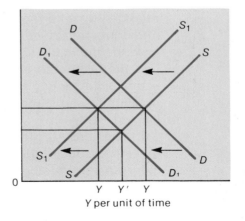

losses occur, returns on investment are below average. So investment is constantly being redirected from less valuable to more valuable uses. Profits and losses thus play a key role in a private enterprise economic system.

THE ECONOMIC FUNCTIONS OF PROFITS AND LOSSES

There is much controversy over profits and the flames of controversy have been fanned high by the inflation that has been with us since the last half of the 1960s. Some of it is the result of ideological conflicts; some of it reflects a misunderstanding of the role that profits and losses play in guiding and directing a private enterprise economy; and some of it comes from deep-seated beliefs that the economic system is not competitive enough to respond to profit and loss incentives. We cannot hope to resolve the first and third sources of controversy. But the competitive model provides an excellent platform for dispelling misunderstandings about what profits and losses are supposed to do.

Patterns of demand for consumers as a group are ever changing. On a week to week, a month to month, or even a year to year basis the pattern appears to change slowly. Yet when demand patterns now are compared with what they were 25 or 30 years ago, the change is quite startling. Many new products have come into existence. Many old ones have disappeared, and substantial shifts have occurred in the proportions in which many are now demanded and supplied.

Profits and losses are the guiding and directing mechanism that rechannels productive capacity in the directions that consumers want it to go. As demand patterns shift, prices rise relative to costs for firms producing the items for which demand has increased. Prices fall relative to costs for firms that produce the items from which demand has turned. The former become profitable and the latter incur losses. Profits are the economic signals reporting the areas where productive capacity should be expanded. Losses signal where it should be contracted.

In the long run the higher than average rate of return on investment in profit-making areas attracts additional investment and productive capacity into them. By the same token the loss-incurring areas repel investors, inducing investment and productive capacity to leave. As capacity expands in the former areas the profits decline toward zero. In the latter areas, as capacity shrinks, prices rise and the losses move toward zero.

In the competitive model there are no restrictions on entry into the production of any good or service. Consequently, productive capacity would be expected to follow changes in demand patterns accurately and with reasonable quickness. Competition among sellers hold prices down sufficiently to prevent sellers from taking advantage of buyers. Similarly, competition among buyers holds prices up enough to prevent buyers from taking advantage of sellers. The competitive system works automatically with no need for government or other direction or control. But, as we shall see in the next chapter, monopoly elements throw sand in the gears. The important question—and one that has not been answered to everyone's satisfaction—is that of how much sand they inject. Is there enough competition so that profits and losses can do their jobs and so that sellers or buyers are not able to take advantage of one another? That is, is the economy *workably* competitive?

SUMMARY

What are the incentives tending to induce the productive capacity of an economy to respond to changing consumer demand patterns over time? The incentives are seen most easily in the competitive market model in which buyers and sellers each are small relative to the markets in which they operate; price fixing does not occur; buyers and sellers are mobile; and buyers and sellers are knowledgeable.

An individual firm in any given industry usually attempts to maximize its profits or minimize its losses. In order to do so it must adjust output to the level at which its marginal cost equals its marginal revenue. Marginal revenue for the firm is equal to the price of the product that it sells since the firm faces a horizontal demand curve for its output at the level of the market price. The marginal cost curve of the firm is its supply curve.

In an economic model made up of competitive industries, the market supply curve of any one industry is the horizontal summation of the marginal cost curves of the firms in the industry. Market price is determined in the market as a whole by the interaction of buyers and sellers. An individual firm sees that price as given and adjusts output so as to maximize profits. Market or industry output is the summation of individual firm outputs.

In industries where economic profits are made, outputs should be expanded; they should be contracted in industries incurring losses. Thus profits and losses signal the changes in productive capacity that should be made in the economy. They also provide the incentives for those changes to be made. Where profits occur the rate of return on investment is greater than the average for the economy. Losses mean a less than average return on investments. Investors in the economy's productive capacity thus have an income incentive to move their investment—and the economy's productive capacity— in response to profits and losses.

QUESTIONS AND PROBLEMS

1. What are the major characteristics of a competitive market? Explain each one.

2. What do you think the objectives of Gulf Oil Corporation should be? ABC Supermarket? Horton's farm in western Kansas?

3. Draw a representative *TR* and *TC* curve for a competitive firm. Below it, using an identical quantity scale draw the corresponding *dd* and *MR* curves, along with the *AC* and *MC* curves. Show the profit-maximizing output on each diagram (they should be the same). Explain *MR* and *MC* in terms of the *upper* diagram. Explain *MR, TC,* and profits in terms of the lower diagram.

4. Show with a set of diagrams the simultaneous determination of market price, individual firm output, and market output for a competitive industry.

5. The technological breakthrough lending to the development of small electric calculators resulted in an upward surge of demand for them and larger profit for the few firms making them. What has happened in the few years since that time to outputs and prices? Why?

Chapter 13

The monopolistic response to demand

A t the other end of the market structure spectrum stand the markets characterized by monopoly. In the extreme case we find *pure monopoly,* defined as a market in which there is only one seller of a product for which there are no good substitutes. In between the extremes of purely competitive markets on the one hand and purely monopolistic markets on the other we find those in which competition and monopoly are commingled. The degree of monopoly or of competition may differ considerably from market to market. These are usually referred to as *imperfectly competitive* market structures. We will look first at pure monopoly and then at imperfect competition.

PURE MONOPOLY

A market of pure monopoly results in different price, output, profit, and efficiency characteristics from those of pure competition. However, there are similarities between the way a monopolistic firm operates and the way a purely competitive firm behaves. It is useful in setting up the monopoly model and in analyzing its results to compare it with a purely competitive firm and market. First, it is important to note how demand and marginal revenue look to a monopolist. Second, we shall consider its profit maximizing conditions. Third, we shall analyze the effects of demand change on the output of the industry. Finally, we shall direct our attention to the "evils" of monopoly in a private enterprise economic system.

Demand and marginal revenue

Whereas a purely competitive firm faces a horizontal demand curve for its output, a firm that is a pure monopolist faces the market demand curve. This is so because the pure monopolist is the only firm selling the product. It is the industry on the selling side. It can sell at various possible prices exactly the amounts that the public will take at those prices. Suppose, for example, that Table 13–1 reflects the market for pizzas. The market demand schedule is composed of columns (1) and (2). They show the quantities of pizzas that consumers will buy at various alternative prices, other things being equal. They also show the quantities that the monopolist can sell at various alternative price levels, other things being equal; that is, they comprise the demand schedule facing the firm.

Table 13–1
Market demand and revenues for a monopolistic seller of pizzas

(1) Price	(2) Quantity per u.t.	(3) Total revenue	(4) Marginal revenue
$10	1	$10	$10
9	2	18	8
8	3	24	6
7	4	28	4
6	5	30	2
5	6	30	0
4	7	28	(−) 2
3	8	24	(−) 4
2	9	18	(−) 6
1	10	10	(−) 8

The *DD* curve of Figure 13–1 (A) provides exactly the same information.

Marginal revenue for a monopolistic seller is defined in the same way that it is for a purely competitive seller. It is the change in the seller's total receipts per unit change in the quantity sold per unit of time. However, for the monopolistic seller marginal revenue is not equal to the product price, as it was for the purely competitive seller—it is less than the product price, except for the increase from a zero sales level to a 1-unit sales level. The reason for the difference between marginal revenue and price can be deduced from Table 13–1. Consider the 3-unit sales level. The price is $8 and total receipts are $24 since each of the three units is sold at that price. Now suppose that the monopolist increases sales by one unit. In order to sell four units it must reduce the per unit price to $7. Although the fourth unit sells for $7 and yields a $7 increase in revenue, the other 3 units, which formerly sold for $8 each, now also sell for $7 each. So, increasing the sales level to four causes a reduction in the firm's revenue of $1 each for each of those 3 units. Subtracting the $3 reduction from the $7 gain leaves the firm with a new increase in revenue or marginal revenue of $4 when it increases sales from 3 units to 4 units per unit of time. Try the same kind of logic for an increase in the sales level from 4 to 5.

Marginal revenue for sales levels from one unit through ten units is listed in column (4) of Table 13–1. It is plotted as *MR* in Figure 13–1(A). If the range of output levels of a monopolistic seller is large, say in the hundreds, a one-unit output

Figure 13–1
Market demand and revenues for a monopolistic seller of pizzas

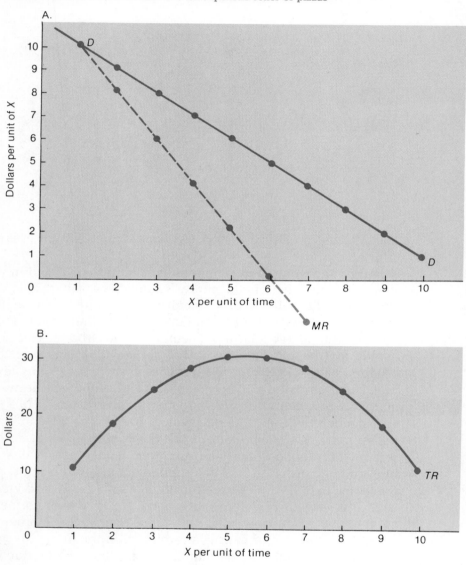

level would not be distinguishable from the vertical axis of the diagram. For all practical purposes then, the demand curve facing the monopolist and the firm's marginal revenue curve both start from a common point on the vertical axis. We will show them as such in the remainder of the diagrams we use.

The total revenue of a monopolist plotted for various sales

levels yields a total revenue curve different in appearance from that of a purely competitive firm. As we noted in Chapter 12, a purely competitive firm's total receipts curve starts at the origin of the diagram and is a straight line sloping upward to the right. This was so because the pure competitor can sell all it desires to sell at the market price, and each addition to the sales level adds an amount equal to that market price to the firm's total receipts. Not so for a monopolist. In order to increase sales a monopolist must decrease its selling price. The result is a total receipts schedule like that of column (3) in Table 13–1 and a total receipts curve such as TR in Figure 13–1(B). Note that output level at which TR is maximum is also the output level at which MR is zero. Can you explain why this is so?

Profit maximization

In order to maximize profits a pure monopolist, like a pure competitor, chooses the output level at which its total receipts exceed its total costs by the greatest possible amount. Figure 13–2(A) shows output level x as the one that accomplishes this objective. From a common sense point of view the slopes of the TC curve and the TR curve must be the same at the profit maximizing output. At an output lower than x the slope of TR exceeds that of TC and the curves will spread farther apart as output is increased up to x. Increases in output beyond x bring the two curves closer together since the slope of the TR curve will be less than that of the TC curve.

What we are really saying is that profits are maximum at the output level at which marginal revenue equals marginal cost. The slope of the TR curve at any given output level *is* marginal revenue for that output. The slope of the TC curve at any given output level *is* marginal cost for that output level. To say that profits are maximum at the output level at which $MR = MC$ is simply another way of saying that profits are maximum at the output level at which the slope of the TR curve equals the slope of the TC curve. Below output x in Figure 13–2, $MR > MC$ and profits will increase with an increase in output. Above output x, $MR < MC$ and profits will decrease with an increase in output.

Total profits are measured in Figure 13–2(A) by the distance TE, which is the same as the distance AB. Total receipts are OE, or xB. Total costs are OT, or xA.

Figure 13–2
Profit maximization by a monopolist

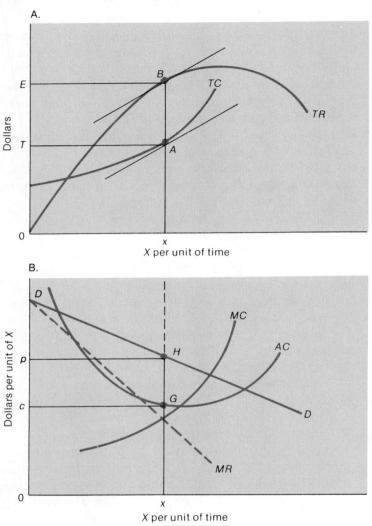

A.

B.

In Figure 13–2(B) we pick up a little more information about the firm's situation. For output x the firm can obtain price $0p$, which is the same as xH. Its average cost at that output is $0c$, or xG. Profits per unit of product are cp or GH. Total profit is profit per unit multiplied by the number of units produced and sold. Total profits are equal to $cp \cdot 0x$, or to the area $cpHG$.

Pay careful attention to the difference in the way total profits are measured in the two diagrams of Figure 13–2. In Figure 13–2(A) the vertical line *AB*, or *TE* is the measure. In Figure 13–2(B) they are measured by the area *cpHG*.

Entry into and exit from the industry

Profits and/or losses provide the same indications in markets of pure monopoly that they do in markets of pure competition as to whether or not the society as a whole desires expansion or contraction of the output of any give monopolized product relative to the outputs of other products. Where profits occur investors earn higher than average rates of return on their investments. Buyers of those products yielding profits value the resources used in producing them more highly than they value those same resources in their alternative uses— that is, they are willing to pay more for such products than it costs to produce them. The profits are the society's way of indicating that it wants the outputs of such products expanded relative to the outputs of other products. Similarly, where losses occur investors are receiving less than average rates of return on their investments. Consumers are not willing to pay as much for such products as it costs to produce them. Resources are worth less to them in producing such items than those same resources are worth in their best alternative uses. The society is indicating that it wants the outputs of these goods and services contracted relative to the outputs of other goods and services. In monopoly as in pure competition, profits and losses provide incentives for channeling investment and, consequently, productive capacity from the loss-incurring to the profit-making areas of the economy.

Successful monopoly over time in a profit-making industry is possibly only if the monopolist can prevent new firms from entering the market. The profits provide incentives for new firms to enter. But for the monopolist to remain a monopolist over the long run, entry into the industry must somehow be blocked. Barriers to entry may exist in imperfectly competitive industries although they may not block entry completely. They do not exist at all in purely competitive industries. Barriers to the entry of new firms into an industry may take one or more of several forms, conveniently classified into *artificial* barriers and *natural* barriers.

The very term "artificial barriers" implies that such barriers could be eliminated if the society were strongly enough inclined to do so. In fact most artificial barriers to entry are established and enforced by governmental units. They include patent rights; tariffs on imports of foreign goods; licensing of businesses that sell certain products (for example, alcoholic beverages and taxicab services); licensing of persons who want to pursue certain occupations such as plumbing, undertaking, or medicine; zoning laws and building codes; direct regulation of entry into many areas of transportation, nuclear energy, broadcasting, and other fields. The list goes on and on. Artificial barriers may also be imposed by the firm (or firms) already in a given market. Price manipulations or predatory pricing may be used. Suppose, for example, that when new firms want to enter an industry in which the existing firm (or firms) is making profits, the existing firm simply cuts prices to levels that the potential entrant cannot meet. Potential entrants, likely to be less efficient than the existing firm or firms, may never be able to gain a foothold in the industry. Still another privately imposed artificial barrier occurs when one firm (or a few firms) own the raw materials needed for making the product. The potential entrant is simply denied access to the resources and thus is unable to enter. Additional

Figure 13–3
The natural monopoly case

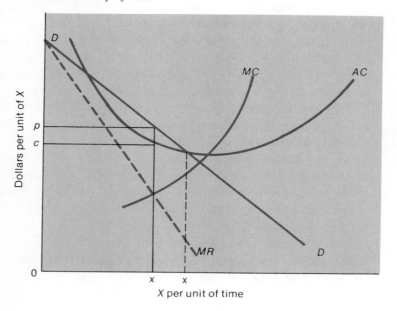

artificial barriers could be listed, but these will suffice for illustrative purposes.

The primary natural barrier to entry exists in the so-called natural monopoly case. In the typical case the firm requires a very sizeable scale of operation in order to produce efficiently. American Telephone and Telegraph Company is an example. The larger the size of the firm and the greater its output level, the lower its average costs will be up to some relatively large limit. The initial firm in such a field has an advantage over potential entrants. For example, in Figure 13–3 the initial firm maximizes profits by producing output x and selling at price p. Profits are $cp \cdot Ox$. What would happen to profits if a new firm with cost curves like those of the existing firm were to come into the market? Industry output would be expanded well beyond x'—the no-profit output for one firm—and both the existing firm and the entering firm would incur losses. Who wants to come into an industry under circumstances like these? In addition to telephone service, natural monopoly is thought to be common in public utilities such as natural gas, electricity, water purification and distribution and the like.

If a monopolist incurs losses like $pc \cdot Ox$ in Figure 13–4 on a long-run basis, it will exit from the industry. The firm's

Figure 13–4
Monopolistic losses

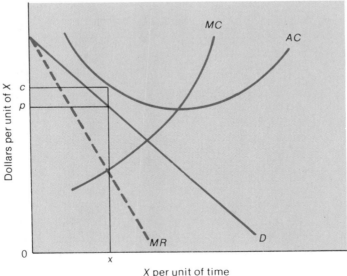

operations are not paying an average rate of return on the investment in it and its owners will seek greener pastures elsewhere. Ordinarily there are no barriers to exit except those that a government may impose. A firm can get out of the industry as soon as it can liquidate its assets unless, as in the case of airlines, buses, or trains, the government forces it to continue service to specified communities.

The "evils" of monopoly

Monopolistic economic "sins" take three unrelated forms in a private enterprise economy. First, the total output of a monopolized product is restricted below what the consuming public would like relative to other goods and services. Second, monopoly prevents productive capacity from being allocated in accordance with consumer demand patterns. Third, monopolistic producers may tend to produce at inefficient output levels. We shall look at these points in turn.

Output restriction.   To obtain an understanding of monopolistic output restriction we start with a purely competitive market in Figure 13–5. The average cost curve of the representative firm is omitted—we do not need it for the present analysis. Ignore the *MR* curve in the market diagram for the moment. The market price of the product is *p*, the representative firm

Figure 13–5
Output restriction under monopoly

A. Firm

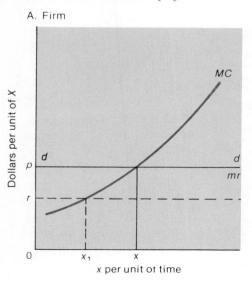

B. Market

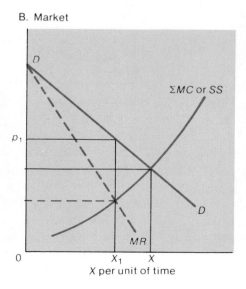

output is x, and the entire market output is X. These reults stem from the profit-maximizing activities of the many firms in the industry. Each firm produces an output level at which its marginal cost equals its marginal revenue, and marginal revenue for each firm is equal to the market price. Thus we can say, correctly, that each firm produces an output at which its marginal cost equals the market price of the product.

What would happen to the market price and output if the industry were now monopolized? Suppose that one firm obtains control of all the production facilities in the industry. What were once individual firms now become production plants for the monopolist. The demand curve facing the individual firm in the diagram on the left disappears, taking with it the firm's marginal revenue curve. The demand curve facing the monopolist is the market demand curve DD in the diagram on the right. Since DD is downward sloping to the right, the marginal revenue curve MR will like below it. The monopolist's marginal cost curve is ΣMC, the horizontal sum of the marginal cost curves of its many plants. The monopolist maximizes profits by reducing industry output to X_1, where its marginal cost and marginal revenue are the same. Market price rises to p_1. To minimize its costs the monopolist produces an output level such as x_1 in each of its plants—that is, where marginal cost in each plant is equal to industry marginal revenue r. The reduction in output and the increase in price resulting from monopolization of the industry is not due to malevolence on the part of the monopolist; it is due to the monopolist's desire to maximize profits—the same incentive that motivates a pure competitor.

Misallocation of productive capacity. In the long run in competitive markets, when profits exist new firms enter until the profit is eroded away and investors in the industry are making an average rate of return on their investments in productive capacity. In monopolized markets entry into such a profit-making industry is blocked; consequently, new firms cannot come in to expand its productive capacity.

Figure 13-6 illustrates the comparative long-run situations of competitive industries and monopolized industries. In Figure 13-6(A) the productive capacity of industry X has settled into a no-profit no-loss condition. Consumers pay a price p_x that just covers average costs of production (including an average rate of return to investors in the industry's productive capacity). By way of contrast, Figure 13-6(B) shows long-run equi-

Figure 13–6
Industry long-run equilibrium

A. Pure competition

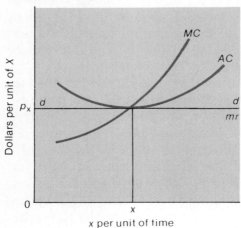

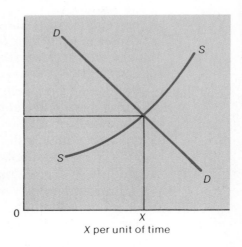

B. Pure monopoly

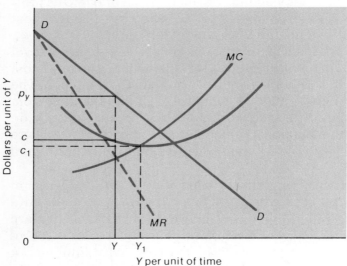

librium for a monopolist. This monopolist makes profits of
$cp_y \cdot OY$. The price that consumers pay for the product is
higher than the average cost of producing it. Investors receive
a higher than average rate of return on their investment. Output
restriction by the monopolist, coupled with blocked entry into
the industry, bring about these results. The society would like

relatively more of the economy's productive capacity to be used in making product Y; that is, productive capacity is poorly allocated with too little of it being used in monopolized industries.

Inefficiency.   Even when monopolists are maximizing their profits they may use the resources of the economy inefficiently. Inefficiency may show up in two ways. In the first place it occurs when an economy does not use units of its resources to produce the product most highly valued by consumers. Thus, the misallocation of resources brought about by the existence of monopoly in some industries is itself a manifestation of inefficiency. In the second place, if there is only one firm in an industry, the profit-maximizing output level may not be the one most conducive to efficiency in production.

Figure 13–6 helps explain the relations among market structures, firm output, and efficiency. In Figure 13–6(A) we have a purely competitive firm and industry in long-run equilibrium. Enough firms have entered so that no firm makes profits or incurs losses. For each firm in the industry the price and the average cost of the product are equal. But, since the demand curve facing a firm is horizontal, the no-profit and no-loss situation means that the firm is producing an output—x in the diagram—at which its average cost is least. At no other output will its average cost be as low as p_x; that is, no other output level can be produced as efficiently as X is produced.

By way of contrast, consider the monopolist of Figure 13–6(B). Profits are maximum at output level Y. Entry into the industry is blocked, so the firm—which is also the industry on the production and selling side—and the industry are in long-run equilibrium. Output Y—the profit-maximizing output—is not the output level at which the firm's average cost is lowest; that is, at which the firm is most efficient. Average costs are lowest at output Y_1 where they are c_1. This output is the monopolist's most efficient output level. But there is no inducement for the monopolist to produce at the most efficient output level. Instead, it is induced to produce the profit-maximizing output.

IMPERFECT COMPETITION

Between the limits of pure competition on the one hand and pure monopoly on the other are the markets that come under the general heading of *imperfect competition*. In any one such market there will be more than one firm; but there will not be enough for it to be purely competitive. Consequently, we find a mixture of competitive and monopolistic characteristics. We will examine demand and marginal revenue; profit maximization; incentives to engage in collusive activities; incentives to break away from collusive arrangements; profits and losses; entry and exit; and the concept of "workable competition."

Demand and marginal revenue

The demand curve facing the firm in an imperfectly competitive market is in most cases downward sloping to the right, like that of a monopolist. Typically one firm is large enough relative to the market as a whole to be able to influence the price of the product; that is, the firm can increase industry output enough to make the price of the product go down, or it can cause the price to rise by withholding the product from the market. General Motors Corporation is surely in such a position; yet the demand curve facing the firm will tend to be rather elastic because there are several firms selling the same product. By cutting the price below that charged by other

Figure 13–7
Profit maximization under imperfect competition

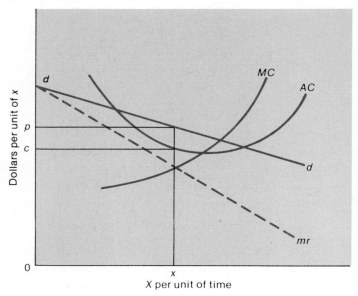

firms, one firm can cut into the market shares of the other firms. So the quantities that one firm can sell tend to be rather responsive to changes in the price that it charges.

If the demand curve facing the firm has a downward slope, the firm's marginal revenue curve lies below the demand curve as Figure 13–7 illustrates. Only if the demand curve were horizontal, like that facing a purely competitive firm, would the marginal revenue curve coincide with the demand curve. So, typically, the demand curve and the marginal revenue curve for the firm operating in an imperfectly competitive market will look something like *dd* and *mr* in Figure 13–7, although they need not be straight lines.

Profit maximization or loss minimization

To maximize profits a firm in an imperfectly competitive market follows the same rules that a pure monopolist and a firm in a purely competitive market follow. It must produce and sell the output at which its marginal costs are equal to its marginal revenue. In Figure 13–7 profits are maximum at output x. The product price is p; average cost at that output is c; and profits are $cp \cdot 0x$.

Loss minimization by an imperfectly competitive firm is identical to loss minimization by a monopolist. If at all possible output levels the firm's average cost exceeds the price it can get for its product, losses are inevitable. They are minimum at the output at which the firm's marginal cost equals its marginal revenue. For a review of loss minimization look again at Figure 13–4.

Profits, losses, entry, and exit

The economic functions of profits and losses are the same in imperfectly competitive markets as they are in the other market structures that we have considered. They provide the signals indicating where the productive capacity of the economy should be expanded and where it should be contracted. In the industries where profits are made, the consumers of the economy are indicating that they value the resources used in producing those products more than they value them in alternative uses; that is, they want the outputs of the profit-making industries expanded. Where losses are incurred, consumers value resources less than in alternative uses—outputs of the products produced in these industries should be contracted.

The conditions of entry into profit-making areas vary a great deal among different imperfectly competitive industries. Entry may be totally sealed off in some instances—for example, the taxicab industry in New York City. In others it may be partially blocked, as in the case of the steel industry. Foreign producers of steel cannot sell in the United States at prices below a calculated "trigger-point" level. In still other industries entry may be relatively open but the production unit size necessary for efficiency may be so large relative to the entire market that only a few firms can exist in the industry. The automobile industry is a case in point.

Restricted or blocked entry into industries where profits are made inhibits a full response of the economy's productive capacity to the pattern of consumer demand. To the extent that entry is restricted or blocked in imperfectly competitive (as well as monopolistic) industries, outputs will be relatively too small, prices will be relatively too high, and profits will be made in the long run.

In some imperfectly competitive industries where entry is open, new firms may enter until profits become zero. Textile industries and the barbering industry provide examples. In a case of this kind where profits are made the entry of new firms reduces the market available to each firm, shifting the demand curve facing the firm to the left. When enough firms have entered to make the demand curve facing each firm just tangent to its average cost curve, as illustrated in Figure 13–8, profits will be zero and entry will cease. The output of a representative firm will be x. The product price and the firm's average cost will be p. Note that in an industry of this type there may be some inefficiency in the sense that an individual firm does not produce the precise output at which its average cost is minimum. However, productive capacity can follow consumer demand patterns with a fair degree of accuracy; output restriction by the individual firm and by the industry is minimal.

Exit of productive capacity from industries where losses are incurred poses no great problem. The return on investment in such industries is less than can be earned elsewhere in the economy. Consequently, as soon as possible, investors

Figure 13–8
A no-profit situation under imperfect competition

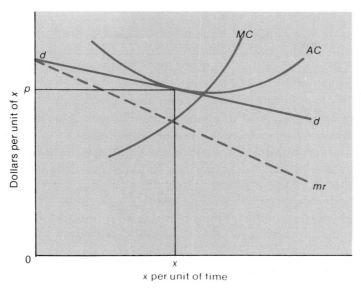

will leave the industry, reducing product output and causing the price to rise until losses are no longer incurred by those firms that remain.

Price and nonprice competition

Contrary to the case of pure competition in which the actions of one firm have no effects on the market as a whole, when one firm in an imperfectly competitive market cuts the price at which it sells or engages in other activities that increase its sales, other firms in the market are affected. In the usual case each firm in an imperfectly competitive market has a significant share of the total market. Firms are vying for market shares and if one firm is successful in increasing its market share, there is less of the market left for others. The other firms find that the demand curves they face have shifted to the left.

There are three major types of action that a firm can take to expand its sales. These are price cutting, advertising its product, and changes in the design and/or quality of the product. All three are common in the world about us. Price cutting tactics are often engaged in by gasoline service stations. General merchandise stores and supermarkets cut prices for their weekend specials and periodic sales. But the firm that seeks to expand its sales by cutting its price faces a serious problem. Other firms can cut their prices, too, thus thwarting the intentions of the price cutter. *All* firms may end up with lower prices and profits than they were making before the price cutting occurred.

Advertising and changes in product design and/or quality are often referred to as *nonprice competition*. When they are used by any one firm in the market they are not as easily followed or copied by other firms and, hence, are less dangerous to the firm that desires to increase its sales. Examples of advertising abound in the news media, on television, and almost anywhere else that one cares to look. The automobile industry furnishes one of the best examples of changes in product quality and/or design with its annual model changes.

Incentives for and against collusion

Because of their dependence on what other firms do in the market, firms operating in imperfectly competitive markets in many instances find themselves surrounded by an atmosphere of uncertainty. They are not sure what other firms in the market are going to do, nor are they sure what effects actions of the other firms will have on them. This uncertainty becomes an incentive for the firms in the market to act jointly or to collude in order to reduce it.

The firms in a market may try to collude in order to obtain monopoly profit. We saw in the competitive case that monopolization of such a market would reduce output, raise the product price, and increase profits. The same reasoning applies in the case of imperfect competition. If the firms of the industry get together and act as a monopoly, they can avoid rivalrous price cutting and milk the industry for monopoly profits.

Collusion among the firms in a market may also be a device for impeding the entry of new firms. Together they may be able to accomplish what no one of them could do individually. At the same time they protect their profits from potential intruders.

A collusive arrangement among several firms tends to be hard to hold together. Suppose that through collusion a monopoly-like price is being charged by each firm. If one firm now cuts its price slightly while the other firms hold to the market price level, the price-cutting firm can pick up some of the other firms' market shares and profits. This temptation is always present. Successful collusion occurs only when the colluders are able to police the market effectively against price cutting.

WORKABLE COMPETITION

The economic world in which we live obviously is not characterized throughout by purely competitive market structures, although there are segments of it in which pure competition in buying, in selling, or in both is approached. Neither is pure monopoly the predominant market form. The largest part of the economy's output is produced and sold under conditions of imperfect competition. The important and persistent questions are (1) how well does it perform now and (2) how well is it likely to perform over time?

To perform in a manner that is acceptable to a society, a predominately private enterprise economy must be "workably competitive." Prices, profits, and losses must be able to guide and direct production reasonably well in accordance with consumer demand patterns. Entry barriers into markets must not be unduly restrictive. Collusive price fixing by buyers and/or sellers must be minimal. But how can we determine the meanings of such phrases as "reasonably well," "not unduly restrictive," and "minimal?" Judgments are involved and the people making them may have access to varying sets of facts and may make different interpretations of what the facts show. In short, workable competition is difficult to define.

From the point of view of market structures, abstracting from governmental interference in the processes of pricing and production, sand in the gears of workable competition comes from two related sources: (1) monopoly and collusive (monopoly-like) pricing and output and (2) restricted or blocked entry into profit-making industries. How well the economy continues to perform over the years to come depends very heavily on the extent to which monopoly elements and collusion can be controlled.

SUMMARY

Reallocation of an economy's productive capacity in response to changing patterns of consumer demand is impeded by monopolistic elements. The extreme monopoly market structure, at the opposite pole from pure competition, is pure monopoly. Between the extremes of pure monopoly and pure competition are markets of imperfect competition.

The pure monopoly firm differs from the pure competition firm in that it faces the market demand curve for its product. The demand curve slopes downward to the right and the marginal revenue curve is below it. Profits are maximum, or losses are minimum, at the output level for which MC equals MR. To remain a pure monopolist the firm must have entry into the monopolized market blocked. Either or both artificial and natural barriers to entry may be established.

Pure monopoly engenders three related economic sins. First, it brings about output restriction in monopolized industries. Second, it results in misallocation of the economy's productive capacity. Third, it may cause inefficiency in production.

Imperfect competition combines competitive and monopolistic elements. What one firm does in a given market affects what other firms in the market are able to do. Price cutting and nonprice competition may bring about an atmosphere of uncertainty causing firms to collude in a monopolistic manner. At the same time, any firm in a collusive arrangement will have an incentive to break away from the group and act independently.

In markets of imperfect competition entry conditions run the gamut from completely open to completely blocked. Thus, depending upon the significance of entry barriers, productive capacity may or may not follow consumer demand patterns quickly and accurately.

For a private enterprise system to operate effectively, it must be workably competitive. It must keep monopolistic elements under such control that output restriction, misallocation of productive capacity, and inefficiency do not unduly inhibit the achievement of high and rising levels of economic performance.

QUESTIONS AND PROBLEMS

1. From the following demand schedule for cartons of cornflakes, complete total revenue and marginal revenue at each sales level as the sales level is increased from one through ten cartons per day. Plot both the demand curve and the marginal revenue curve.

Price	Quantity	TR	MR
$50	0	___	___
45	1	___	___
40	2	___	___
35	3	___	___
30	4	___	___
25	5	___	___
20	6	___	___
15	7	___	___
12	8	___	___
9	9	___	___
6	10	___	___

2. Using a *TR* and an *MR* curve explain profit maximization by a monopolist. Do the same thing using per unit diagrams.

3. Does output restriction by a monopolist mean that a monopolistic firm pursues different objectives from those of a competitive firm?

4. In what ways does imperfect competition differ from pure monopoly? Pure competition?

5. List and explain the major means by which entry into an industry is restricted. Of what significance for the operation of the economy is entry restriction?

6. Do you think we should restrict the importation of textiles from the Peoples Republic of China? Automobiles from Japan? Why or why not?

Chapter 14

The pricing and employment of resources

A n economy's resources—its labor and its capital—are owned by its households. Households earn their incomes by selling or hiring out the services of the resources that they own. So the prices that households can obtain for their resources and the amounts per time unit that they can place in employment are of great importance to them.

The classification of resources into labor and capital categories is nothing more than an analytical convenience. There are many different kinds of labor and many different kinds of capital, each of which can be thought of as a different resource. In this chapter we use common labor as an example, but the principles that we develop are applicable to the pricing and employment of any resource. We consider first the demand for a resource. Next we look at its supply. Third, we consider pricing and employment levels of a resource.

RESOURCE DEMAND

Demand for any one kind of resource originates with the firms that use it as an ingredient in producing their products. They are its purchasers or buyers. In purchasing resources, as in selling their product outputs, the primary objective of firms is assumed to be profit maximization. In order to maximize profits a firm must follow a pattern in resource purchases similar to the one it uses in producing and selling its product output. If the use of additional units of a resource will add more to the firm's total revenues than they add to its total costs, the firm's profits will be increased (or its losses will be decreased) if the employment level per unit of time is expanded. Similarly, if decreases in the amount of the resource used per unit of time will subtract less from total receipts than they will subtract from total costs, profits are increased by reducing the employment level of the resource.

Marginal revenue product

The change in a firm's total receipts resulting from a one-unit change in its level of employment of a resource is called the *marginal revenue product*, or *MRP*, of the resource to the firm. The computation of the marginal revenue product of common labor for a hypothetical shirt factory is illustrated in Table 14–1. In column (1) we show alternative possible employment

Table 14–1
Marginal revenue product and marginal resource cost of a resource

(1) Labor, person-days (l)	(2) Total product, shirts (x)	(3) Marginal physical product (MPP$_L$)	(4) Product price* (p$_x$)	(5) Marginal revenue† (MR$_x$)	(6) Total receipts† (TR)	(7) Marginal revenue product (MRP$_L$)	(8) Resource price, marginal resource cost (MRC$_L$)
1	13	13	$15.00	$15.00	$195	$195	$30
2	25	12	14.00	12.92	350	155	30
3	36	11	13.06	10.91	470	120	30
4	46	10	12.17	9.00	560	90	30
5	55	9	11.36	7.22	625	65	30
6	63	8	10.63	5.62	670	45	30
7	69	6	10.14	5.00	700	30	30
8	73	4	9.86	5.00	720	20	30
9	75	2	9.73	5.00	730	10	30
10	75	0	9.73	5.00	730	0	30

* Rounded to the nearest cent.
† Average of marginal revenues for the increments in product shown in the MPP$_L$ column.

levels of labor in workers per day. The total output obtainable with each quantity of labor is listed in column (2). The firm is assumed to be imperfectly competitive (or monopolistic) in selling its product, so in column (4) the market price of shirts for larger sales volumes is lower than it is for smaller ones. Total receipts in column (6) are found by multiplying the output of shirts at each level of employment by the corresponding product price for each output level. Marginal revenue product of labor at each level of employment is then determined as the change in total receipts that a 1-unit change in the employment level brings about at that employment level. For example, a change in the employment level from 4 to 5 workers per day in column (1) increases total receipts in column (6) by $65; that is, the MRP_L at an employment level of 5 workers per day in $65 and is so recorded in column (7). The other numbers of column (7) are computed in a similar manner.

The marginal revenue product of labor at each employment level can also be thought of as the marginal physical product of labor multiplied by the marginal revenue per unit of product at the corresponding output levels. Consider, for example, an increase in the employment level from 5 to 6 workers per day. The marginal physical product of labor is 8 shirts. Each of those 8 shirts adds $5.62 to the firm's total receipts, that is, the MR_x is $5.62.[1] So

$$MRP_L = MPP_L \cdot MR_x = \$8 \cdot \$5.62 = \$45.$$

At each employment level in Table 14–1, note that in column (7) MRP_L for each level of employment is equal to the MPP_L of column (3) multiplied by the MR_x of column (5) at that level of employment.

Marginal resource cost

On the cost side of the picture, the change in a firm's total costs resulting from a one-unit change in the employment level of a resource is called the *marginal resource cost* of that resource. A firm that is a pure competitor in the purchase of a resource can take as much or as little as it desires at the

Figure 14–1
Marginal revenue product, marginal resource cost, and profit maximization

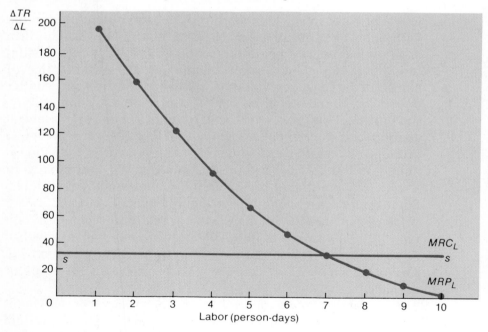

1. We note from Table 14–1 that in moving from 5 to 6 workers per day total product increases by 8 shirts and total receipts of the firm increase by $45. Thus MR_x, the increase in total receipts per one unit increase in output is $45 ÷ 8 or $5.62 for each of the 8 shirts added to the firm's output and sales.

market price of the resource. If the price of labor is $30 per unit, at any employment level a 1-unit change in that employment level changes total costs of the firm by $30. Thus marginal resource cost, or MRC_L, is equal to the resource price or p_L under these circumstances. The marginal resource cost and the price of labor are listed in column (8) of Table 14–1 and are plotted as MRC_L in Figure 14–1.

Profit maximization

How much labor should a firm employ in order to maximize its profits (or minimize its losses)? Consider an employment level of 1 unit per day in Table 14–1 and Figure 14–1. It adds $195 to the firm's total receipts and only $30 to total costs so the firm will have $165 more profit by employing it than it would have by not employing it. If the firm moves to an employment level of 2 units of labor, $125 more can be added to profits. In fact, whenever, MRP_L is greater than MRC_L, an increase in the employment level will bring about an increase in profits. The firm maximizes profits at the 7-unit employment level at which MRP_L equals MRC_L. At the employment level a 1-unit increment in labor adds the same amount to the firm's total receipts that it adds to total costs and therefore adds nothing to profits. Since the increment in labor from the 6-unit to the 7-unit employment level adds nothing to profits, it follows that profits are also maximum at the 6-unit employment level. However, for consistency and to make the conditions for profit maximization easier to remember, we consider the employment level at which the marginal revenue product of the resource is equal to its marginal resource cost as the true profit maximizing level. In Figure 14–1, the quantity of labor that maximizes the firm's profits occurs at the intersection of the MRP_L and MRC_L curves.

The firm's demand curve

The firm's demand curve for a resource should show the quantities of it that the firm will purchase at different possible prices, other things being equal. The "other things" in the definition are: (1) the quantities of other resources employed, (2) the firm's techniques of production, and (3) the demand for the firm's output. Assuming that these "things" remain constant assures us that the marginal revenue product curve for the resource will hold still while we consider the quantities that the firm will take at different resource prices.

Whatever the market price of the resource happens to be, the firm will want to employ the quantity that maximizes profits with respect to the resource. Thus at the price of $30 per unit the firm of Table 14–1 and Figure 14–1 purchases 7 units of labor. If the price were $20, it would want 8 units—the amount at which MRP_L equals MRC_L. If the price were $65, the firm would want 5 units. Whatever the price is, the firm will want the quantity at which MRP_L equals MRC_L and p_L. Consequently, the firm's MRP_L curve is also its demand curve for the resource.

The market demand curve

The market demand curve for a resource shows what all firms employing it will take at all possible prices, other things being equal. To obtain it we sum horizontally the individual firm demand curves for the resource. In Figure 14–2 let Firm 1 and Firm 2 be two of several firms employing labor. If the price of labor were p_L, Firm 1 would take quantity l_1 and Firm 2 would take quantity l_1'. The quantities taken by other firms would be determined similarly. In the market diagram quantity L_1 is the sum of l_1, l_1', and the quantities that other

Figure 14–2
Construction of the market demand curve

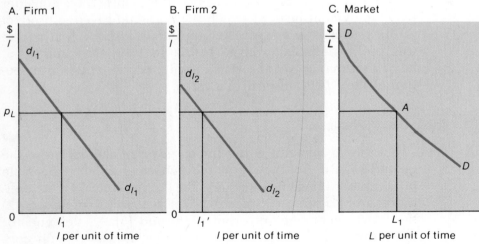

firms would want to employ at that price. Price p_1 and quantity L_1 locate point A on the market demand curve. Other points comprising DD are located in the same way. It is not necessary that the individual firms demanding labor produce and sell the same product in order for their demand curves for labor to be summed horizontally. Firm 1 may be producing copper and Firm 2 may be producing steel. Other firms may be producing still different products.

RESOURCE SUPPLY

The *market supply curve* of a resource indicates the quantities per unit of time that resource owners will place on the market at all possible prices, other things being equal. It usually slopes upward to the right like SS in Figure 14–3, indicating that larger quantities will be placed on the market at higher prices than at lower prices. We would expect this to be the case for particular kinds of labor—carpenters for example as well as for resources of their kinds. At higher wage rates for carpenters more people will want to work in that occupation than would at lower wage rates. The same thing will usually hold for bricklayers, plumbers, machinists, economists, and

Figure 14–3
The market supply curve

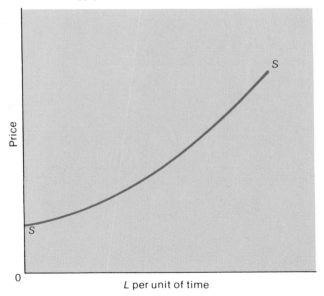

Price

S

S

0

L per unit of time

other labor resource categories. Many kinds of resources, particularly capital resources, are the outputs of production units or firms. The higher their prices are, the more profitable it is for firms to produce them and the greater the outputs of them will be. Coal, crude oil, wheat, and many other items provide examples.

The *supply curve of a resource to a firm* is usually horizontal at the level of the going market price. In most cases any one firm is a relatively small user of any one resource and is not able to affect its price significantly. It tends to be more or less a pure competitor in resource purchasing. A horizontal resource supply curve to the firm generates a marginal resource cost curve to the firm that coincides with the supply curve. In Figure 14–1 *ss* represents the labor supply curve to the firm and the firm's marginal resource cost curve when the market price of labor is $30 per unit.

RESOURCE PRICING AND EMPLOYMENT

Equilibrium price and employment level

The market price and employment level of a resource are determined by the same kinds of forces that determine the price and quantity exchanged of any other item. In Figure 14–4(B) we put the market demand curve of Figure 14–2 and the market supply curve of Figure 14–3 together. The equilib-

Figure 14–4
Determination of the price and employment level for labor

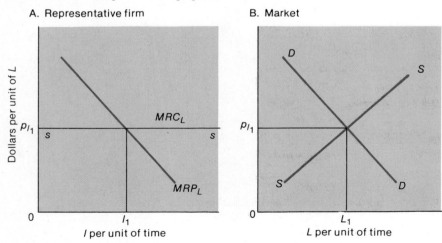

rium price or wage rate for labor will be p_{l_1} and the quantity employed will be L_1. If the price were below p_{l_1}, a shortage would occur inducing employers to bid against each other for the available supply until the price rises to p_{l_1}. If the price were greater than p_{l_1}, there would be a surplus or unemployment. Unemployed units of labor would have incentives to reduce their asking prices until at wage level p_{l_1} the unemployment would disappear.

The situation facing one of the many firms using labor is depicted in Figure 14–4(A). The firm must pay the market price p_{l_1}. The market price determines the level of the ss and MRC_L curve to the firm. Together with the firm's MRP_L curve they present the same picture as did Figure 14–1; however, we can now see how the resource price that the firm must pay, taken as given at \$30 in Figure 14–1, is determined. The firm maximizes profits by employing l_1 units of labor per unit of time. The employment levels of all firms using this kind of labor add up to L_1 units at the p_{l_1} price.

The effects of price floors

Resource markets do not always operate smoothly and efficiently. The establishment of minimum prices or price floors for some resources creates problems. Suppose the sellers of a certain kind of resource are dissatisfied with the equilibrium price. They take joint action or agree among themselves not to sell at that price, but rather to sell only at a higher price level. Examples of this sort of action are abundant. Labor unions do it; farmers do it; the OPEC oil countries do it. Sometimes the sellers are able to get legislation passed to require by law that no one sell below a given and fixed price floor. Farm price supports and minimum wages are cases in point.

An effective price floor, regardless of how it is set, always generates a surplus or unemployment of the resource for which it is set. Suppose in Figure 14–5 that L represents unskilled labor. The equilibrium price is p_{l_1} and the equilibrium levels of employment are l_1 for a representative firm and L_1 for market as a whole. There is neither a surplus nor a shortage. Full employment exists.

Now suppose that either through union action or through a minimum wage law a price floor is set at p_{l_2}—no firm is allowed to purchase labor services at a lower wage rate. The supply curve facing the firm and the firm's marginal resource

Figure 14–5
Effects of a resource price floor

A. Representative firm

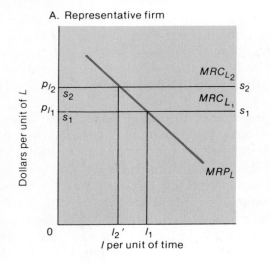

B. Market

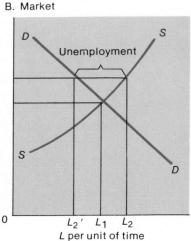

cost curve are shifted upward to s_2s_2 and MRC_{L2} by the action. The quantity of labor that maximizes the firm's profits is now l_2' instead of l_1; thus the higher wage rate induces the firm to decrease its level of employment. As all firms employing unskilled labor reduce their individual levels of employment, the market level drops to L_2'. On the other hand the higher wage level provides incentives for more units of labor than before to seek employment. A surplus of labor or unemployment amounting to $L_2'L_2$ is generated.

The analysis is essentially the same for wheat as it is for labor. At support prices above the equilibrium price level, firms that use wheat will buy less than they will buy at the equilibrium price. At the same time a support price induces farmers to place more on the market than they will at the equilibrium price. The inevitable result is a surplus.

If a price floor is set *below* the equilibrium price level, it is ineffective. The higher equilibrium price prevails. Minimum prices are at lower limits below which they are not allowed to fall. They are not maximum prices.

The effects of price ceilings

An effective price ceiling for a resource always creates a shortage of that resource. The market for domestically produced crude oil is a current example. In Figure 14–6(B) let

Figure 14–6
Effects of a resource price ceiling

A. One refiner

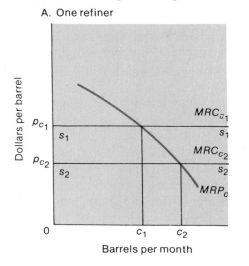

B. Market

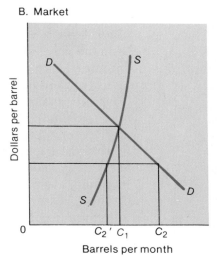

DD represent the demand for crude oil. The domestic supply curve is SS.

In the absence of price ceilings or maximum prices fixed by law, domestic producers would place C_1 barrels per day on the market at the equilibrium price p_{c_1}. One individual refiner would maximize profits by purchasing c_1 and all refiners together would take the entire amount C_1 at that price. There are no shortages and no surpluses.

Now suppose that a price ceiling is placed on oil at p_{c_2}. It would be most profitable for the single refiner to expand its purchases to c_2 barrels per day. All refiners together want quantity C_2; however, producers will place only C_2' on the market. A shortage exists and a representative refiner will not be able to get as much as c_1, much less c_2. The analysis can be extended to any resource. An effective price ceiling always means that a shortage will occur. The only way to eliminate the shortage is to let the price rise to its equilibrium level.

RESOURCE PRICES AND HOUSEHOLD INCOME DETERMINATION

The households of the economy are the ultimate owners of its resources and the resources owned by any one household determines its income. Specifically, the income of a household depends upon (1) the quantities of resources that it can place in employment and (2) the prices that it receives for them. As we have seen, in the absence of price ceilings and price floors the price of any one resource is determined by the forces of demand and supply, and at the equilibrium price, units of it will be fully employed.

But the incomes yielded by equilibrium prices are not always satisfactory to resource owners. For example, in a university community, secretarial pay is usually thought to be unduly low. The reason for this is relatively simple—the supply of secretarial services is great relative to the demand for them. The remedy for relatively low prices and low incomes is generally thought to be a price floor or a minimum wage. But such a minimum price will result in unemployment. Those who retain their jobs will indeed receive higher incomes. Those who are made unemployed by, or who are unable to find employment at, the minimum price level will now have incomes of zero. Is the minimum wage a satisfactory solution to the problem?

It is not even certain that a minimum price for a resource above the equilibrium level will increase the total amount paid by buyers for that resource. Whether the total expenditures of buyers (and the total income of all owners) of the resource increase, decrease, or remain the same depends upon the elasticity of demand for it. In Figure 14–7 suppose that the supply curve for labor is S_1S_1. The equilibrium price is p_1 and the quantity employed is L_1. If a minimum price of p_1' is put into effect, the employment level drops to L_1'. Demand is elastic for the price increase and the total outlay of buyers (income of sellers) will decrease. On the other hand, if the supply curve were S_2S_2, the equilibrium price and quantity is in the inelastic segment of the demand curve. A price floor raising the price to p_2' would increase the total income of all sellers of the resource; however, the owners of unemployed units receive zero incomes from those units.

We can be reasonably certain of the real income effect for the economy as a whole if a minimum resource price is effective. To the extent that an effective minimum resource price generates unemployment of that resource, the total output or real net national product will be reduced below what it would be if the resource were fully employed. It thus appears likely

Figure 14–7
Elasticity of demand and income earned by resource owners

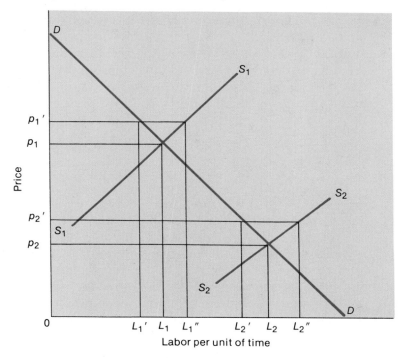

that effective minimum resource prices result in gains for the households owning the units of those resources that remain employed. But the income gains of such households will be at the expense of (1) households owning the unemployed units of those resources and (2) the net national product of consumers in general, who now have less to consume.

THE VALUE OF A RESOURCE

How much are units of a resource worth? This question perplexes many people. We observe that a major league baseball player, or an opera star, earns $100,000 per year. Those who are not baseball fans tend to believe that the ballplayer is overpaid. Those who dislike opera think the opera star is overpaid. Others believe that both are overpaid. On the other hand, most resource owners think they are underpaid for the resources that they sell. But beliefs of these sorts are simply unsubstantiated opinion. We need a more reliable means of measuring the value of a resource. To obtain it we must ask who does the valuing and what determines the values that they set. Three groups important in the valuing of resources can be identified: (1) the purchasers or employers of the resource, (2) the buyers of what the resource produces; that is, the whole set of consumers in the economy, and (3) the owners of the resource. Essentially, the first two groups generate demand for the resource while the third provides the supply of it.

Value to employers

The value of a resource to its employers or purchasers is represented by the highest price they are willing to pay for any given quantity. For any one purchaser the unit value of the resource at any given employment level is its *marginal revenue product*—what any one unit contributes to the firm's total receipts. The firm will not pay a higher price. Further, the value of the resource to the firm—its marginal revenue product—varies, depending upon the quantity that the firm employs. In Table 14–2 suppose that the firm employs 7 units of labor. It will not be willing to pay more than $30 per unit for it. If the firm were employing 6 units, however, it would be willing to pay a higher price per unit—$45 in this case. This is so because at the lower employment level each unit of labor is more valuable to the firm—its marginal physical

Table 14–2
Marginal revenue product and value of marginal product of a resource

(1) Labor, person-days (l)	(2) Marginal physical product (MPP$_L$)	(3) Product price (p$_x$)	(4) Marginal revenue (MR$_x$)	(5) Marginal revenue product (MRP$_L$)	(6) Value of marginal product (VMP$_L$)
1	13	$15.00	$15.00	$195	$195.00
2	12	14.00	12.92	155	168.00
3	11	13.06	10.91	120	143.66
4	10	12.17	9.00	90	121.17
5	9	11.36	7.22	65	102.24
6	8	10.63	5.62	45	85.04
7	6	10.14	5.00	30	60.84
8	4	9.86	5.00	20	39.84
9	2	9.73	5.00	10	19.46
10	0	9.73	5.00	0	0.00

product is greater and so is the marginal revenue from the sale of the smaller total product output level.

The market demand curve of Figure 14–4 shows the values that all employers together place on a resource at different possible levels of employment. The market demand curve is the horizontal summation of individual firm MRP_L curves and at any given market quantity, say L_1, each firm employs a quantity such as l_1, placing a value per unit on the resource equal to its MRP at that employment level.

Value to sellers

The value of units of a resource to the sellers of it is the least price they will accept for any given quantity of it. This set of values is summed up by the market supply curve. Most suppliers would be willing to sell larger quantities at higher prices than they would be willing to sell at lower prices. Most individual suppliers have reservation prices below which they will not sell at all. The combined sellers' valuations of different resource quantities is summed up in an upward sloping market supply curve for the resource, which shows the minimum prices or values at which various alternative quantities will be placed on the market.

At the equilibrium price—price p_{l_1} in Figure 14–4—the value placed on the resource by employers and by sellers is the same. Employers are just willing to purchase quantity L_1 and sellers are just willing to place that quantity on the market. If the quantity were greater, the value placed on each unit by sellers would exceed that placed on it by buyers, and the latter simply would not pay the price that sellers require. If the quantity were smaller, the value placed on the resource by buyers would exceed that placed on it by sellers.

Value to consumers

The value of units of a resource to consumers of the goods and services that it helps to produce is called the *value of marginal product* or *VMP* of the resource. The computation of the value of marginal product of labor, along with how it differs from the marginal revenue product of labor, is illustrated in Table 14–2. Suppose the firm is employing 6 units of labor initially and then moves to an employment level of 7 units. The 1-unit increase in employment increases the total output of shirts by 6 units. Each of these sells for $10.14 so the value to the consuming public of the extra six shirts is $60.84; that is, VMP_L at the 6-unit level of employment by the firm is $60.84. At an 8-unit level of employment VMP_L is $39.44. The other entries in column (6) are computed in a similar way, reflecting at each employment level the value of a unit of labor to consumers.

Since the producer of shirts in Table 14–2 exercises some degree of monopoly—faces a downward-sloping demand curve for its product output—the MRP_L is less than the VMP_L. This difference means that consumers place a higher value on a unit of labor than does the producer or employer of labor. It always occurs when sellers of a product exercise some degree of monopoly. As we learned in Chapter 12, a firm facing a downward sloping demand curve for its product MR_x will be less than p_x. Consequently, $MPP_L \cdot p_x$, or VMP_L, will be greater than $MPP_L \cdot MR_x$, or MRP_L at any given level of employment of labor. However, if the producer-employer were a purely competitive seller of goods, VMP_L and MRP_L would be equal. The same results are obtained for any resource; they are not confined to the labor resource.

SUMMARY

Resource prices, like other prices, are determined by supply and demand in competitive resource markets. Resource demand originates with producers. For the firm it is the firm's marginal revenue product curve for the resource. Market demand for a resource is the horizontal summation of individual firms' marginal revenue product curves for it. At the equilibrium price of a resource there is neither a shortage nor a surplus.

When the price of a resource is controlled, above or below the equilibrium price, surpluses or shortages will occur. An effective price floor will always cause surpluses of a resource to appear. An effective price ceiling will always generate a shortage.

The income of a household is determined by the quantities of resources that it can place in employment and the prices received for those resources. A price floor set for a resource in order to augment the incomes of the households that own it will always result in unemployment and will succeed in increasing the total income received by all of its owners only if demand for the resource is inelastic. Price floors help those resource owners who succeed in keeping their resource units employed at the expense of resource owners whose resources become unemployed because of the floor and the consuming public.

QUESTIONS AND PROBLEMS

1. Define marginal revenue product of a resource. How is it related to the marginal physical product of the resource?

2. Explain in a common sense way how a firm can determine the profit-maximizing employment level of a resource.

3. Show with a diagram and explain the following for common labor:

   a. A firm's demand curve.
   b. The market demand curve.
   c. The market supply curve.
   d. The market price.
   e. The supply curve to the firm.
   f. The firm employment level.
   g. The market employment level.

4. Show and explain what effective minimum wage rate will do to the results of question 3.

5. Are consumers currently paying a price for gasoline that measures its value to them? How do you know?

Chapter 15

Resource allocation

In addition to being a key element in the determination of
the incomes of resource owners, resource prices serve to
allocate resource units among their various uses. This alloca-
tory function tends to be overlooked by advocates of minimum
resource prices and of "equal pay for equal work." We shall
discuss first the "correct" allocation of units of a given resource. Second, we shall consider the response of the price
system to an "incorrect" allocation or a misallocation of the
resource. Last, we shall examine the impediments that tend
to prevent the correct allocation of a resource from occurring.
Again, unskilled labor will be used as a representative resource example.

THE "CORRECT" ALLOCATION

From the point of view of economic efficiency or economic
welfare units of any given resource are correctly allocated
among different uses when the allocation is such that the resource is making its maximum contribution to net national
product. The allocation is correct if every unit of the resource
is in the use in which it is most valuable. There exists no
other use to which a unit of the resource could be transferred
that is more valuable than the one in which it is currently
being used.

For the allocation of a resource among its various uses to
be correct or most efficient, the value of marginal product of
the resource must be the same in all of those uses and there
must be no use for it in which its value of marginal product
would be greater. Suppose in Figure 15–1 that unskilled labor
can be used (1) on a wheat farm and (2) in a home construction
firm. The current employment levels are l_1 units of labor on
the farm and l_2 units of labor in the construction firm. The
value of marginal product of labor is \$20. In either use a unit
of labor contributes an amount to the economy's total output
valued by consumers at \$20. Nothing could be gained by con-
sumers if a unit of labor were transferred from the home construction firm to the wheat farm. In fact, such a transfer would
make consumers worse off. They would lose \$20 worth of hous-
ing and their gain would be a little less than \$20 worth of
wheat since the VMP_L^w curve for labor on the wheat farm slopes
downward to the right.

Suppose on the other hand that the wheat farm of Figure

Figure 15–1
Correct and incorrect allocations of a resource

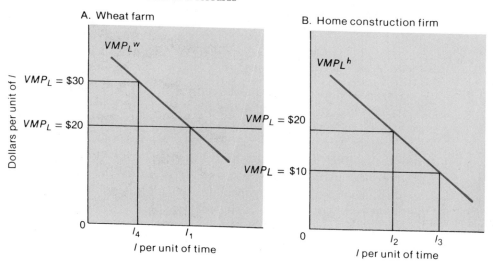

A. Wheat farm

B. Home construction firm

15–1 employs l_4 units of labor and that the construction firm employs l_3 units. The value of marginal product of labor on the farm is \$30 while in the construction firm it is \$10. The transfer of a unit of labor from construction to the farm would increase net national product and consumer welfare. Loss of the unit of labor to the construction firm brings about a reduction in the economy's total output valued by consumers at \$10. Adding the unit of labor to the farm's labor force adds output to the economy that consumers value at just slightly less than \$30. Consumers gain almost \$20 of product by the transfer. All such transfers of unskilled labor from lower value of marginal product uses to higher value of marginal product uses increase net national product. Only when all possible transfers of this kind have been made and the value of marginal product of the resource is the same in all its uses will unskilled labor be making its maximum contribution to net national product and consumer welfare.

RESPONSE TO MISALLOCATION

At any given point in time some misallocation of units of a resource are likely to exist. Demands for the resource in different uses grow at different rates. Or demand may grow in one use while it declines in another. Supplies of the resource may be fed into one use more rapidly than into another. These and many other forces cause misallocations to occur. How does the economy respond to misallocation?

Price differences

Suppose that for unskilled labor we think of a rural market and an urban market, separate from one another over a short-run time horizon, say six months, but between which migration can occur in the long run. Suppose also that the supply of labor relative to demand for it is greater in the rural area than in the urban area. Suppose further that the users of unskilled labor sell their products under conditions of pure competition, so that product prices are equal to their respective marginal revenues and the value of marginal product for the resource in each of its uses is equal to its marginal revenue product.

The foregoing conditions are pictured in Figure 15–2. The employment level in the urban area is l_u and the value of marginal product of labor for each firm that employs it is VMP_{Lu}. In the rural area the employment level and the value of marginal product of labor are l_r and VMP_{Lr}, respectively. The higher value of marginal product of labor in the urban area is the evidence of its misallocation. The price employers

Figure 15–2
Market response to incorrect allocation

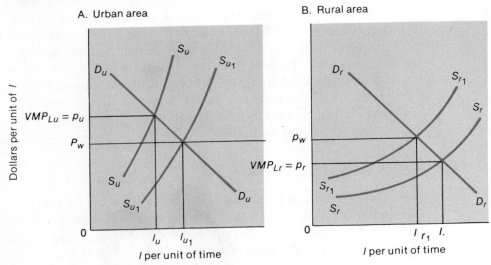

will pay for labor in the urban area is p_u and is higher than the price p_r paid in the rural area. A unit of labor is more valuable to employers and to consumers when used in the urban area. In summary, misallocation of a resource occurs if its value of marginal product differs in alternative uses of it and, since in each use the resource is paid a price equal to its value of marginal product, the misallocation results in price differences paid for the resource among its various uses.

Incentives for reallocation

The price difference for the resource between the urban and the rural area in Figure 15–2 provides an incentive for its owners to reallocate it, headed toward correction of the initial misallocation in the long run. The higher prices in the urban area mean higher incomes for resource owners selling in the urban market. Labor owners seeking to maximize their incomes, will transfer units of labor from the rural to the urban area as soon as they perceive the earnings differential and are able to make the transfer.

Migration of labor from the rural to the urban area would be expected to continue until wage rates are approximately the same in each area. As the migration occurs, the supply curve of labor in the urban area shifts to the right toward S_{u_1} while that of the rural area shifts to the left toward S_{r_1}. When enough labor has been moved so that the wage rate and value of marginal product for labor is p_w in *both* areas, the migration will cease and labor will be correctly allocated. The value of marginal product of labor will be the same in all uses in both areas.

Effects of reallocation on net national product

When resource units are reallocated from lower to higher value of marginal product uses, the reallocation increases net national product. For each such transfer of a resource the loss in net national product from its withdrawal from the lower paying, lower value of marginal product use is offset by the gain in net national product from its employment in the higher paying, higher value of marginal product use. For example, the withdrawal of a diesel tractor from a use where it adds $5,000 worth of farm products per year to the economy's output, and the transfer of it to a construction use where it adds $10,000 worth of roads per year, results in a net gain to the economy of $5,000 worth of product per year. The $5,000 per year net gain is the difference between the *VMP* of tractors used in farming and the *VMP* of tractors used in road construction. Generally, transfers of resource units from lower paying uses to higher paying uses are also transfers from lower value of marginal product uses to higher value of marginal product uses and serve to increase net national product.

IMPEDIMENTS TO "CORRECT" ALLOCATIONS

Between the cup and the lip, slips may occur. There are often stumbling blocks in the way of a smooth efficient reallocation of a misallocated resource. Some of the most common impediments are (1) monopoly in product sales, (2) price fixing, and (3) entry barriers to certain occupations or employments.

Monopoly in product sales

It comes as no surprise that monopoly in product sales will prevent resource units from being allocated correctly. We know intuitively that industries restricting output are likely to use too little of any given resource relative to industries in the more competitive segments of the economy. But, specifically, why is this so?

Monopolistic restriction of the quantity of a resource used results from the difference between the marginal revenue product and the value of marginal product of the resource. For a monopolistic seller of product, employing a given amount of the resource, value of marginal product exceeds the marginal revenue product. This difference was explained in Chapter 14 and was illustrated numerically in Table 14–2. Plotted diagrammatically the two curves look like MRP_L and VMP_L in Figure 15–3(A). In review, for a monopolistic seller of product the product price is greater than the firm's marginal revenue at any given level of product sales. The value of marginal product of labor equals $MRP_L \cdot p_x$ whereas the marginal revenue product of labor equals $MRP_L \cdot MR_x$ at the level of employment generating the given sales level. Consequently VMP_L is greater than MRP_L. By way of contrast, the value of marginal product and the marginal revenue product of a resource used

Figure 15–3
Monopolistic causes of misallocation

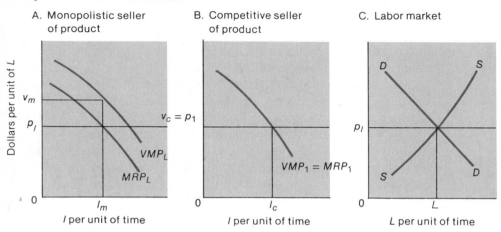

A. Monopolistic seller of product B. Competitive seller of product C. Labor market

by a competitive seller of product are the same since MR_x and p_x are the same for such a firm. We show this result in Figure 15–3(B).

In the situation depicted in Figure 15–3, labor is misallocated. Figure 15–3(A) shows a representative user of labor that is a monopolistic seller of product; Figure 15–3 (B) shows a representative user that is a competitive seller of product; and Figure 15–3(C) shows the market for labor in its entirety. Each of the firms purchases the quantity of labor that maximizes profits—the quantity at which its marginal revenue product is equal to the price of labor (marginal resource cost to the firm) as determined by the market as a whole. The value of marginal product of labor for the competitive firm is v_c. For the monopolistic firm it is v_m, so units of the resource are not correctly allocated.

Net national product would be increased by transferring units of labor from competitive firms to monopolistic firms. However, the price system will not bring this reallocation about. The *price* paid labor by both types of firm is the same, at level p_l, so no incentives exist for resource owners to move labor from the lower to the higher value of marginal product uses. They cannot increase their incomes by doing so. Thus where some users of a resource are monopolistic sellers and others are competitive sellers, the result is a misallocation of the resource that the price system will not correct.

Price fixing

If some of the owners of a resource are able to act together and set a minimum price for the part of the resource supply that they own, the result may be a more or less permanent misallocation of the resource.

Consider two labor markets—one rural and one urban—that are separate from each other in the short run, but are close enough for migration to occur between them in the long run. Let supply relative to demand be greater in the rural than in the urban market as illustrated in Figure 15–4. The price and value of marginal product of labor are p_u in the urban market. In the rural market they are at level p_r. The price differential would draw labor from the rural to the urban market in the long run thus correcting the misallocation.

Suppose the workers in the urban area, finding that an inmigration of labor from the rural area lowers their wage rates and their incomes, decide to organize a union. Suppose also that when they have done so, they act with great restraint and demand only the going urban wage rate p_u. Employers in the urban area are likely to find the demand reasonable and a collective bargaining contract is signed setting the urban wage rate at p_u.

Workers who now try to migrate from the rural to the urban area in response to the wage differential find no jobs. At wage rate p_u urban employers will hire L_u workers only—and these positions are filled by the already existing labor force. The

Figure 15–4
Price fixing as a cause of misallocation

A. Urban market

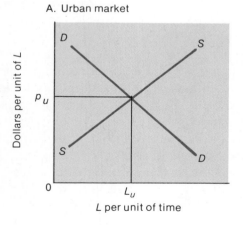

B. Rural market

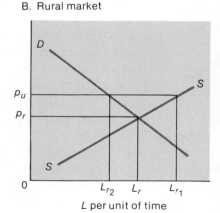

rural workers are thus forced to remain permanently in the lower paying, lower value of marginal product rural area.

The situation is the same in any skill or occupation where the same members of the occupation have organized and succeeded in establishing a minimum price for their labor above what the unorganized persons in the occupation receive. The minimum price limits the number that will be hired by the employers of the organized workers since their value of marginal product must be equal to the level of the minimum price. The non-organized workers are delegated to lower paying, lower value of marginal product jobs. The price system is unable to perform its function of moving resource units toward a more productive allocation pattern.

Can't the unorganized lower paid workers organize and improve their situation? Suppose they do so and succeed in pushing the wage rate in the rural area up to p_u in Figure 15–4. Employers in the rural area now find that to maximize profits they must employ a smaller amount of labor, L_{r_2}. But L_{r_1} workers desire employment at that wage level. Unemployment amounting to $L_{r_2} L_{r_1}$ in the rural area will occur. The L_{r_2} workers who remain employed are definitely better off. But what about the $L_{r_2} L_{r_1}$ workers who want to work at wage rate p_u?

Blocked entry

In many instances the owners of resources in relatively high paying, high value of marginal product uses take direct actions to block or partially block the entry of additional resource units into those uses. They do so in order to preserve their incomes—larger supplies of the resources would reduce resource prices and values of marginal product. They would also reduce incomes of the initial resource owners. Among the devices used to impede or block entry into such occupations are apprentice programs, rigorous examinations for admissions to the profession or occupation, and the requirements that those who practice the profession or occupation be licensed. In almost every case the action taken by those in the group is defended by the group as necessary to "protect the public." It will seldom, if ever, be defended on grounds protecting the incomes of those already in the occupation or profession.

The medical profession historically has done much to control entry. Through the American Medical Association, the profession accredits (or fails to accredit) medical schools. Members of the profession control entry into those schools that are accredited. And the graduates of medical schools must be licensed by state medical boards (staffed by medical doctors) before they can practice. At the present time roughly three out of every five "qualified" applicants for medical training are accepted by the limited number of accredited medical schools.

Licensing laws enable members of an occupation to use the government—usually the state—to help them limit entry. One must pass an examination and obtain a license in most states to be a real estate broker, a lawyer, an undertaker, a plumber, a barber, or to enter many other occupations. If it appears to those in the occupation that "too many" are coming into it, "standards" for admission can be raised. In virtually every case the licensing board for an occupation is composed of members of the occupation.

Obviously, controls on entry into specific occupations hold national income below what it would be in their absence. Persons denied entry to the higher paying, higher value of marginal product occupations are forced to remain in lower paying, lower value of marginal product occupations in which their contributions to net national product are smaller. The economy as a whole is thus denied the net increase in the value of output that results whenever a resource unit transfers from a lower to a higher value of marginal product use.

SUMMARY

Resource prices provide the mechanism for allocating resource units among their various uses. Units of any given resource are "correctly" allocated when the value of marginal product of the resource is the same in all of its alternative uses, there is no use in which its value of marginal product is greater.

In a competitive market, the price of a resource is equal to its value of marginal product when the firms using it maximize their profits. Misallocation of units of the resource results in differences in its price. The price differences provide incentives for owners of the resource to transfer units of it from the lower paying to the higher paying uses, or from lower value of marginal product uses to higher value of marginal product uses. Such transfers increase net national product and tend to be continued to the point at which units of the resource are correctly allocated.

Impediments to the correct allocation of units of a resource may take the form of (1) monopoly in product sales, (2) price fixing, and (3) blocked entry into occupations or professions. Monopoly permits resource owners to move their resource units from lower paying to higher paying uses until the resource price is the same in all uses. However, the difference between the value of marginal product and the marginal revenue product of the resource results in some degree of misallocation even after allocation has made the resource price the same in all uses. Price fixing and blocked entry force some resource units to remain in lower paying, lower productivity uses.

QUESTIONS AND PROBLEMS

1. In University City non-union carpenters are paid $6.00 per hour. Union carpenters are paid $9.00 per hour. Under these circumstances would you expect that carpenters are "correctly" allocated? Explain in detail.

2. How does the price system, when it is free to do so, react to a misallocation of resources?

3. Suppose that the price of diesel fuel is controlled by the government and is selling at the ceiling price in both Kansas and Colorado. There is a shortage in Colorado but not in Kansas. What is wrong? How would you recommend it be corrected? Defend your recommendation.

4. What happens to *NNP* when units of a resource move from lower to higher *VMP* uses? How do you know?

5. In what way may licensing laws cause *NNP* to be lower than it would be in their absence?

Chapter 16

Economic justice and equity

CHECKLIST OF ECONOMIC CONCEPTS

Equity or justice
Commutative justice
Distributive justice
Median income
Negative income tax

W̱e turn in this final chapter to a question that is very important to almost all of us. Is our economic system equitable or just in its treatment of different individuals and/ or families? We will not be able to answer the question definitively because the concept of equity or justice means different things to different people. Even though a state of affairs is thought to be equitable by one person, the same state of affairs may well be deemed inequitable by another. But at the very least we can bring our tools of economic analysis to bear on the subject and, perhaps, we can whittle away at the edges of the problem, narrowing the scope of disagreement.

WHAT IS EQUITY?

The first task is to define the terms as they are used in this chapter. We use the concepts of equity and justice interchangeably. We discuss that which may be equitable or just as well as that which may be inequitable or unjust. In general these terms are used with respect to how people are rewarded by the economic system. An important step toward clear thinking is to differentiate between the concepts of *commutative justice* and *distributive justice*.

Commutative justice

An economic system is said to yield *commutative justice* if it pays resource owners what their resources are worth when those resources are used in production processes. Units of any given resource, like common labor, are paid what they are worth if the price paid for the resource is equal to its value of marginal product; that is, if the price paid is equal to the value placed by consumers on the marginal physical product of the resource.

Commutative justice is an objective concept. This means that it is defined in a way that does not depend on peoples' values or their prejudices. With statistical techniques the marginal physical product of a resource in any one use or in a number of uses can be determined quite accurately. The price per unit that is paid for it by its users can be observed to see whether or not commutative justice is achieved. If the facts are accurate and are known all persons with access to the facts reach the same objective conclusions.

In a private enterprise market economy, does the price system lead toward commutative justice; that is, does it pay people what their resources are worth? It is certain that thoroughgoing commutative justice does not occur; however, it is doubtful that there are largescale or widespread deviations from it. If units of a resource are paid less than they are worth by one employer, there will be other employers who will pay them what they are worth. If there are no other employers willing to pay them what their owners think they are worth, the evidence is strong that the resource owners should revise their thinking with regard to what the resource units are really worth. Competition among employers for resource units tend to assure that by and large resource units are paid approximately what they are worth.

Distributive justice

The big issue in the realm of economic equity is that of distributive justice. The concept of distributive justice is much more elusive than that of commutative justice and, in fact, it is not susceptible to unambiguous definition. Distributive justice or equity refers to the justness of the distribution of income among the households of the economy. Whether or not any given distribution is equitable cannot be objectively determined.

One problem that arises in trying to arrive at a definition of distributive justice is that households are a very heterogeneous lot. The most obvious difference among them is that they vary in size. If this were the only difference, it would be easy to correct for it by considering comparative per capita incomes instead of comparative household incomes. But persons also vary in age, health, educational levels, place of residence, vigor, laziness, capacities to enjoy, and many other characteristics that make corrections for the differences virtually impossible. So how can we determine what distribution of incomes among households is just?

Another problem, even more serious, is that different observers have different ideas as to what constitutes distributive justice. It all depends on who is making the judgment. That which one person thinks is equitable will be thought inequitable by another.

Our inability to define distributive justice with objective

precision does not mean that we can say nothing useful about it. Most people, but not all people, will agree that the incomes of some households in the United States are too low for them to afford minimum acceptable standards of nutrition, housing, clothing, education, and the like. They will also agree that something should be done about it—that there should be some redistribution of income toward the poor. Such a redistribution is generally thought to constitute a movement toward distributive justice, even if this term cannot be defined in an objective way.

INCOME INEQUALITY

The extent of income differences

The distribution of money income in the United States for 1976, as determined by the U.S. Bureau of the Census, is presented in Table 16–1. The data are rough. Money income includes amounts earned in wages, dividends, and interest; social security and public assistance benefits; unemployment compensation, government and private pensions, and other periodic income. It does not include nonmoney income such as food stamps, health benefits from the government, subsidized housing, income in kind from business, or farm income in the forms of housing and goods produced and consumed on the farm. Deductions have not been made for personal income taxes, social security taxes, union dues, medicare pre-

Table 16–1
Income distribution in the United States: Families and unattached individuals (1976)

Total money income	Families		Unattached individuals	
	Number (000)	Percent	Number (000)	Percent
Under $5,000	5,842	10.4	10,146	47.2
5,000 to 9,999	11,124	19.6	6,025	28.1
10,000 to 14,999	11,481	20.2	3,109	14.5
15,000 to 19,999	10,824	19.1	1,284	6.0
20,000 to 24,999	7,326	12.9	459	2.1
25,000 to 49,999	9,013	15.9	364	1.7
50,000 and over	1,098	1.9	71	0.3
Total	56,710	100.0	21,459	100.00
Median income	$14,958		$5,375	

Source: U.S. Department of Commerce, Bureau of the Census, Current Population Reports, *Money Income in 1976 of Families and Persons in the United States*, Series P-60, no. 114 (July 1978).

miums, and the like. The data give us a rough general view of the distribution of income.

The *median* income level is a convenient benchmark for thinking about the distribution of income. It is the income level that exactly divides the population—the same number of families or unattached individuals above as there is below. Median family income for 1976 was $14,958 while that for unattached individuals was $5,375. These data are rough measures of what the economy is capable of doing—what it could provide if there were no deviations from the median. Families are clustered in the $5,000 to $25,000 per year brackets with over 70 percent of them falling within that range. Unattached individuals are largely in the under $10,000 brackets.

Although there may be much disagreement over the meaning, seriousness, or importance of the existing range of incomes, it has one dimension that is disliked universally—there are people living in poverty in an economy that is capable of supporting its entire population at a level well above the poverty line. In 1976 the poverty line was defined by the federal government as an annual income level of $5,815 for a nonfarm family of 4 persons with appropriate adjustments for family size and location. During that year some 24,975,000 persons, or 11.8 percent of the U.S. population lived in poverty. It is this characteristic of income distribution on which we focus our attention.

The cause of income differences

From the point of view of economic analysis the causes of poverty are straightforward enough. As we noted in Chapter 14 in a private enterprise system a household earns its income by selling or hiring out the services of the labor and the capital that it owns. A household with relatively inferior or small amounts of labor power and which receives relatively low prices for it receives a relatively low level of income from labor. A household with relatively inferior or small amounts of capital receives a relatively low level of income from capital. By and large, then, households fall below the poverty line because the resources they have available are not worth much in the processes of production. We beg the question of the very inportant sociological and psychological factors that put them in this position. These fall largely outside the scope of the discipline of economics. But we can look at some of the economic factors that are at work.

Differences in labor resources owned.   Differences in labor resources owned by households are determined basically by (1) differences in physical and mental inheritance and (2) differences in the opportunities for developing those characteristics that are inherited. We will consider these in turn.

Differences in what we inherit physically and mentally are so obvious that they need no elaborate explanation. In a society of manual workers the poor would be those who inherit the weak bodies. In our society, mental abilities can compensate in varying degrees for relatively poor physical inheritances. Unfortunately, some people inherit both weak bodies and weak minds.

Differences in opportunities for developing and training that which is inherited mentally and physically account for a substantial part of the differences in labor resources owned by different households. Many of those born into poor families and/or minority group families encounter disadvantages relative to the children of the rich. In the first place, the community attitudes toward and expectations for the children of the poor are considerably less conducive to educational and economic achievement than the attitudes and expectations that surround the children of the rich. In addition, children of relatively more affluent families have access to better schools and better opportunities to put their labor resources to work than children growing up in the less affluent areas of the society.

Painting with a rather broad brush, it appears that differences in innate or inherited physical and mental characteristics are random accidents of birth. In addition the opportunities for developing the characteristics that different persons inherit vary rather widely and tend to favor those lucky enough to be born in more affluent circumstances.

Differences in capital resources owned.   Some of the differences in income that exist among households of the society are attributable to differences in capital resources owned among those households. These differences develop from (1) differences in material inheritance, (2) differences in propensities to accumulate, and (3) differences in luck.

Differences in the inheritance of capital resources account for many differences in incomes among households. In any community a number of the affluent households simply inherited their wealth from their parents and have managed to keep it intact. On the other hand, most of the poor families inherited little or nothing in the way of capital resources.

However, there are many who are born poor but do not stay that way. Over their productive years people have varying propensities to amass capital resources—or to dissipate those they inherit. Some who start poor accumulate capital resources and become rich. A few who start rich end up poor. We differ a great deal in our abilities and in our desires to build up stocks of capital resources.

Pure unadulterated luck plays some role in generating differences in capital resources owned by different households. The typical case is that in which valuable minerals—oil, uranium, coal, and the like—are discovered on an otherwise barren piece of land owned by a poor household.

Differences in capital resources owned are, of course, closely related to differences in labor resources owned. A good income from labor resources owned can and frequently does spark stronger propensities to accumulate capital resources. On the other hand, it is very difficult for a common laborer with a family, at the edge of subsistence, to accomplish any accumulation of capital resources at all.

TOWARD LESS INEQUALITY

The criticism most often leveled against private enterprise economic systems is the allegation that they distribute income unequally; that is, they do not provide acceptable measures of distributive justice. The problem in a nutshell is this: with some exceptions (notably in the case of discrimination) a private enterprise economy yields commutative justice; that is, it tends to pay people what they are worth. But the system does little or nothing to lessen the differences in what the resources available to different households are worth. Some households have large quantities of valuable resources and large incomes. Some have small quantities of not-so-valuable resources and incomes that are judged by the society to be inadequate. There is no automatic mechanism that leads toward acceptable measures of distributive justice.

If the distribution of resource ownership and income is unsatisfactory to the society then it is a function of government,

representing the values of the society, to bring about the appropriate (or at least some) redistribution. Laws against robbery
preclude the have-nots from taking directly from the haves,
but governments as coercive institutions can accomplish the
same result by levying taxes on those who are more wealthy
and subsidizing those who are poor. If the government is to
engage in income redistribution, most of us want it accomplished as efficiently as possible. Two avenues seem to be
open for government anti-poverty programs. First, government
policies can be directed toward improving the qualities and
increasing the quantities of resources owned by the poor. Second, the government can transfer purchasing power from taxpayers to the poor.

Increasing the productivity of the poor

One of the most important steps toward increasing the productivity of the poor is to make sure that they have access
to educational opportunities that are at least as good as those
available to the rest of the society. If we are really interested
in helping the children of the poor break out of the poverty
rut, we will make sure that the primary and secondary schools
they attend are not inferior to those attended by the rest of
the population. In fact we may very well want more educational attention directed toward them than to the children of
the well-to-do to overcome the social and psychological handi-
caps that may confront them. In addition, vocational education
and retraining programs may be useful in increasing the productivity of the adult poor.

Educational programs will not produce instant results. Neither will they increase the productivity and incomes of *all*
the poor. Nevertheless, they constitute one of the great equaliz-
ers in our society.

Another important measure in increasing the productivity
of the poor is the improvement of labor market information.
Unemployed persons or persons in relatively low-wage occupations and areas often do not know where better opportunities exist. Frequently those in the areas where unemployment
is low and wages are high are reluctant to publish this information for fear that an influx of labor will "spoil" what they
have. A system of federal employment exchanges for observing and reporting labor market conditions is already in existence, but its performance leaves much to be desired.

There are additional ways of increasing the productivity of the poor. Hopefully, anti-discrimination measures contribute toward this end, enabling qualified persons to break into professions or occupations that were closed to them by discriminatory practices. Examples include blacks breaking into positions where they may be supervising whites, and practicing professions—medicine, dentistry, accounting, law, etc.—in which their clients may be white. Occupational and professional mobility of groups that have traditionally been discriminated against was greatly enhanced by opening previously segregated schools at all levels to students of all groups.

Income transfers

Even under the best of circumstances policies designed to increase the incomes of the poor cannot eliminate all poverty. Some people are too old and some are too young to take advantage of them. Some are not healthy enough in either mind or body. Some may be victims of structural problems in the society. Any comprehensive or reasonably complete anti-poverty program must include direct income transfers to those whose productivities cannot be increased sufficiently to enable them to earn minimum acceptable income levels.

A great problem with using government transfers of income to alleviate poverty is that they often are used to subsidize the nonpoor as well as the poor. This occurs largely because special interest groups manage to worm their way into the ranks of those eligible for subsidization and politicians have a way of catering to the voting powers of special interest groups.

A very large part of present government income transfers is toward the aged through Social Security payments and Medicare. What could be more humane than taking care of the old? The fact is that many of the elderly people in our society are perfectly capable of supporting themselves, including the costs of their medical care. But Social Security payments and Medicare payments are made to them anyway whether they are poor or not.

Other special interest groups receiving substantial subsidies that may or may not be related to poverty include veterans and farmers. Recipients of veteran's medical benefits, pensions, educational allowances, and the like are not restricted to veterans who are poor. Subsidies to farmers are much more generous to skilled, highly productive and high income farmers than they are to the farming poor. But both veterans and farmers are highly visible, politically powerful groups.

Some government income transfer programs are aimed directly at the poor and, except for cases of misrepresentation and poor administration, they hit their target. Among these are Aid to Families with Dependent Children, Unemployment Compensation, the Food Stamp Program, and the like. The primary problem with programs like these is that they do not provide their recipients with incentives to produce and earn income. They tend to do just the opposite, they encourage people not to look for earning opportunities. Unemployment Compensation tends to be an exception since the time period for which it can be received is fixed.

A negative income tax

There is much dissatisfaction with current government income transfer programs. The major sources of dissatisfaction were mentioned above. First, they subsidize many persons who are not poor. Second, some of the poor do not meet eligibility requirements of programs limited to particular special interest groups and are left out. Third, they provide built-in disincentives to their recipients to get work and earn incomes. As a consequence of such dissatisfaction, considerable support has developed for direct income transfers in the form of *negative income taxes.* Although several versions of the negative income tax have been developed by economists, their common elements are contained in the one that we present below.

The negative income tax plan is usually built on the base of a guaranteed annual income for each household in the economy. Such an income base might be $5,000 for a family of four with appropriate adjustments for households of different sizes. But it can be set at whatever levels the society deems appropriate. If the household earns income during the year, it will have a total disposable income greater than the base. The essence of the plan is the more the household earns the more the household will have to spend *and the less will be the subsidy it gets from taxpayers.* At some level of earning the subsidy will disappear and the household becomes like any other household at or above the zero-subsidy income level.

A numerical example of how a negative income tax plan would work is provided by Table 16–2. The schedule is for a family of four, and it is assumed that the guaranteed income base for any such family will be $5,000. We assume a "negative tax rate" of 60 percent in computing the total amount of a family's subsidy or negative tax—the total subsidy being the base of $5,000 minus 60 percent of income earned. A family's total disposable income per year will consist of income earned plus the annual subsidy or negative tax.

The negative tax ranges from the $5,000 base down to zero depending on how much a family earns. If a family's earnings are zero it is the full $5,000 base—$5,000 minus 60 percent of zero equals $5,000—and disposable income amounts to the $5,000 subsidy. If a family earns $1,000 its subsidy amounts to $5,000 minus 60 percent of $1,000 or $4,400 and its disposable income is $5,400. At an earned income level of $5,000 a family receives a subsidy of $2,000 and has a disposable income of $7,000. A family that earns $8,333.33 has just earned its way out of a subsidy.

The negative income tax plan has several advantages over currently existing income transfer programs of the government. First, it would enable the government to concentrate on subsidizing the poor rather than subsidizing special interest groups such as the elderly, farmers, veterans, and the like. If the society deems it desirable, socially or politically, to subsidize special interest groups, such subsidization outside the negative income tax plan would be possible but it would show up for

Table 16–2
The negative income tax*

Income earned	Negative tax†	Disposable income‡
$ 0	$5,000	$5,000
1,000	4,400	5,400
2,000	3,800	5,800
3,000	3,200	6,200
4,000	2,600	6,600
5,000	2,000	7,000
6,000	1,400	7,400
7,000	800	7,800
8,000	200	8,200
8,333.33	0	8,333.33

* Based on a guaranteed income of $5,000.

† Income base ($5,000) minus 60 percent of income earned.

‡ Income earned plus negative tax.

what it is rather than being given to those groups under the guise of mitigating their poverty.

Second, it would be simple to administer. The administrative structure already exists. Everyone files income tax returns and the Internal Revenue Service processes them. Negative tax payments could be mailed to those entitled to them just as income tax refunds are at the present time. Or, for any given year advance declarations of estimated income and negative taxes could be made; negative tax payments could be mailed out on a quarterly or monthly basis; and the necessary adjustments between the recipient and the IRS could be made at the end of the year when households' income tax returns for the year are filed.

Third, the complexity of the present welter of programs confronting the needy would be reduced. At the present time a poor family may need to check out some 30 to 40 programs to see which ones it is eligible for. One needs a university degree with a field of specialization in poverty problems to be knowledgeable of the intricacies of the various programs, and this most of the poor do not have.

Fourth, the negative income tax system contains incentives to earn. Any household that earns income has a greater disposable income than it would have if it did not earn. By way of contrast, a household on direct relief—Aid to Families with Dependent Children, for example—finds that if it earns income its welfare payments will be cut almost correspondingly, leaving it no better off than it would be if it earned nothing.

Despite the glowing picture just painted of a negative income tax plan, we should inject a note of caution. Current experiments conducted with them indicate that the incentive effects of such a plan are not strong. In addition a bill putting a negative income tax plan into effect must be written by and passed by Congress. It may become enormously complex in the process. Finally, such a plan would be administered by professional bureaucrats. Still, when compared with current income transfer programs, it has much appeal.

PRIVATE ENTERPRISE AND ECONOMIC JUSTICE

The most ubiquitous single criticism leveled against a private enterprise type of economic system is that it does not provide economic justice for the households that comprise it.

We hear, see, and read that in a private enterprise or "capitalistic" system the rich get richer and the poor get poorer. Government intervention and/or a socialistic type of economic system are often thought to be necessary to correct the alleged abuses of the private enterprise system.

Neither available data nor economic logic support the contention that socialistic systems provide a greater measure of justice or that a private enterprise system is incapable of providing whatever degree of economic justice we desire.

By and large it appears that a private system does reasonably well in providing commutative justice. It tends to pay households for their resources about what those resources are worth in production processes. For the most part the poor in a private enterprise economy are those who own small quantities of resources that produce little of what consumers want. Discrimination and monopoly are the primary forces interfering with the achievement of commutative justice, but the distortions introduced by them do not appear to be unduly large. A major function of government in a democratic, predominately private enterprise economy is to ensure that equality of opportunity and workable competition exist.

The private enterprise economy tends toward neutrality insofar as distributive justice is concerned. In providing commutative justice it provides relatively little income to those households short on resources and relatively much income to those households owning large quantities of highly productive resources. It provides some incentives for those who are poor to increase the qualities and the quantities of the resources that they own, but it may provide limited opportunities for them to pursue those incentives. Government can do much to bring about greater measures of distributive justice *within the framework of the private enterprise system*. It can pursue policies designed to increase the productivities of poor households. To the extent that these policies succeed, they benefit almost everyone in the economy. Government can transfer purchasing power from taxpayers in general toward persons at the bottom of the income scale. But in doing so it should exercise care not to destroy incentives and to interfere as little as possible with the price signals that organize and guide the operation of the economy.

It is important that we understand the private enterprise system for what it is, not for what it is alleged to be. It uses

markets, prices, and profits to organize economic activity
rather than leaving the organizing to the discretion of government bureaucrats. It can accommodate about as much income
redistribution as can a socialistic system. In addition, it can
accommodate much higher levels of individual freedom and
initiative than can any socialistic system.

SUMMARY

A criticism most often levied against the private enterprise
type of economic system is that it is unjust or inequitable.
In examining the issue of justice or equity it is first necessary
to examine the meaning of the terms. In economics the concept
of justice or equity refers to how the system rewards its inhabitants. Commutative justice is an objective concept referring
to whether or not persons are rewarded in accordance with
the contributions their resources make to the economy's output. Distributive justice is a subjective concept referring to
how people share in the output of the economy. Most critics
are concerned with distributive justice.

Income distribution data for the U.S. economy indicate that
about 11 percent of the population lives in poverty. Income
differences result from differences in labor resources owned
and in capital resources owned by different households. The
households living in poverty are those that own relatively
small quantities of low-quality resources.

A reduction of poverty means essentially a reduction in
income inequality or a greater measure of distributive justice.
In a private enterprise economy, poverty reduction requires
policies to (1) increase the productivity of the poor and (2)
income transfers to the poor who cannot be made sufficiently
more productive. It appears that a negative income tax type
plan would accomplish income transfers more efficiently and
more on target than does the welter of present transfer programs of the government.

A private enterprise type of system seems to do reasonably
well in providing commutative justice. It is neutral on the issue
of distributive justice. However, it appears that if the government will focus on the poverty problem as such instead of
enacting policies that favor and transfer income to special
interest groups, the private enterprise system can provide a
measure of distributive justice at least as satisfactorily as can

a socialistic system. And it can preserve and enhance individual freedom and individual initiative as well.

QUESTIONS AND PROBLEMS

1. Define commutative justice. Is it an objective or a subjective concept? Explain.

2. Define distributive justice. Is it an objective or a subjective concept? Explain.

3. What are the major economic causes of income differences? Explain each in some detail.

4. Suppose that a negative income tax plan is put into effect in the economy in place of other income transfer programs. The guaranteed family income base is $4,000 and the negative tax rate is 50 percent. How much is the negative tax if a family's earned income is zero? $1,000? $2,000? $3,000? $4,000? At what earned income level will the negative tax be zero?

5. Must an economy be socialistic in order to achieve a "satisfactory" measure of distributive justice?

Index

This book has been set Videocomp in 11 point and 10 point Vermilion, leaded 2 points. Part numbers and titles and chapter numbers and titles are set in 36 point Vermilion Bold. The maximum size of the type page is 30 picas by 47½ picas.

417
469

466-68
78-80
483

408 6-59
69
70
75